THE
HOBBIT
ENCYCLOPEDIA

Damien Bador Vivien Stocker
Coralie Potot Dominique Vigot

FRANCES
LINCOLN

Dedication

To J.R.R. Tolkien for having invented the extraordinarily rich world
that is Middle-earth, and to his son Christopher, thanks to whom
this universe of stories is now even better known.

Quarto

First published in 2023 by Frances Lincoln
an imprint of The Quarto Group.

One Triptych Place,
London, SE1 9SH
United Kingdom
T (0)20 7700 6700
www.Quarto.com

Originally published in French under the title:

La grande encyclopédie du Hobbit
© Editions Le Pré aux Clercs, 2013

and this edition: © Editions Hors Collection, 2022
© English language translation Quarto Publishing, 2023

Text authors: Damien Bador, Coralie Potot, Vivien
Stocker and Dominique Vigot

Translation: Alayne Pullen and Matthew Clarke
in association with First Edition Translations Ltd,
Cambridge, UK

Editing: David Price in association with First Edition
Translations Ltd, Cambridge, UK

Graphic design: Nord compo

Original illustrations: Xavier Sanchez and
Sandrine Gestin

Artworks: Leslie Boulay

A catalogue record for this book is available from
the British Library.

ISBN 978-0-7112-8898-0

Ebook ISBN 978-0-7112-8899-7

10 9 8 7 6 5 4 3 2 1

Printed in China

Acknowledgements

Our sincerest thanks go first to the editors, without whom half this volume would never have seen the light of day: Elisa Bes, Solveig Boissay, Benjamin Bories, Aurélie Brémont, Lucie Brice, Julien Carbon, Gaëlle Coudurier-Abaléa, Romain Escarbassière, Gwenc'hlan Hamon, Sébastien Marlair, Audrey Morelle and Romain Paulino. We would also like to thank those of them who lent their support by proofreading the articles, to whom we must also add Cloé Dottor, Éric Flieller and Maxime Priou, along with those unnamed individuals of all ages who were kind enough to offer their opinions. This project was made possible through the help and support of two French-speaking associations that have been working for several years to promote Tolkien in France: Elbakin.net and Tolkiendil. It was through Tolkiendil that most of us met, and we have communicated and worked via the Tolkiendil forum.

This publication also represents the combined work of three illustrators to whom we owe a debt of gratitude: Leslie Boulay, Sandrine Gestin and Xavier Sanchez. We would like to thank too Éditions Le Pré aux Clercs, and in particular Isabelle Lerein and Carola Strang whose faith in us enabled us to make this ambitious idea a reality.

We should also like to give special thanks to Vincent Ferré and Daniel Lauzon for the part they have played in translating Tolkien's works into French and their efforts to make one of the greatest English writers better known on this side of the Channel.

Contents

Introduction

'In a hole in the ground, there lived a hobbit.' Who, today, does not recognise this sentence? Yet it seems unlikely that John Ronald Reuel Tolkien could have imagined that it would be so well known more than eighty years after it was written. It is a sentence that came to the author in a moment of sudden inspiration while sitting in front of a blank page, marking a student's work. Of course, Tolkien had no conscious idea of what a Hobbit might be or of the adventures that might befall him. The story advanced step by step as the hero, now known as Bilbo Baggins, travelled onwards along the Great East Road in the direction of the Lonely Mountain, beneath which lay the dragon Smaug.

A literary childhood
When Tolkien began writing about Bilbo's adventures, he was probably not expecting that his tale would be published. He was better known at that time for his university work on English language and literature than for his fiction, and had only published a few

poems in magazines and anthologies. However, his magical inspiration went back a long way. In one of his letters, Tolkien recalls the first story he wrote, when he was just seven years old – a tale that featured a large green dragon. It was his mother, Mabel Tolkien who first introduced him to English literature and who taught him the basics of Latin, French and German. Tolkien was particularly keen on the fairy tales of George MacDonald and Andrew Lang, and it was there that he first encountered the Arthurian and Scandinavian legends that would later come to fascinate him. At King Edward's School in Birmingham, he learned Greek and began learning Old English and Old Norse, the language once spoken in Scandinavia. This enabled him to read the heroic poem *Beowulf* and the Norse sagas. In 1911, just before leaving for Oxford University, he discovered the *Kalevala*, a collection of epic Finnish poetry compiled by Elias Lönnrot. Three years later, Tolkien acquired several works by the writer and medievalist William

Morris, including a translation of the *Völsunga Saga* and the fantasy novel *The House of the Wolfings*, of which he was particularly fond. He then decided to embark on his first large-scale narrative. He decided to take a story in the Kalevala – the tragedy of Kullervo, which he had found particularly striking – and to rewrite it in the style of Morris. However, Tolkien did not complete this project, abandoning the story before its conclusion, a practice that was commonplace for him. In fact, the story was not finally published until 2010, thanks to the efforts Verlyn Flieger,[1] an American university professor. However, Tolkien would re-use the idea of interspersing elements of poetry into narrative in his later stories, notably in *The Hobbit*. Graduating from Oxford in 1915, it was not long before he signed up to serve in the British army and to fight in the war then raging on the continent of Europe. He joined the Lancashire Fusiliers and arrived in France in June 1916. He was soon sent to the Front and served at the Battle of the Somme. After a few months, he developed trench fever, a disease transmitted by the lice which flourished in the makeshift bunkhouses, and he had to return to England to be hospitalised.

---

1 – 'The Story of Kullervo' *and* 'Essays on Kalevala', *Tolkien Studies: An Annual Scholarly Review vol. 7, West Virginia University Press, 2010, p. 211–278*

2 – *These appeared under the title* The Legend of Sigurd and Gudrún *in 2010.*

The first *Silmarillion* : a springboard for *The Hobbit*

During his convalescence in hospital at Great Haywood in Staffordshire, Tolkien began writing *The Book of Lost Tales*, an early version of the stories that would make up the core of his Legendarium. Very different in their form from his later work, they are light in nature, closer to Victorian and Edwardian fairy tales than to *The Lord of the Rings*. Not entirely satisfied with their form, Tolkien embarked on a series of rewrites from which eventually emerged the concept of *The First Age of Middle-earth* – a story punctuated by the wars between the Elves and Morgoth, the first Dark Lord. At the same time, he devoted a lot of energy to developing his Elvish languages, which he constantly reworked. These early prose works were soon followed by a series of major narrative poems focusing on the story of Túrin, the dragon slayer, and on that of the lovers Beren and Lúthien, whose love succeeds in triumphing over Morgoth's malice. The character of Lúthien, in particular, was directly inspired by Edith Bratt, whom the author married in 1916, after a long and complicated love story.

In the early 1930s, Tolkien interrupted his work on these poems to return to Scandinavian literature, notably the *Eddas* and the *Völsunga Saga*. He wrote two long alliterative poems on the legend of Sigurd who killed the dragon Fafnir, on the Valkyrie Brynhild, and on Gudrún, who in turn marries Sigurd and Attila the Hun.[2] After completing these, he began work on an epic poem about the

end of the reign of Arthur, but ultimately abandoned it and decided to return to his tales of Middle-earth.[3] At the same time, Tolkien continued with a range of academic work. In 1922, he published *A Middle English Vocabulary*, under the direction of Kenneth Sisam, who had been his tutor at Oxford. In 1925, with E.V. Gordon, one of his former students at Oxford, he published an edition of the medieval poem *Sir Gawain and the Green Knight*, heavily inspired by Celtic legends. There followed numerous lexicographic articles which sought to decipher various fragments of forgotten Anglo-Saxon mythology through certain English toponyms and archaic expressions, the original meaning of which had become obscured. The same year, he was elected Professor of Anglo-Saxon at Oxford.

The Hobbit: the novel that brought early success

Even with all this frantic activity, Tolkien still proved to be an attentive father to his four children. He enjoyed telling them stories of his own invention. Some of these he put down on paper, such as *Roverandom*, written in 1927 but not published until 1998. And his adventures of *Mr Bliss*, published in 2009, were illustrated by Tolkien himself. Around 1929 or 1930, he began telling his children a new tale, the hero of which was the Hobbit who had made his first appearance on that blank examination page.

From the start, Tolkien took inspiration from his tales of the First Age of Middle-earth to enrich the atmosphere of his narrative – a technique he had already employed, though to a lesser extent, in *Roverandom* and *The Father Christmas Letters*. These adventures were soon recorded on paper. The first version of the tale, which ends with the first chapter, is very different from the version we know now: most of the characters have very different names from those that appear in the published Hobbit: for example, Smaug is called Pryftan, Gandalf is Bladorthin and Thorin is Gandalf! After an extensive revision, the story then continues quite straightforwardly up to the death of Smaug and the Dwarves settling at Ravenhill. Tolkien then stops and starts the story again from the beginning, incorporating the changes made along the way, and including new adventures. In early 1933, Tolkien asked his friend C.S. Lewis to read the manuscript, and then one of his former students, Elaine Griffiths, who worked for the publishers George Allen & Unwin. Three years later, Griffiths spoke about *The Hobbit* to one of her friends, Susan Dagnall, who also read it and decided that it deserved to be published by Allen & Unwin. Tolkien polished the story during the summer of 1936. Stanley Unwin, the publisher, then asked his ten-year-old son Rayner to read it and review it for the modest sum of one shilling. The boy was enthusiastic

---

3 – *This appeared under the title* The Fall of Arthur *in 2013.*

and warmly recommended it for all children between five and nine years old.

Discussions with the publisher continued over the coming months, as Tolkien was extremely punctilious about the proofs of his book. He also wanted to include maps and illustrations, which would increase the printing costs. In fact, Unwin was convinced by Tolkien's talents as an illustrator and eventually persuaded him to produce the artwork for the book jacket. The book was finally published in September 1937. Reviews were very positive and the first print run of 1,500 copies sold out in just a few months. In the United States, the book was published in March 1938 by Houghton Mifflin and enjoyed the same success as it had had in the United Kingdom. By December 1937, Unwin had asked for a sequel to *The Hobbit*. Tolkien offered him an unfinished version of *The Silmarillion*, but this did not suit the publisher at all.

The second *Hobbit*: the Consecration of Tolkien

Tolkien therefore returned to work, but made little progress with his story. He rewrote the first chapter of what would become *The Lord of the Rings* several times, not really knowing whether the hero of this new narrative should be Bilbo or one of Bilbo's family. The crux of the plot also escaped him until he thought in greater detail about the magic ring that Bilbo had acquired and considered what its origin could be. Gradually, the story fell into place, although Tolkien surprised himself by including characters whose real identity and whose motivations were unknown to him, which often led to new developments in the plot. The story grew richer, grew longer and became increasingly dark. Tolkien went through several periods when he doubted whether he would reach the end of this new novel; in fact, this led him to write the short autobiographical tale *Leaf by Niggle* in 1942. Tolkien then decided to revise *The Hobbit* and connect it better to *The Lord of the Rings*; this second edition was published in 1951. His new novel was finally completed in 1949, but Tolkien held back its publication as he was trying to have it published alongside his as yet incomplete *Silmarillion*.

Realising that his efforts were fruitless, he accepted Unwin's offer to publish *The Lord of the Rings* in three volumes, which appeared in 1954 and 1955. The final volume was actually delayed by Tolkien, who provided large amounts of material for the appendices, notably regarding the Dwarves and the Quest of Erebor. Again, success was immediate, and the first print run soon sold out. The critics were never indifferent to the work: some were openly enthusiastic, some had mixed feelings, while others were downright hostile. In 1960, the American publishers Ace Books discovered that the book was not protected by copyright law in the US, as it did not fully comply with American regulations of the time. The pirate edition published by Ace Books was vigorously challenged by Tolkien, who asked readers to buy only the authorised editions. With his publisher's agreement,

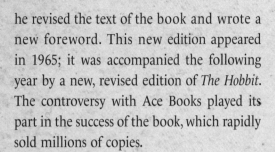

he revised the text of the book and wrote a new foreword. This new edition appeared in 1965; it was accompanied the following year by a new, revised edition of *The Hobbit*. The controversy with Ace Books played its part in the success of the book, which rapidly sold millions of copies.

After *The Lord of the Rings*

However, Tolkien had by no means abandoned his academic work. In 1945, he was elected Professor of English Language and Literature at Merton College, Oxford. He worked tirelessly on the publication of medieval English texts such as *Ancrene Wisse*, in collaboration with his colleague N.R. Ker. Tolkien was a perfectionist and several of his publications would only appear posthumously; these included translations of *Sir Gawain and the Green Knight*, *Pearl* and *Sir Orfeo*, published by his son Christopher in 1975. The same is true of *Finn and Hengest*, published in 1982 by Alan Bliss, one of his former students. At the same time, Tolkien returned to *The Silmarillion* and tackled several novels taking place in the First and Second Ages of his Legendarium. With the exception of *The Children of Húrin*, eventually published by Christopher Tolkien in 2007, the rest remained unfinished. In 1959, Tolkien retired from the university. He then devoted his time entirely to writing *The Silmarillion*, but went on to spend more and more time exploring the philosophical foundations of his work.

The success of *The Hobbit* and then *The Lord of the Rings* meant that Tolkien's reputation soon reached beyond the narrow confines of philological studies. The first translation of *The Hobbit* was published in Sweden in 1947, and *The Lord of the Rings* appeared in a Dutch version in 1956-57. New impetus to the translation effort was given by Tolkien himself who in 1967 wrote *A Guide to the Names in the Lord of the Rings* to give practical help and guidance to translators, although the first French edition, which finally appeared in 1969 (as *Bilbo le Hobbit*) retained the original place-names. By 2023, *The Hobbit* had been translated into more than sixty languages, the most recent including editions in Silesian, Ukrainian, Korean, Breton and Mongolian, although perhaps the translation which might have pleased the author most was that into his beloved Icelandic, in 1978. His death in Bournemouth on 2 September 1973, meant he did not live to see the only translation so far into an extinct language, the Latin edition published in 2012 (as *Hobbitus ille*). *The Lord of the Rings* has a handful fewer translations than *The Hobbit*, but by 2023 had reached just short of 60 translations, including most recently into Azerbaijani, Bengali, Uzbek and Afrikaans. After his father's death, Christopher Tolkien gave up his post as a lecturer at New College, Oxford to devote his time to publishing Tolkien's yet unpublished writings. His adaptation of *The Silmarillion* appeared in 1977, soon

followed by *Unfinished Tales* in 1980. Interestingly, this work contains the final version of 'The Quest of Erebor,' which relates the journey of Thorin and Company from the viewpoint of Gandalf. From 1983 onwards, Christopher Tolkien decided to publish all his father's manuscripts about Middle-earth, except for those on *The Hobbit*. This major work, entitled *The History of Middle-earth*, consists of twelve volumes, the final volume not having been published until 1996. In 1988, the editor and scholar Douglas Anderson published *The Annotated Hobbit*; his annotations to Tolkien's text tell the story of the publication and revisions of *The Hobbit*. An appendix, added in 2002, also contains a longer version of 'The Quest of Erebor.' Following this, in 2007 John Rateliff, an author of role-playing games and a Tolkien expert, published drafts of *The Hobbit* in his book *The History of the Hobbit*. And in 2011, *The Art of The Hobbit by J.R.R. Tolkien*, by Wayne Hammond and Christina Scull, appeared; this includes all the illustrations Tolkien had produced for his first novel.

Adapting *The Hobbit* — a long-established story

In 1953, a first stage adaptation of *The Hobbit* was performed at St Margaret's School in Edinburgh. As early as 1957, Tolkien received expressions of interest in a film adaptation of *The Lord of the Rings*, but after reading the proposed script, Tolkien rejected this project, appalled by the changes to the plot and to the nature of his characters. In the 1960s, The Beatles approached Tolkien with a view to producing their own adaptation of the story, but Tolkien was opposed to this and nipped the project in the bud. However, in 1962, financial necessity drove the author to sell the rights to adapt *The Hobbit* and *The Lord of the Rings* to the producer Bill Snyder. After several failures with the studios, Snyder produced a twelve-minute short that had little to do with the original story, with the sole aim of reselling the adaptation rights at a good price. They were eventually bought by the producer Saul Zaentz, who brought the filmmaker John Boorman on board to direct the first film adaptation of *The Lord of the Rings*, but the project was never completed.

However, *The Hobbit* was adapted for other media: in 1967, a musical adaptation of *The Hobbit* written by Humphrey Carpenter, Tolkien's future biographer, was performed at New College School in Oxford; Tolkien himself attended the last performance. The following year, Tolkien approved a stage adaptation by Patricia Gray; further adaptations followed in 1990 and in 1994. In 1968, a first radio adaptation was broadcast on BBC Radio 4. This was followed by two more versions for radio, in German (1980) and in Czech (1996); also, several audiocassette recordings were produced in the United States. In 1975, a first board game – The Battle of Five Armies – was created by Larry Smith; this paved the way for numerous board and card games. The first computer game – *The Hobbit* – was developed by Beam

Software in 1982. This, too, was the first in a long line of games. Finally, a comic strip in three volumes, illustrated by David Wenzel, was published in 1989 by Eclipse Comics. It was not until 1977 that Arthur Rankin and Jules Bass made a cartoon adaptation of *The Hobbit* for the NBC network; this was quite well received by the critics, despite the graphics deviating significantly from what Tolkien described. It was followed by two cartoon adaptations of *The Lord of the Rings* which met with mixed success. In 1979, the BBC broadcast a television adaptation of *The Hobbit* with the action narrated by several narrators. In the USSR a television adaptation was produced by the Leningrad TV-5 channel in 1985, infringing copyright. It was not until 1995 that Peter Jackson thought about adapting Tolkien's two novels for the cinema. The first project, including a first film on *The Hobbit* and two for *The Lord of the Rings*, failed due to distribution rights issues. It would take several years to convince a producer to embark on such a costly project. Robert Shaye, founder of New Line Cinema, was finally persuaded, but asked that *The Lord of the Rings* be adapted into three films. Filming began in October 1999 in New Zealand. The first film was released in December 2001 and the other two followed, each a year apart. They enjoyed enormous commercial success and revived interest in Tolkien worldwide. By 2006, the studios were planning to adapt *The Hobbit* as two films. Financial disputes led to considerable delay for the project, and filming only began in March 2011. In July 2012, Jackson announced that he would in fact make three films. The first part was finally released in December 2012 and the other two parts followed, at one-year intervals.

In 2022, Amazon Studios and New Line Cinema released *Rings of Power*, an eight-part television series for Netflix covering the major events of the Second Age, including the rise of Sauron, the forging of the Rings of Power and the drowning of Númenor. *The War of the Rohirrim*, an animated film directed by Kenji Kamiyama, with a 2024 release, covers the war of the Rohan against the Dunlendings, some 200 years before the events of *Lord of the Rings*, including the legendary defence by Helm Hammerhand of the fortress that later took his name as Helm's Deep.

Why an encyclopaedia of *The Hobbit?*

Today, Tolkien's work is enjoying unprecedented popularity, but is still plagued by a double problem. Paradoxically, the enormous success of *The Hobbit* and *The Lord of the Rings* often overshadows Tolkien's other works. But even translated, Tolkien's works do not necessarily contain an accessible synthesis of a character or an event. Added to this, there is the distorted view that can be created by Peter Jackson's films, which often deviate from Tolkien's plot. We therefore hope that our knowledge of Tolkien's work, supported by long involvement in the Tolkienian media community, may be useful to all those who wish to know more about the universe

invented by Tolkien. It is to you, the reader of this encyclopaedia, that we wish to offer the benefit of our extensive reading, research and ongoing discoveries of the immense potential offered by the simplest of Tolkien's heroic novels: *The Hobbit*.

This encyclopaedia has been designed to act as a tool, giving you easy access to information scattered throughout Tolkien's Legendarium. You will find the characters and peoples who play a part, directly and indirectly, in Bilbo Baggins' adventure, as Tolkien conceived it. We also explore the languages and writing systems for which the world of Middle-earth is famous. This book also gives an insight into the main objects that play a part in the Hobbits' adventure. Described too are the principal events that enable us to place the Quest of Erebor in the context of the Third Age of Middle-earth. Finally, we look at some of Tolkien's sources of inspiration drawn from medieval texts or borrowed from modern writers. We hope that this new perspective, this window on to fantasy, will help you to gain an even greater appreciation of the rich imagination that J.R.R. Tolkien demonstrated so abundantly.

Chronology

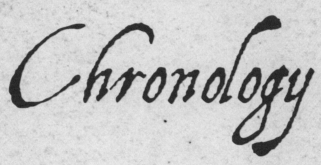

Public life	Year	Writings
Born in Bloemfontein, in the Orange Free State, now South Africa	1892	
Arrives in Birmingham, England	1895	
Meets Edith Bratt, who will become his wife	1905	
Begins his studies at Oxford	1911	
	1914	*The Story of Kullervo*
Marries Edith; serves at the Battle of the Somme	1916	
Birth of John, his first son	1917	*The Book of Lost Tales*
Appointed lecturer at the University of Leeds; birth of Michael, his second son	1920	
Elected Professor of English Language at Leeds; birth of Christopher, his third son	1924	
Elected Professor of Anglo-Saxon at Oxford University	1925	*The Children of Húrin; Roverandom*
Birth of his daughter Priscilla	1929	
	c. 1930	*The Hobbit*; first texts of *The Silmarillion*
Instrumental in the reform of the English Language and Literature programme at Oxford	1931	*The Legend of Sigurd and Gudrún; Mythopoeia; The Lay of Leithian*

	1934	*The Fall of Arthur*
	1936	*Beowulf: the Monsters and the Critics*
	1937	Publication of *The Hobbit*; start of *The Lord of the Rings*; *The Quenta Silmarillion*; *Farmer Giles of Ham*
	1939	*On Fairy-stories*; *Leaf by Niggle*
	1944	*The Notion Club Papers*
Elected Professor of English Language and Literature at Oxford	1945	
	1949	Completion of *The Lord of the Rings*
	1951	Start of the revision of the texts of *The Silmarillion*
Awarded honorary degrees by the University of Liège and the National University of Ireland	1954	Publication of *The Fellowship of the Ring* and *The Two Towers*
	1955	Publication of *The Return of the King*; lecture entitled *English and Welsh*
Retires from Oxford University	1959	
	1962	*The Adventures of Tom Bombadil*
	1964	*Smith of Wootton Major*
	1967	*The Road Goes Ever On*
Death of Edith	1971	
Appointed doctor *honoris causa* by the University of Oxford; appointed Commander of the Order of the British Empire (CBE) by Queen Elizabeth II	1972	
Death of J.R.R. Tolkien in Bournemouth	1973	
Posthumous publications by his son Christopher	from 1977	

List of abbreviations

To facilitate reading, abbreviations have been kept to a strict minimum.
Their meanings are found below.

- add.: addendum
- app.: appendix
- c.: circa
- ch.: chapter, chapters
- dir.: under the direction of
- ed.: edition
- F.A.: First Age of Middle-earth
- Fth.A.: Fourth Age of Middle-earth
- ill.: illustration
- no, nos: number, numbers
- p.: page, pages
- publ.: publisher
- S.A.: Second Age of Middle-earth
- v.: verse
- T.A.: Third Age of Middle-earth
- vol.: volume

The works of J.R.R. Tolkien, and those edited and published by his son Christopher, are often divided into books and chapters. Thus, 'The Lord of the Rings, V, 1' refers to the first chapter, entitled 'Minas Tirith', of the fifth book of this novel.

Characters

Azog and Bolg

'Nár turned the head and saw branded on the brow in Dwarf-runes [...] the name AZOG. That name was branded in his heart and in the hearts of all the Dwarves afterwards.

(The Lord of the Rings, app. A, III).

Azog and his son Bolg are important leaders of the Orcs of the Misty Mountains, and their history is closely linked to that of the Dwarves of the line of Durin, the founders of the underground kingdom of Moria. Towards the middle of the Third Age, when Moria is a powerful and prosperous kingdom, Sauron's power is once again felt. At this time, the Dwarves are digging deeply and eagerly under Caradhras and awake a Balrog that had been hidden deep within the mountains since the fall of Morgoth. The Balrog kills King Durin, and the Dwarf people are decimated or flee. Most of those who escape flee north and Thráin I, Durin's heir, comes to Erebor, where he finds the Arkenstone and becomes the first King under the Mountain. Durin's folk eventually settle permanently under the Lonely Mountain in the reign of Thrór. There they prosper for many years, their numbers swelling with the arrival of the Dwarves from the Grey Mountains. Gradually, word of Erebor's riches reaches the dragons who live on the Withered Heath. The most powerful of them, Smaug the Golden, comes down from the north and descends upon the Lonely Mountain. He ravages the Dwarves' kingdom, amassing gold and riches in the heart of the mountain and settles there. Many Dwarves escape during the Sack of Erebor, including King Thrór, his son Thráin II and his grandson Thorin II Oakenshield. Many years later, Thrór gives his son the last of his treasure, one of the Seven Dwarven Rings, and sets off alone with his faithful servant Nár.

They leave Dunland, where they are living at the time, and head north, travelling as far as Azanulbizar in Dimrill Dale. As they approach Moria, they find the gate open. Nár begs the king to be wary, but Thrór enters all the same, and disappears. Some days later, the Orcs who had taken over Moria throw

Thrór's decapitated body onto the steps at the gate. With a hot iron, the leader of the Orcs himself brands his name on Thrór's forehead: AZOG. He throws Nár a purse of coins to pay him for acting as messenger, and sends him back to his people with these words: 'If beggars will not wait at the door, but sneak in to try thieving, that is what we do to them.'

The murder of Thrór leads to the Great War between the Dwarves and the Orcs. Thráin rallies his family and allies and, one by one,

> *The murder of Thrór leads to the Great War between the Dwarves and the Orcs.*

attacks all the Orc strongholds in the Misty Mountains. The Dwarves are victorious time after time, the fire of vengeance burning within them. They track Azog to Moria. There, below the East Gate, the bloody battle of Azanulbizar is waged. It is during this battle that Thorin earns his nickname of Oakenshield when, needing to replace his broken shield, he takes an oak branch and uses it as a club and shield. Azog kills Náin, King of the Dwarves of the Iron Hills, but his son, Dáin II Ironfoot kills Azog by cutting off his head. The Dwarves take the purse that Azog had thrown to Nár and stuff

it between his teeth, and then stick his head on a pike in revenge.

Many years later Bolg, Azog's son, becomes leader of the Orcs of the Misty Mountains, after the death of the Great Goblin, killed by Gandalf during the crossing of the mountains with Thorin and Company. Having learnt of Smaug's death, Bolg gathers a powerful army to seize his gold. He marches on Erebor, still harbouring hatred for the Dwarves since the Battle of Azanulbizar. It is on the slopes of the Lonely Mountain that the Battle of the Five Armies takes place, pitting Orcs and Wargs against the Elves of Mirkwood, the Men of the Long Lake and the Dwarves of the Iron Hills. During the battle, Thorin is mortally wounded, and his nephews, Kili and Fili, are killed protecting him. But Beorn, who, assuming the form of a bear, has come from the Vales of Anduin to take part in the battle, prevents the Orcs from finishing off Thorin. Enraged, he then returns to the battle and crushes Bolg, thus ensuring victory for the Free Peoples.

Baggins Family

'The Bagginses had lived in the neighbourhood of The Hill for time out of mind, and people considered them very respectable [...] because they never had any adventures or did anything unexpected.' *(The Hobbit, Ch. 1)*

The Bagginses, who are related to the Tooks and the Brandybucks, are one of the most respected families in The Shire. Though not as rich as their Took cousins, the Bagginses have the advantage of being more predictable. With them, there were no adventures, no surprises. But all this changed when the respectable Bungo Baggins married Belladonna, the daughter of the Old Took. Bungo built the luxurious smial of Bag End, under Hobbiton Hill, for his wife. The hole was then left to their son, Bilbo Baggins, who proved himself worthy of his Took ancestry by setting off in 2941 T.A. on an adventure with the Wizard Gandalf and the Company of Thorin Oakenshield to reclaim the treasure stolen by the dragon Smaug. On his journey, Bilbo encounters many creatures, from Trolls to Goblins, even including the strange creature Gollum, from whom he steals the One Ring, which has the power to make anyone who puts it on their finger invisible.

In 2980 T.A., Bilbo adopts his favourite young cousin Frodo Baggins, who has been orphaned at the age of twelve. His father, Drogo Baggins, was a distant cousin of Bilbo and, despite his entirely respectable and ordinary ancestry, was a keen sailor. One day, while sailing on the Brandywine river, he drowned. So what was an extraordinary pastime for a Hobbit ended up costing Drogo his life and that of his wife, Primula Brandybuck, too.

The adoption of the young Frodo does not go down well with Bilbo's closest cousin, Otho Sackville-Baggins, who should have succeeded him at Bag End. By marrying Lobelia Bracegirdle, whose family cultivated pipe-weed, Otho has become a major landowner in the South Farthing. However, his own wealth is not enough for him, and his keenest desire is to own Bag End. Consequently, during the Quest of Erebor, Otho and Lobelia try to acquire the luxurious smial when it is put up for auction.

The return of Bilbo, fit and well, marks the end of their aspirations, which are dashed once and for all when Bilbo makes Frodo his heir.

In 3001 T.A., Bilbo leaves the Shire again to retire to Rivendell and leaves all his possessions to Frodo, including the Ring. When Gandalf tells Frodo of his suspicions about the Ring, in 3018 T.A., he too leaves the Shire. Before he goes, he sells Bag End to Lobelia, now a widow, who buys it at a good price for her son Lotho. Frodo carries the Ring from the Shire to Mordor, where it is finally destroyed. When they return to the Shire, Frodo, Sam Gamgee, Meriadoc ('Merry') Brandybuck and Peregrin ('Pippin') Took find their country ravaged by Saruman, who uses Lotho Sackville-Baggins to satisfy his thirst for vengeance and then has him murdered when he becomes a nuisance. After dealing with Saruman, the Hobbits restore order in the Shire and free Lobelia from his dungeons. She then returns to Bag End with Frodo, thus putting to an end the enmity that had long existed between them.

Frodo becomes deputy mayor of Michel Delving, but the wounds he received during the course of his journey do not heal and he becomes ill. He finally decides to leave the Shire and Middle-earth together with Bilbo, who sets sail for the Undying Lands in 3021 T.A. with Gandalf and the Elves Elrond and Galadriel. The story of Bilbo and Frodo Baggins is passed down to future generations via *The Red Book* in which Bilbo, then Frodo, have recorded their adventures.

Balin

'If Balin noticed that Mr Baggins' waistcoat was more extensive (and had real gold buttons), Bilbo also noticed that Balin's beard was several inches longer, and his jewelled belt was of great magnificence. (The Hobbit, Ch. 19).

Balin is a Dwarf of the Line of Durin and takes part in the Quest of Erebor with Thorin Oakenshield. He is the eldest of the company of Dwarves after Thorin, and one of the few to have known the Lonely Mountain before the arrival of Smaug the dragon.

Balin is the second Dwarf to knock on Bilbo Baggins' door for the surprise party being organized in Bag End by the wizard Gandalf. He has a long, white beard and a scarlet hood. During the Quest, he befriends the Hobbit and is the only one to dare accompany him into the secret tunnel of Erebor. Later, he volunteers to rescue Bilbo from the darkness of the treasure chamber, then shows the way to the guard post at Ravenhill. It is there that Roäc, son of Carc, leader of the great ravens of the Mountain, recognizes him and greets him, along with Thorin. His role in the Company is that of watchman and wise counsellor.

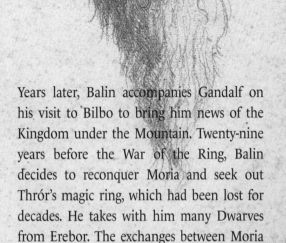

Years later, Balin accompanies Gandalf on his visit to Bilbo to bring him news of the Kingdom under the Mountain. Twenty-nine years before the War of the Ring, Balin decides to reconquer Moria and seek out Thrór's magic ring, which had been lost for decades. He takes with him many Dwarves from Erebor. The exchanges between Moria

and Erebor last only a short time and the story of this quest is revealed years later in the Book of Mazarbul. After five years spent bringing the ancient Durin kingdom under the Misty Mountains back to life, exploiting the mithril lodes and endeavouring to restore the chambers abandoned since the awakening of a Balrog in the depths, the Dwarven colony is wiped out by Orcs. On 10 November 2994 T.A., Balin is killed by an Orc arrow in Dimrill Dale, the same valley where his father perished 195 years earlier. Balin, son of Fundin, king of Moria, is then buried in a white stone tomb in the Chamber of Records. Balin is a character who soon becomes familiar: he is one of the first to arrive at Bilbo's house, and then returns with Gandalf to see him. He is also mentioned at the Council of Elrond, when Glóin recounts his quest to Moria and the lack of recent news. With his brother Dwalin, he is also a travelling companion of Thráin II on his journey to Erebor and the one who brings the news of Thráin's disappearance to Thorin. Balin's life is a succession of adventures: as a seven-year old, he survives the Sack of Erebor; as a young man, at the age of thirty-six, he experiences the War of the Dwarves and Orcs; at seventy-eight, he accompanies Thráin on his journey to see Erebor once again. Forty-eight years then go by and his thirst for adventure has not been quenched, so he leads a new quest to retake the ancient kingdom of Khazad-dûm and settle there. Thirty years later, it is at his tomb in the Mazarbul Chamber that Gandalf has the revelation that Moria has been invaded by Orcs and by Durin's Bane.

Often accompanied by his brother Dwalin, Balin is a Dwarf of high lineage who remains loyal to the House of Durin, always in the vanguard when it comes to restoring the past glory of his people. Over the 230 years of his life, he experiences the Kingdom under the Mountain in Erebor, the Wandering Exile to Dunland, the war against the Orcs below the Misty Mountains, the return to Dunland before settling in the Blue Mountains, the adventures of Thráin's last journey to the wooded depths of Mirkwood, the long journey made by Thorin and Company from Eriador to Erebor and, finally, the last journey to Moria. He rubs shoulders with four kings of the Durin Line, from Thrór to Dáin II. Unlike most of the Dwarves of Thorin and Company, Balin's name does not come from the *Völuspá*, part of the *Poetic Edda*; various theories have been put forward to explain where Tolkien may have drawn it from.

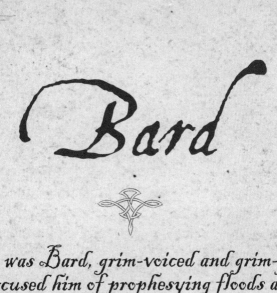

Bard

'Their captain was Bard, grim-voiced and grim-faced, whose friends had accused him of prophesying floods and poisoned fish, though they knew his worth and courage.' (The Hobbit, Ch. 14).

In 2941 T.A., when the dragon Smaug attacks Lake-town, Bard is the first to sound the alarm. He is captain of a company of archers who are the last to hold out against the creature as it burns down the town. Unfortunately, his companions leave the tall, black-haired warrior alone amid the flames. It is then that an old thrush comes to him and alights on him. A descendant of Girion, the last lord of Dale, Bard realizes that he can understand the bird's language. It reveals to him that there is a weak point in Smaug's armour under his left armpit, which had been spotted by Bilbo Baggins. Bard draws back his bow and with his final arrow – the famous Black Arrow, passed down to him by his ancestors and said to have been made in the forges of the Lonely Mountain – pierces the side of the dragon, who falls dead over the ruins of Lake-town.

With Smaug vanquished, the townspeople give vent to their anger towards the Master, who had fled the town instead of defending it, and are sad to see that Bard is gone. But suddenly Bard emerges from the water into which he had plunged when the dragon fell. The townspeople applaud him and claim him as their king, but he remains in the service of the Master. Faced with a town in ruins and its survivors in need, the hero seeks help from the King of the Woodland Elves, Thranduil, who arrives five days after the dragon's death. With the treasure of Erebor now released from its dragon guardian, Bard and Thranduil set off with their troops to the mountain to take possession of it. However, they find Thorin and Company are there and alive. Bard pleads his case with Thorin Oakenshield, but the latter refuses to hand anything over. Thus begins the siege of Men and Elves around the mountain. Bilbo, weary of the siege, gives the Arkenstone to Bard without Thorin's knowledge, thus enabling him to offer an exchange for part of

the treasure. The course of the conflict then shifts with the arrival of the Orcs and Wargs; the Battle of the Five Armies begins as the Dwarves of Dáin Ironfoot, who had come to support Thorin, join forces with the Men and Elves against their common enemies. After the battle and Thorin's death, Bard places the Arkenstone in Thorin's tomb. With the stone returned to its people, Dáin honours the agreement made by Thorin and entrusts a fourteenth part of the treasure to Bard, who divides it between the Master of Lake-town, for the reconstruction of the town, and the Elf King, to whom he gives the Emeralds of Girion and two chests of gold and silver. In 2944 T.A., Bard rebuilds Dale and becomes its king. Its people are known as Bardings and enjoy good relations with the neighbouring Dwarves and Elves. Whenhe dies, thirty-three years later, he is succeeded by his son Bain.

In his first drafts, Tolkien had planned that Smaug would be killed by Bilbo, but then he created Bard, a character who at first seems negative and sinister, then suspicious and severe, though honest and courageous. Tolkien drew inspiration for the character from Wiglaf in *Beowulf*. They have much in common: they only appear late in the story and, although seemingly of modest status, are of royal descent and the last defenders against the dragon when all their companions have fled. Both also play their part in a dragon's death before becoming king.

Beorn

'If you must know more, his name is Beorn. He is very strong, and he is a skin-changer.' (The Hobbit, Ch. 7).

After the members of the Quest of Erebor leave the Misty Mountains, Gandalf leads them to the place where Beorn lives. The Wizard takes care to warn them that Beorn can be irritable and dangerous, as well as mysterious in nature. In fact, Beorn is a Man known to be a skin-changer: he is able to transform himself into a bear. In his human form, Beorn is very tall, a giant as far as the Hobbit Bilbo Baggins is concerned, and powerfully muscular, with a thick black beard. He retains his tall stature when he is in bear form.

Beorn lives alone in a low, long house somewhere in the Vales of Anduin, between the Misty Mountains and Mirkwood, near to the stony eyot of Carrock. Not only did he give the island rock its name, he also carved steps there to make it easier to meet with the local bears when transformed into bear form. Beorn raises cattle and horses. He also owns many dogs and talks with them, and they serve him at table. Gandalf informs the Dwarves that Beorn is not a meat eater and feeds almost exclusively on cream and honey. To avoid provoking the hostility of this moody skin-changer, Gandalf introduces himself as a close friend of the Wizard Radagast, with whom Beorn is on good terms. Gandalf also ensures that Thorin and Company arrive only in pairs, to avoid troubling Beorn, who rarely invites anyone to his home. Although somewhat surprised by these constant arrivals, Beorn eventually welcomes them wholeheartedly when he learns that they have just crossed the Misty Mountains and escaped the Orcs, who are Beorn's sworn enemies. He offers them not only room and board, but also provisions and valuable advice. He lends them ponies for the rest of their journey. Beorn later intervenes in the Battle of the Five Armies: when the Orcs seems about to claim victory, he bursts on to the battlefield in bear form. Striking terror among the Orcs, he brings down their leader, Borg, before taking the wounded Thorin Oakenshield to safety. After this battle, Beorn becomes ruler of the entire

region between the mountains and the forest; the people who come to populate this land become known as Beornings. They defend the region from the Orcs and the Wargs and allow travellers to cross the ford of Carrock on payment of a toll. Beorn dies before the region is again subjected to conflict in the War of the Ring. His son Grimbeorn takes over from him.

Beorn's character is strongly Scandinavian in inspiration. He displays many of the characteristics of the Berserkers, the warriors of Scandinavian sagas known for their murderous frenzy. The word *beorn* means 'warrior' in Old English but derives from a Germanic term meaning 'bear', a meaning retained in the Norse word *björn*. Beorn also owes much to two characters whose names also reference bears: Beowulf and Bödvar Bjarki, and to the latter's family. Bödvar Bjarki – whose name means 'little bear' – appears in the *Saga of Hrólf Kraki*; when asleep he is able to produce a double in the form of a bear that is formidable in battle, thus presenting a similarity with Beorn's intervention in the Battle of the Five Armies. Beorn is also inspired by other members of Bödvar Bjarki's family: like his brother Elk-Fródi, he is a loner and, like his other brother Thórir, he ends up leading a people that carry his name.

The hero of the poem *Beowulf* has a name that means 'bee wolf', in other words, 'bear'. The connection between Beorn and Beowulf is further strengthened by one of the illustrations Tolkien created for *The Hobbit*: Beorn's Hall. It shows a long, wooden hall with a central nave containing a hearth and side aisles bounded by beams, following the traditional model of the Germanic hall and very similar to the description of King Hrothgar's hall in *Beowulf*.

Beorn is, in fact, a Man known to be a skin-changer: he is able to transform himself into a bear.

Bilbo Baggins

'Bilbo, their only son, although he looked and behaved exactly like a second edition of his solid and comfortable father, got something a bit queer in his makeup from the Took side, something that only waited for a chance to come out.' (The Hobbit, Ch. 1).

Born in 2890 T.A, Bilbo Baggins is the son of Bungo Baggins and Belladonna Took. While the Bagginses had always been a respected family with an uneventful history, the same could not be said of the Tooks. For Hobbits, their behaviour was so reckless that they were suspected of having a fairy among their ancestors. Bilbo Baggins appeared to have inherited the home-loving temperament of his father and led a peaceful life in the upmarket smial (or Hobbit-hole) of Bag End, built years ago by Bungo Baggins for his wife. Nothing out of the ordinary ever happened in Bilbo's life. Like any Hobbit, he enjoyed good food and good quality pipe-weed. Each day went by like the next, without anything unusual disturbing the tranquillity of this respectable Hobbit, until he reached the age of fifty-one, when the Wizard Gandalf determined otherwise.

In the year 2941 of the Third Age, Gandalf comes to Bilbo with a strange proposal: he is looking for a burglar to join the Company of Thorin Oakenshield who, with twelve Dwarven companions, is seeking to recover the treasure from the Kingdom of Erebor and take revenge on Smaug, the dragon who drove his family out. Reluctant at first, Bilbo finally agrees and sets off for the Wilderland with the Wizard and the Dwarves. Scarcely have they left the Shire when Bilbo receives his first mission: to discover the origin of a light shining not far from the Company's encampment. He sees three Trolls sitting around a campfire and tries to pick their pockets, but is caught, and his companions are obliged to come to his rescue. Once freed by Gandalf, the Company explores the Trolls' hideout, where they discover some fine booty, including valuable Elven swords, one of which is small enough to suit Bilbo. After resting in Rivendell, the home of Elrond, Thorin's Company set out to cross the Misty Mountains, where they are captured by Goblins. Brought before the Great Goblin, they are saved by Gandalf, who guides them to the exit. As they flee, Bilbo is knocked unconscious and is left behind. When he awakes, he finds himself alone in the tunnel and, while groping in the darkness, discovers a ring. Searching for a way out, he encounters a small, slimy creature – Gollum – and competes with him in a riddle contest. After a dubious victory, Bilbo flees the furious Gollum. Placing the ring on his finger, he realizes that it has the power to make its wearer invisible, enabling him to follow Gollum to the exit and to find his companions.

Bilbo faces many more dangers before the Company reaches the densely wooded Forest of Great Fear, where Gandalf leaves them in order to attend to other business. It is in the darkness of the forest, when the Company is once again scattered, that Bilbo demonstrates the true extent of his abilities. Alone, face to face with a giant spider, Bilbo slays the foul creature with his sword, to which he then gives the name Sting. Having put the rest of the spiders to flight, he frees his companions, now only twelve in number. Thorin has been captured by the Woodland Elves and the same fate soon befalls them. Taking advantage of the commotion, Bilbo slips the ring on his finger and disappears. Invisible to the Elves, he uses his advantage to study the underground palace, taking note of the few entrances and exits, and eventually works out a plan. While the guards are drinking heavily during the king's banquet, Bilbo steals their keys and frees his companions from their jail and from the Elf Kingdom.

After a short rest at Lake-town, the Company reach the Lonely Mountain, where Bilbo, Fili and Kili eventually find a hidden path leading them to the secret door they were seeking. On Durin's Day, when moonlight and sunlight combine, Bilbo discovers how to open the door and enters the dragon's lair for the first time, stealing a cup from him. But Smaug realizes that the cup has been stolen and remains on guard, trying to trap Bilbo on his second visit. While conversing with the dragon, Bilbo notices a weak point in the creature's scaly armour, under his left armpit. After Bilbo emerges from the mountain, the dragon leaves Erebor and sets off to attack Lake-town, where he is killed by Bard. The Dwarves are then free to take back their treasure and their home. Among the treasure, Bilbo finds the Arkenstone, the jewel that Thorin so ardently desired, but he says nothing to him about it.

The mountain is soon besieged by Men and Elves claiming their share of the booty. When he realizes that it will be impossible to reason with Thorin, Bilbo meets those laying siege and offers them the Arkenstone to assist in their negotiations with the Dwarves. Dismissed by Thorin, who sees him as a traitor, Bilbo joins the Men and Elves, who are now accompanied by Gandalf. At the same time, Thorin's cousin, Dáin Ironfoot, arrives on the scene with his army. War is inevitable when the Orcs and Wargs descend on the mountainside. Men, Elves and Dwarves then join forces to confront the enemy: this is the Battle of the Five Armies. Bilbo joins the ranks of the Elves, but is knocked unconscious by a stone and does not take part in the fighting. He regains consciousness in time to hear Thorin, who is mortally wounded, apologize and bid him farewell.

Bilbo returns to his normal life and decides to tell the story of his adventures in what will become *The Red Book of Westmarch*. After his return, he is seen in a very different light, especially as he continues to stay in touch with the Elves and Dwarves. In 2980 T.A., his life takes another new turn when he adopts his young cousin (or nephew), Frodo Baggins, after Frodo's parents have drowned. He makes him his heir and, when he leaves the Shire in 3001 T.A. to take to the road again, he leaves all his possessions to Frodo, including his ring. After returning to the Lonely Mountain, Bilbo settles in Rivendell and remains there throughout the events of the War of the Ring. In 3018 T.A., the Council of Elrond takes place and Bilbo meets up again with Frodo, who has brought the ring to Rivendell. The Council recognizes this ring to be the One Ring forged by Sauron in the depths of Mount Doom, and its fate is sealed – it must be destroyed in the place it was created. Frodo volunteers to carry the Ring to Mordor, and Bilbo gives him his sword, Sting, along with his mithril chain mail shirt, a gift from Thorin. When Frodo returns, in 3019 T.A., Bilbo gives him his book, and Frodo decides to add his own story to it before leaving it to his faithful companion, Samwise Gamgee. Then, in 3021 T.A., Bilbo embarks on a final journey, along with Frodo, as they have been granted the honour of taking part in the last ride of the Guardians of the Ring and to live among the Elves on the other side of the Sea. The name Baggins probably comes from the English word 'bagging', which is a snack eaten between meals carried by workmen in a bag. The first name Bilbo was probably inspired by contemporary characters such as Pombo in Lord Dunsany's *The Injudicious Prayers of Pombo the Idolater* (1912), and Gorbo, one of E.A. Wyke-Smith's Snergs. Tolkien indeed acknowledges Snergs as 'a race of people only slightly taller than the average table but broad in the shoulders and of great strength,' (*The Annotated Hobbit*, p. 21) as a source of inspiration for his Hobbits and is known to have had a particular affection for *The Marvellous Land of Snergs* (1927).

Dismissed by Thorin, who sees him as a traitor, Bilbo joins the Men and Elves, now accompanied by Gandalf.

We can also see a resemblance between Bilbo and Mole from Kenneth Grahame's novel *The Wind in the Willows*. Mole is a very busy character who keeps his burrow in good order, just as Bilbo takes pride in his Hobbit hole.

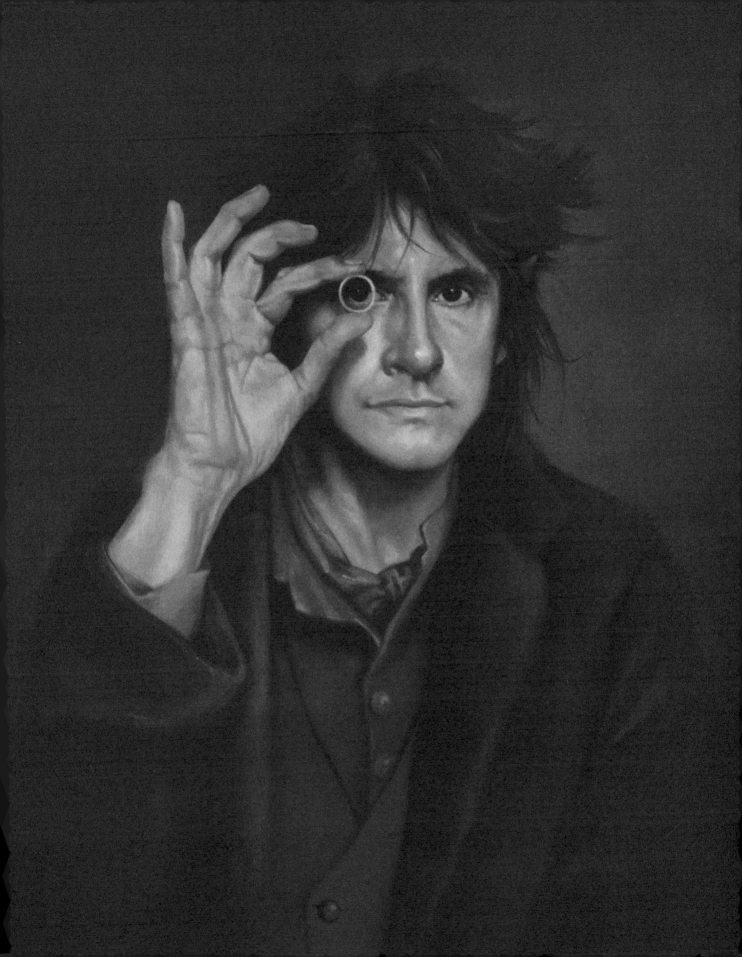

Bilbo Baggins

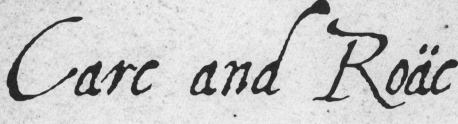

Carc and Roäc

He was an aged raven of great size. He alighted stiffly on the ground before them, slowly flapped his wings, and bobbed towards Thorin. (The Hobbit, Ch. 15).

After fleeing the Lonely Mountain, from where the dragon Smaug had taken flight to destroy Lake-town, Thorin and Company, accompanied by Bilbo Baggins, take shelter on Ravenhill. The hill was called this because a pair of ravens from an ancient race of crows, Carc and his wife, known for their wisdom, had taken up residence there long ago. The Dwarves and the Hobbit see an unusually large number of

Old Roäc was the leader of the great ravens of the Lonely Mountain.

birds flying above them and the old thrush, who had previously helped Bilbo enter the mountain, seeks out a raven and brings him to them. This large raven is visibly aged, almost blind, with a balding head, and can barely fly. Gifted with the power of speech, he introduces himself to Thorin Oakenshield and Balin as Roäc, son of the dead Carc. Born in 2788 in the Third Age, old Roäc is 153 years old at the time of the Quest of Erebor, and is the leader of the great ravens of the Lonely Mountain. Though few in number now, they still remember Thrór, the King under the Mountain and grandfather of Thorin, as a great friendship had existed between the Dwarves and the Ravens in his time. Roäc has news, first announcing the death of Smaug to Thorin – information he received from the thrush who had witnessed the event. He also tells him of the imminent arrival in Erebor of the Woodland Elves and of the Lakemen, all of them in pursuit of a share of the treasure no longer guarded by the dragon. Roäc, in his wisdom, also offers Thorin advice, the venerable bird being manifestly keen to promote as much peace as possible among the Dwarves and other peoples of the region. Thorin then tells him to send some

of his ravens to seek help from Thorin's relatives and, in particular, to ask Dáin Ironfoot and his troops to come as quickly as they can, in view of the coming confrontation. Roäc fulfils this mission and thereafter the ravens continue to serve as informants and messengers to Thorin and Company.

In Middle-earth, the ravens are gifted with speech and the individuals are known by their names, in this case Carc and Roäc. The names of these two birds are rendered in the way they are known in the language of their people and are derived directly from onomatopoeic renderings of the birds' calls. Although in many European traditions, the raven is traditionally considered as a bird of ill omen, in *The Hobbit* Tolkien chose to give this creature a positive and even benevolent role, providing both tactical and moral support to the Dwarves. The messenger and informant role that Tolkien gives to the ravens can be compared with the qualities of *Huginn* 'thought' and *Muninn* 'memory' attributed to the two ravens in the service of Odin, the king of the gods of Norse mythology, to whom the birds report everything that they see and hear as they travel across the world. In fact, Odin is known as the god of ravens, those pre-eminent scavengers, because he is also the patron of warriors killed in combat.

Dáin II Ironfoot

There now Dáin son of Náin took up his abode, and he became King under the Mountain, and in time many other Dwarves gathered to his throne in the ancient halls. (The Hobbit, ch.18).

Dáin is the cousin of Thorin Oakenshield, born in the Iron Hills to the east of Erebor. After the death of the dragon Smaug, Thorin uses Roäc's messenger ravens to call on Dáin to stand guard against treasure hunters. Dáin answers the call of the line of Durin's heir by sending 500 battle-ready Dwarves. As soon as they arrive, the Battle of the Five Armies begins. At the end of it, as Thorin's heir, Dáin becomes King under the Mountain.

The life of Dáin, son of Náin, is closely associated with the battles fought by the Dwarves: he excels in the last battle of the War between the Dwarves and Orcs by killing Azog, who had felled his father in front of his eyes. He is only thirty-two at the time and becomes Lord of the Iron Hills.

One hundred and forty-two years later, at the death of Thorin Oakenshield, he becomes Lord of Erebor and King of Durin's Folk under the name Dáin II Ironfoot.

In 3017 T.A., he learns that Sauron the Necromancer is looking for Bilbo Baggins and his Ring and instructs Glóin to warn him. Later, when the War of the Ring breaks out in both the north and south, Dáin lives up to his reputation by taking part in the fighting, axe in hand, despite being 252 years old. He dies fighting alongside Bard the Bowman's grandson Brand at the Battle of Dale against Sauron's allies.

It is interesting that Dáin is spoken of as a warrior fighting in the service of the older Dwarven branch: the people of the Iron Hills answer the call to avenge the death

of Thrór, the brother of his grandfather Grór, and it is Dáin who defeats Azog, not Thráin or Thorin. Dáin predicts to Thráin that the ancient kingdom of Moria will not be freed by their power alone. He again answers Thorin's call against the armies of Elves and Men, before joining forces to fight the Orcs and Wargs. Once King of Erebor, he respects Thorin's commitments, thanks the Lord of the Eagles for his help by crowning him with gold, and reigns with wisdom and justice over Durin's Folk. Many Dwarves come to join him; Dáin ensures his kingdom prospers and maintains a strong friendship with the Kings of Dale.

Though he appears many times, the reader does not hear Dáin express himself until after the Battle of Azanulbizar; elsewhere he

Dáin answers the call of the Line of Durin's heir by sending five hundred battle-ready Dwarves.

is quoted only indirectly and is never seen talking with Bilbo Baggins. His name, like that of most Dwarves, is derived from Norse mythology and comes from the *Dvergatal*, the list of Dwarf names in the *Eddas*.

Elrond

'In those days of our tale there were still some people who had both Elves and heroes of the North for ancestors, and Elrond the master of the house was their chief.' *(The Hobbit, Ch. 3)*.

As Tolkien points out, the half-Elven Elrond plays a minor but crucial role in the plot of *The Hobbit*, though this does not prevent him being seen as a figure of comparable importance to Gandalf. When Frodo, Bilbo's heir, meets Elrond seventy-seven years after the Quest of Erebor, he describes him as an ageless figure, with bright grey eyes, a face marked by many memories, dark hair held back by a silver band, and as strong as an experienced warrior should be. Elrond and his twin brother Elros are the sons of Eärendil and Elwing, both descended from Elven nobles and Men. They were born near the Mouths of Sirion, in Beleriand, shortly before the end of the First Age. While still children, they were taken by the sons of Fëanor, who ravaged the Havens of Sirion in order to seize the Silmaril of Elwing. One of them, Maglor, took pity on the twins and raised them. After the fall of Morgoth, Sauron's former master, the Valar force the two brothers to choose between their Elven

and their human parentage. Elros chooses Men and becomes the first king of Númenor. After many generations, it is from Elros that the first kings of Arnor and Gondor, Elendil and his sons Isildur and Anárion, will descend. Elrond chooses the Elves and becomes herald to the Great King Gil-galad. In the Second Age, Elrond lives first in Lindon, to the west of Eriador, where he stands up against the coming of Annatar, who is none other than Sauron in disguise. When the latter's duplicity is revealed and he attacks the Elven kingdom of Eregion, Elrond is sent at the head of an army to rescue the Elves of Ost-in-Edhil. He manages to join forces with Celeborn, husband of Galadriel, who fought the enemy but could not prevent the fall of the city. Pressed by Sauron's troops, he gathers the survivors but is soon forced to retreat north. His army is saved by a diversion created by the Dwarves of Khazad-dûm and the Elves of Lórien. Elrond falls back to the Vale of Rivendell, where he

successfully withstands a three-year siege. After the intervention of the Númenóreans, Gil-galad and Elrond catch the army besieging Rivendell in a pincer movement and annihilate it.

After Sauron's defeat, the first White Council is held in Rivendell, which becomes the main stronghold of the High Elves in Eriador and Elrond's home. Gil-galad entrusts him with Vilya, the Ring of Air, and makes him

Elrond and his twin brother Elros are the sons of Eärendil and Elwing, both descended Elven nobles and Men.

vice regent in Eriador. It is at this Council that Elrond meets Celebrían, daughter of Galadriel, who will become his wife in 109 of the Third Age. During the War of the Last Alliance, Elrond accompanies Gil-galad's army and is present at the last battle on the flanks of Mount Doom. He witnesses the death of Gil-galad and of Elendil, as well as the defeat of Sauron and Isildur's capture of the One Ring. He advises Isildur to throw it into the lava, but he refuses. Elrond returns to Rivendell, while Isildur spends two years restoring Gondor. After Isildur is ambushed and killed near the Gladden Fields, Elrond foretells that Narsil, Elendil's sword, will not be reforged until the Ring is found and Sauron returns.

During the Third Age, Elrond makes his home a refuge and a place of learning. He becomes the most celebrated of the Masters of Knowledge and his talents as a healer are well known. He is one of the few to know the origin of the Wizards and is part of the new White Council. He comes to the aid of the Dúnedain of the North, and after the fall of their kingdom gives shelter to the Heirs of Isildur, children and old men, because he can tell that they have a major role to play in the future. His wife Celebrían bears him three children: the twins Elladan and Elrohir, and a daughter, Arwen Undómiel. In 2509, Celebrían is attacked by Orcs on her way back from a visit to Lórien and receives a poisoned wound. Healed by Elrond, she decides, all the same, to travel to Valinor the following year. Her two sons become ruthless enemies of the Orcs, often hunting them down in the company of the Heirs of Isildur. After the death of Arathorn II in one of these battles, his wife Gilraen takes their son Aragorn to Elrond, who adopts him and names him Estel, to conceal his true parentage. Ten years later, Thorin and Company reach Rivendell and receive a warm welcome from Elrond, who provides them with assistance in crossing the Misty Mountains. Elrond deciphers the runes on the swords Orcrist and Glamdring and discovers that there are lunar runes on Thrór's map. When Aragorn reaches the age of twenty, Elrond reveals his true name to him and gives him the Shards of Narsil. Aragorn meets Arwen in the gardens at

Rivendell and falls in love with her. Elrond is gravely distressed by this and forbids the marriage unless Aragorn becomes King of Arnor and of Gondor. Aragorn tells him that he will rise higher than all his ancestors since the time of Elendil or will be the last of his race. On 20 October 3018, Frodo crosses the Ford of Bruinen, pursued by the Nazgûl who want to seize the Ring. Elrond unleashes a sudden flood, which sweeps the Nazgûl away. He then endeavours to save Frodo, who has been seriously wounded by the Wizard-King. Elrond goes on to preside over the Council that bears his name; he reveals that the Elves will no longer be able to stand up to Sauron if the other Free Peoples are defeated. The decision is therefore made to destroy the Ring, and Elrond approves the choice of Frodo, who dedicates himself to this mission. He sends out Elves as scouts to assist in the initial stages of the journey and provides the Nine Walkers with equipment and provisions. Elrond then dispatches his sons to find Aragorn, who is unsure which route to follow after Saruman's defeat. He instructs them to remind Aragorn of the words of Malbeth the Seer, urging them to follow the Paths of the Dead. At the last debate, after the Battle of the Pelennor Fields, Elrohir reveals that, like Gandalf,

Elrond advises attacking Mordor to divert Sauron's attention and assist Frodo's mission. After Sauron's fall, Elrond and Arwen come to Minas Tirith. Elrond gives Aragorn the Sceptre of Arnor and grants him his daughter's hand in marriage. He then returns from there in the company of Gandalf and the Hobbits. Three years after the fall of Sauron, Elrond decides to leave for Valinor with the other Guardians of the Rings. At the Grey Havens, a ship built by Círdan the Shipwright awaits him. With the departure of the Guardians, the Third Age of Middle-earth comes to an end. Elrond's sons remain in Rivendell for many years; the date of their leaving is not known.

The name Elrond, which means 'starry dome', was given to him by his mother in memory of King Thingol's throne room. It is considered to be prophetic and indeed anticipates the gift of the Ring Vilya by Gil-galad. In his letters, Tolkien states that 'Elrond symbolizes throughout the ancient wisdom, and his House represents Lore – the preservation in reverent memory of all tradition concerning the good, the wise, and the beautiful. It is not a scene of *action* but of *reflection*. Thus it is a place visited on the way to all deeds, or "adventures".

Galadriel

'Galadriel! Galadriel!
Clear is the water of your well;
White is the star in your white hand;
Unmarred, unstained is leaf and land
In Dwimordene, in Lórien
More fair than thoughts of Mortal Men.'

(The Lord of the Rings, III, 6).

Galadriel is an Elf born in Valinor, the Undying Lands to the west of Middle-earth. A woman strong in body and mind, she is known for her long, golden hair with streaks of silver, which earns her the name Alatáriel ('maiden crowned with radiant garland'), given to her by her husband Celeborn. She then chooses to bear the name Galadriel, a translation of Alatáriel in the Elven Tongue Sindarin. Her father, Finarfin, names her Artanis ('noble woman') and her mother names her Nerwen ('man maiden'), because she is taller and stronger than most other Elves, male and female.

When some of the Elves of Valinor go into exile in Middle-earth, she chooses to join them, mainly with the thought of founding her own domain. During the First Age, she lives in Beleriand, more specifically in

Doriath, the kingdom of her great uncle Elu Thingol, where she meets Celeborn. They marry and have a child, Celebrían, who later becomes the wife of Elrond Half-Elven and the mother of Arwen.

At the start of the Second Age, most of the land of Beleriand is submerged by the sea. Galadriel then rejects the pardon of the Valar and so cannot return to Valinor. She is one of the last Elves of Middle-earth to have known the land of Aman. Galadriel and Celeborn together cross the Blue Mountains, travelling eastwards and settle in Eriador, near Lake Nenuial. They then move to Eregion where they befriend the Dwarves of Moria and the Elves of Celebrimbor, who is a relative of Galadriel. Celebrimbor falls in love with Galadriel and gives her one of the Three Rings forged by the Elves – Nenya, the

Ring of Adamant, made of mithril. Galadriel and Celeborn then leave together to live for a time in Rivendell and later by the sea in Belfalas.

At this time, a small, wooded kingdom known as Lórinand lies to the east of the mines of Moria, and is governed by the Elf Amroth. Galadriel likes this place and stays there from time to time. When, in 1980 T.A., the Balrog of Moria, a creature of fire and shadow, is released by the Dwarves, the region of Lórinand is devastated and Amroth disappears. Galadriel and Celeborn decide to repopulate the kingdom, settling there permanently with their retinue and naming it Lothlórien or Lórien. Galadriel becomes the Lady of Lórien, thus fulfilling her long-held dream. The power of the Ring Nenya protects her domain for many centuries, making it timeless. When trouble begins to arise in the south of Mirkwood, Galadriel calls representatives of the Elves and Wizards to attend a Council. This is the first meeting of the White Council, which takes place in 2463 T.A.. Galadriel wants Gandalf to head the Council, but he refuses, and the role finally goes to Saruman. The Council then identifies the source of the trouble as the fortress of Dol Guldur, the seat of Sauron the Necromancer, who survived his defeat at the end of the Second Age. In 2941 T.A., when Bilbo Baggins and Thorin and Company cross Mirkwood and head to the Lonely Mountain, Galadriel and the other members of the White Council determine to drive Sauron out of Dol Guldur. The last meeting of the White Council is held shortly afterwards, in 2953 T.A..

At the time of the War of the Ring, the Lady of Lórien is feared by her neighbours in Gondor and Rohan, and is often, though wrongly, considered to be a powerful, dangerous and malevolent witch. However, she welcomes the members of the Fellowship of the Ring after their crossing of Moria and the fall of Gandalf. She advises Frodo Baggins on his continuing mission and offers each member of the Fellowship a useful gift. During his time in Lórien, the terrible visions shown to Frodo in the Mirror of Galadriel lead him willingly to offer Galadriel the One Ring, but she knows to resist this temptation. After the War of the Ring, she razes Dol Guldur to the ground once and for all. In 3021 T.A., as the power of the Elves and that of Nenya gradually wanes after the destruction of the One Ring, Galadriel leaves Middle-earth. Accompanied by Elrond, Gandalf, Bilbo and Frodo, she sets off for Valinor, while her husband Celeborn chooses to settle for a time in Rivendell. It is not known if he joins her later. By Tolkien's own admission, the character of Galadriel owes much to the Virgin Mary, which is not surprising given the author's strong Catholic faith, passed on to him by his mother Mabel Tolkien. Galadriel also shares something in common with the Lady of the Lake of Arthurian legends: her relationship with water through her mirror and her magical powers of protection.

Gandalf

*'[...] [...] and last came one who seemed the least,
less tall than the others, and in looks more aged,
grey-haired and grey-clad, and leaning on a staff.'*
(Unfinished Tales and Legends, IV 2).

Gandalf, or Olórin as he was originally called, was a Wizard, a member of the order of the Istari. He appears to Men and Elves as an old man with a long, grey beard and grey hair, leaning on a stick, and wearing a large, blue, pointed hat. He wears a long grey cape, a silver scarf and tall black boots. Travelling through Middle-earth on foot, on horseback or sometimes driving a cart, he befriends the Free People, who know him by various names: he is called Mithrandir, the Grey Pilgrim, among the Elves; Tharkûn, the Staff Man, among the Dwarves; among Men he is Gandalf, the Elf with a Staff; he is also known as Incánus.

Around the year 1000 T.A., Olórin is sent to Middle-earth by the Valar to fight the return of Sauron, along with the other Istari. Of the life he lived in Valinor, little is known. He is believed to have lived in the gardens of the Vala Lórien and to have been a close friend of the Valië Nienna, who taught him compassion and patience. When the Valar decide to send emissaries to combat Sauron, Olórin is appointed by Manwë and Varda as their representative. When he lands at the Grey Havens, the Elf Círdan sees him as a more important messenger than his predecessors and offers him Narya, the Elven Ring of Fire, sensing that Gandalf will have need of it in the coming fight. In his wanderings around the north-west regions of Middle-earth, he befriends the Free Peoples, and especially the great Elven nobles Elrond and Galadriel. In 2063 T.A., he makes his way to the tower of Dol Guldur, which Sauron occupied a few years earlier, and manages to drive him away. In 2460 T.A. however, Sauron returns to his stronghold in the guise of the Necromancer. Concerned about his power, the White Council meets three years later. This Council is composed of Elrond, Galadriel, Círdan, Gandalf and Saruman, head of the Istari. Despite Galadriel's wish

to see Gandalf lead the Council, Saruman is chosen for this role. As the Council decides not to take action against the Necromancer, Gandalf resumes his wanderings. He visits the Shire at the time of the Old Took, Bilbo Baggins' ancestor, and becomes friends with him. In 2850 T.A., Gandalf again visits Dol Guldur, where he discovers that the Necromancer is in fact Sauron, who is rebuilding his power. Exploring the dungeons of the tower, he finds the father of Thorin Oakenshield, Thráin II, close to death. Thráin gives him Thrór's map and the key to the secret door to the Lonely Mountain. After this, Gandalf begins to suspect Sauron's goal: to start a war in order to take control of Middle-earth, specifically by attacking Rivendell and Lórien, the most appealing targets. Gandalf guesses, too, that Sauron may use the dragon Smaug as a weapon to open a passage for his armies north of the Misty Mountains. He then begins to devise a plan to get rid of Smaug. In March 2941 T.A., while on his way to the Shire after many years away, he meets Thorin Oakenshield, who invites him to his home in the Blue Mountains. There he explains to him his wish to reclaim the kingdom of Erebor and take revenge on Smaug. Gandalf then devises the secret Quest of Erebor to be led by Thorin. On 25 April, he travels to the Shire, where he meets Bilbo Baggins whom he eventually persuades to join Thorin and Company on this quest. During the first half of the expedition, Gandalf accompanies the Dwarves and rescues them from the pitfalls they encounter. It is during this period that

he discovers the sword Glamdring and kills the Great Goblin, chieftain of the Orcs of the Misty Mountains. Arriving at the edge of Mirkwood, Gandalf abandons the Quest to join the White Council, persuading its members to attack Dol Guldur. Sauron, who has anticipated the attack, flees Dol Guldur for Mordor. Meanwhile, Bilbo and Thorin's Company reach Erebor and Smaug is killed by Bard the Bowman. The Wizard then heads north in time to take part in the Battle of the Five Armies, which sees Men, Dwarves and Elves pitted against Orcs and Wargs. He then accompanies Bilbo as he makes his way home. After this, Gandalf resumes his wanderings in Middle-earth, but continues to visit Bilbo from time to time. He also takes the opportunity to establish new relationships, as with Aragorn in 2956 T.A..

In 3001, at Bilbo's farewell party, Gandalf begins to suspect that the ring discovered by Bilbo during his Quest with the Dwarves is far more than a magical trinket. For seventeen years, he endeavours to trace the history of this object. In 3018 T.A., Gandalf returns to The Shire convinced that this ring is none other than the One Ring lost by Sauron. Leaving Frodo, Bilbo's nephew, Gandalf sets off once more. At midsummer, he is imprisoned by Saruman at Orthanc. In September 3018, he manages to escape with the help of the eagle Gwaihir, who leaves him in Rohan. There he tames one of the King of Rohan's horses, the Meara Shadowfax, then rides to the Shire, but arrives a few days after Frodo has left. He sets off again in the direction of Rivendell, hoping

Gandalf returns to the Shire convinced that this ring was none other than the One Ring lost by Sauron.

to catch up with the Hobbits, who are now accompanied by Aragorn.

Gandalf reaches Elrond's home a few days later, just ahead of Frodo. He takes part in the Council of Elrond, at which the Fellowship of the Ring is formed. When crossing the mines of Moria, Gandalf falls to his death while fighting the Balrog, which confronts him on the summit of Zirakzigil, but also dies. However, Gandalf is sent back to Middle-earth by Eru Ilúvatar, to complete his mission in the guise of Gandalf the White. He takes part in the great battles of the War of the Ring until the fall of Sauron. After crowning Aragorn, he escorts the four Hobbits to the outskirts of the Shire. On 29 September 3021,

he leaves Middle-earth with the other Guardians of the Rings for Valinor. The character of Gandalf appears to have its origin in Josef Madlener's painting *Der Berggeist*, which dates from the late 1920s. Tolkien had a postcard of this painting showing an old man with a long beard, wearing a cloak and hat, sitting at the foot of a tree and stroking a fawn. On the envelope containing this card, Tolkien wrote 'Origin of Gandalf.' Gandalf can also be seen to relate to the magician Merlin.

But for his chief inspiration, we should look not so much to Merlin and the Arthurian legends as to the Norse *Edda* and the god Odin. In one letter, Tolkien explicitly states that he thought of Gandalf as a wanderer similar to Odin.

Both characters also share aspects of physical appearance: Odin is often described as an old man wearing a hat or a hood and blue coat, and leaning on a stick The name Gandalf, too, is taken from the Norse *Poetic Edda*, specifically from the poem *Völuspa*.

Girion

'[…] the necklace of Girion, Lord of Dale, made of five hundred emeralds green as grass, which he gave for the arming of his eldest son in a coat of dwarf-linked rings the like of which had never been made before, for it was wrought of pure silver to the power and strength of triple steel. (The Hobbit, Ch. 12).

Girion is the last Lord of Dale before the Quest of Erebor. He dies in 2770 T.A., when the dragon Smaug attacks and destroys this town of Men, along with the Dwarven kingdom of Erebor. At the time of his death, he has a wife and at least one son, still a child, both of whom manage to escape, thus preserving his lineage. One hundred and seventy-one years after Girion's death, his descendant Bard succeeds in killing Smaug by targeting the weak point in the dragon's armour with his final arrow. This arrow, the Black Arrow, has been passed on to him by his father, who himself received it from his ancestors. It is reputed to have been forged in the Dwarven forges of Erebor and must therefore have come from Girion's armoury. Very little information is available about Girion. Apart from his status as the last Lord of Dale and ancestor of Bard, we know that

Girion possessed a magnificent necklace of emeralds, which Bilbo Baggins spots in the dragon's treasure hoard when he penetrates the heart of Erebor. After the Battle of the Five Armies, Dáin II returns the necklace to Bard who, in turn, offers it to Thranduil, the Elven King, to thank him for his help in rebuilding Lake-town after its destruction by Smaug.

In his drafts, Tolkien first imagines that it will be Bilbo who kills the dragon. The

Girion is the last Lord of Dale before the Quest of Erebor. He dies in 2770 T.A., when the dragon Smaug attacks and destroys this town of Men.

creation of the character Bard complicates matters, as his status as a descendant of Girion gives him legitimate claims to part of the treasure. After the episode of Smaug's death, Tolkien took a break from writing the novel: it appears that he had not envisaged the Battle of the Five Armies, but rather a peaceful resolution of the conflict between Thorin Oakenshield, the Men of Lake-town and the Elves of Mirkwood. Bilbo was to give Bard the 'Gem of Girion' and to accept in exchange Thorin's claims to the treasure. Tolkien finally decided to replace this 'Gem of Girion' with the Arkenstone and created the emerald necklace to act as this once lost and now rediscovered inheritance.

Among Smaug's treasure, there is also mention of spears once intended for the great King Bladorthin, who died long before without ever paying for or receiving the spears he had ordered from the Dwarves. Like Girion, King Bladorthin is not mentioned anywhere else in Tolkien's work. The reference to his death may suggest that he was a Man, although his name is clearly Elven in origin. It is also unclear whether he is supposed to be an ancestor of Girion or of the king of the neighbouring country of Dale. In drafts of *The Hobbit*, Bladorthin was the name given to the Wizard accompanying the Dwarves – the future Gandalf. It may therefore have meant 'wanderer, grey pilgrim', before this meaning was given to the Elven name for Gandalf, Mithrandir.

Gollum

'He was Gollum – as dark as darkness, except for two big round pale eyes in his thin face.' (The Hobbit, Ch. 5).

Gollum, or Sméagol as he was originally named, was born around 2440 T.A.. Related to the Hobbits, he grew up in a matriarchal family living on the shores of the Anduin river, between the Misty Mountains and Mirkwood. In 2463 T.A., while on a fishing trip on the Anduin river with his friend Déagol, Déagol is pulled into the depths by a fish. On the riverbed, he finds a golden ring; it is the One Ring lost hundreds of years earlier by King Isildur, who had seized it from Sauron during the War of the Last Alliance. Fascinated by the Ring, Sméagol tries to persuade Déagol to give it to him as a birthday gift, but Déagol refuses. Sméagol strangles him and takes possession of the Ring before concealing Déagol's body. When Sméagol wears the Ring, he becomes invisible. With this power, he steals and terrorizes his fellows, eventually making himself unwelcome even within his own family. He begins talking to himself or to his 'treasure' and starts producing guttural sounds that earn him the nickname 'Gollum'. He is eventually banished from his family by his grandmother. He then heads to the Misty Mountains and enters them via the tunnels dug by the Orcs. There he discovers a cave with a lake and a small island, on which he settles. The power of the Ring corrupts him but keeps him alive far longer than normal. His appearance changes; he becomes even smaller and slimier, with eyes adapted to the darkness and webbed feet. He feeds on fish from the lake and on Goblins lost in the tunnels.

In 2941 T.A., Sauron, in the guise of the Necromancer, casts his shadow over

When Sméagol wears the Ring, he becomes invisible. With this power, he steals and terrorizes his fellows

Mirkwood. The Ring, attracted by its master, slips from Gollum's finger while he is walking through the tunnels, but he does not notice. By a fortunate coincidence, it is picked up by Bilbo Baggins, who is lost in the tunnels and, having no immediate use for it, puts it in his pocket. Bilbo continues on through the tunnel and eventually arrives at Gollum's cave. Gollum, hungry but curious, challenges Bilbo to a game of riddles. If Bilbo loses, Gollum can eat him, but if Gollum loses, he will have to show the Hobbit the way out of the Misty Mountains. In the end, Bilbo wins the game by asking him what he has in his pocket – a question that Gollum is unable to answer. However, Gollum has no intention of keeping his promise. He returns to his island to retrieve his ring of invisibility so that he can launch a surprise attack on Bilbo, and it is then that he realizes that his treasure has disappeared. He guesses that it is the object that Bilbo has in his pocket. He crosses the lake again intending to kill Bilbo, and pursues him but goes past the Hobbit without seeing him because, meanwhile, Bilbo has put the ring on his finger and become invisible. Gollum then heads towards the eastern exit of the Orc cave, convinced that Bilbo is going in that direction. Bilbo finally manages to find his way out of the Misty Mountains by following Gollum without his knowledge, leaving the poor creature on the threshold, unable to follow him outside.

Three years later, however, Gollum decides to leave, determined to get back his ring. Following in Bilbo's footsteps, he heads east, to Lake-town.

There, spying on the villagers, he learns that Bilbo is a Hobbit from the Shire. In 2951, he turns back, but not knowing the direction of the Shire, he heads south towards Mordor. In 3008, he is captured by Sauron, who extracts information from

him about Bilbo before releasing him nine years later, just before The War of the Ring. He is captured by Aragorn on Gandalf's orders and taken to Thranduil's kingdom, where he is imprisoned and questioned by

the Wizard. Gandalf then leaves him in the custody of the Woodland Elves. However, while walking in Mirkwood, his guards are attacked by Goblins, allowing Gollum to escape. He travels west and enters the caves of Moria and remains there until the Fellowship of the Ring passes through. He follows them, then joins Frodo and Sam as they cross the Emyn Muil hills. He then acts as their guide as far as Cirith Ungol, where

Before *The Hobbit* appeared, Tolkien had created a prototype of Gollum in a poem called 'Glip', named after the creature who appears in it. Glip has the same physical characteristics as Gollum: eyes that shine in the night, a gaunt and slimy physique, etc. The first edition of *The Hobbit* presents Gollum as a relatively sympathetic and honourable creature. In the game of riddles, he offers his Ring as a gift and when he loses

he betrays them and tries to kill Sam in order to seize the Ring. He follows them stealthily, attacks Frodo in the heart of Mount Doom and dies by falling into the lava, destroying the One Ring in the process.

and discovers that his Ring has disappeared, he apologizes and offers to lead Bilbo out of the Misty Mountains. In 1951, during the writing of *The Lord of the Rings*, this version was replaced by the better-known one in

which Gollum is vicious and greedy. Tolkien then turned the version with a benevolent Gollum into a lie told to the Dwarves by Bilbo to explain how he won the Ring.

There are many assumed or proven inspirations for the character of Gollum. He can be compared with Grendel, a monstrous creature who causes terror at the court of King Hrothgar in the medieval text *Beowulf*, which Tolkien greatly admired. Gollum and Grendel possess physical similarities and share a nocturnal, underground, amphibious way of life. The biblical character of Cain has also been suggested as an inspiration for Gollum: each causes the death of one of their relatives and this is followed by rejection by their family. Another Hebrew inspiration can be found in the character of Golem in the *Talmud*, which inspired the Golem legend of Judah Loew ben Bezalel, the great rabbi of Prague. Both creatures obviously have a similar name and deceptive appearance. In modern literature, Gollum can be compared with the character of Gagool, an ape-like sorceress who appears in Rider Haggard's *King Solomon's Mines*, published in 1885, which Tolkien read and enjoyed in his youth. Gagool's physical characteristics, her manner of speaking and her egocentric attitude are particularly striking in relation to Gollum. His relationship with the Ring can also be compared to that of Gypsy Ben – a character in the novel *Mid-winter: certain travellers in Old England* by John Buchan, published in 1923. Like Gollum, Gypsy Ben personifies a ring, calling it his 'darling dear', and like Gollum, he is eventually killed by falling into a ravine. Lastly, Tolkien appears to have been influenced by the Morlocks, the monstruous-looking, degenerate humans that appear in H.G. Wells' 1895 novel *The Time Machine*. The Morlocks have dull, white skin and eyes that reflect the light; they fear light and are like human spiders; they eat the Eloi, just as Gollum devours Goblins and infants.

Legolas

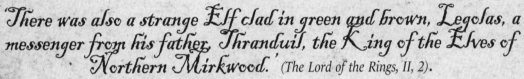

'There was also a strange Elf clad in green and brown, Legolas, a messenger from his father, Thranduil, the King of the Elves of Northern Mirkwood.' (The Lord of the Rings, II, 2).

Legolas is a Sindar Elf from Mirkwood, the region crossed by Bilbo Baggins and the Dwarves of Thorin and Company, who spend some time in the king's jails. Legolas does not appear in Bilbo's story, but he is the son of King Thranduil and is therefore probably present when Bilbo and the Dwarves spend time among the Elves. Legolas is tall and fearless. The colour of his hair is unknown, but the Sindar and the Nandor, from whom he is descended, generally had brown hair, although Thranduil, his father had golden hair. He is usually dressed in green and brown, colours reminiscent of his kinship with the Woodland Elves, and is armed with a dagger, although he is primarily known as an excellent bowman. Like most Elves, he has a natural attraction to music and song, which he practises a great deal.

In 3018 T.A., at the Council of Elrond, Legolas announces to the representatives of the Free People that Gollum, who was being held captive by his people, had managed to escape with the help of the Orcs. At the end of the Council, he joins the Fellowship of the Ring, where he represents the Elves as a Free People. Despite the enmity between their two peoples, Legolas gradually becomes friends with one of the Dwarves, Gimli, son of Glóin. Following the dissolution of the Fellowship, Legolas, Gimli and Aragorn set off in pursuit of the Uruk-hai, who have captured the Hobbits Merry and Pippin. Legolas then follows Aragorn throughout the War of the Ring. After the destruction of the One Ring, Legolas and Gimli together enjoy discovering the beauty hidden below ground and concealed within the branches of the trees. At the start of the Fourth Age, Legolas guides some of his people to Ithilien and brings this region devastated by Sauron back to life. As the years pass, Legolas finds the call of the sea ever stronger, as Galadriel had predicted. Finally, in 120 Fth.A., at the death of

King Elessar, Legolas leaves Middle-earth, accompanied by Gimli, hoping to reach the Undying Lands. Their friendship remains a remarkable one and is considered to be one of the greatest friendships between the two Peoples.

The name Legolas is a form derived from the Sindarin 'laegolas', a word composed of 'laeg/leg,' meaning 'green', and of 'golas', 'collection of leaves,' 'foliage'. As a Woodland Elf whose name means 'Green Leaf', it is only natural that Legolas should be the spokesman for Tolkien's love of trees in *The Lord of the Rings*. It is indeed through Legolas's wonder at the forests of Middle-earth, and especially Fangorn Forest, that Tolkien's particular affection for growing things is most apparent.

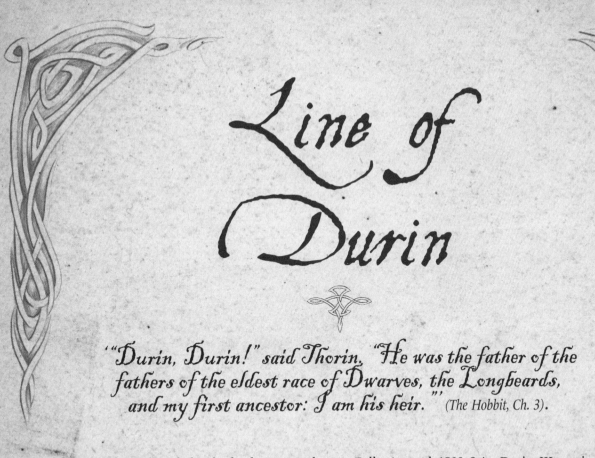

Line of Durin

"Durin, Durin!" said Thorin. "He was the father of the fathers of the eldest race of Dwarves, the Longbeards, and my first ancestor: I am his heir." (The Hobbit, Ch. 3).

The Longbeard clan is also known as the House of Durin, as it was founded by Durin I, the Deathless. Their kingdom of Moria, which they called Khazad-dûm in Khuzdul, meaning Delving of the Dwarves, was founded in the First Age, before the first Men arrived from the East. This ushered in a mutually profitable economy by providing the Dwarven towns and cities with food in exchange for the Dwarves' excellence in construction and craftsmanship.

With the end of the First Age and the submergence of Beleriand, many Dwarves from the cities of Nogrod and Belegost came to Moria under the Misty Mountains. The establishment of an Elf kingdom in Eregion in 750 of the Second Age, and the great friendship that developed with the Dwarves of Moria, marked the peak influence of Durin's Folk. Around 1500 S.A., Durin III receives one of the Seven Rings of Power forged by the Dwarves. When Eregion is destroyed by Sauron's troops, the Dwarves launch a counterattack which allows the routed Elven armies to escape north and take refuge in Rivendell Valley. They then seal their fortress against Sauron's forces. The wealth of Moria comes principally from the mithril they extract there, but in the Third Age, the Dwarves are forced to dig deeper and deeper to find it. In 1980 T.A., they awake an ancient demon, a Balrog, who kills Durin VI and his son Náin and puts the Dwarven People to flight.

Under the leadership of Thráin I, a group of survivors found a new kingdom in Erebor, the Lonely Mountain, in 1999 T.A., and Thráin I becomes the first King under the

Mountain. In 2210, his son Thorin moves the seat of royalty to the Grey Mountains, where the largest group of Durin's Folk in exile live. The House of Durin becomes rich again over more than three centuries, before misfortune befalls it. Durin's Folk are again driven out by a scourge of ancient times: dragons want to seize the Dwarves' treasure and, in 2589, Dáin I is killed, together with his youngest son Frór. His sons Thrór and Grór abandon the Grey Mountains to the dragons; one goes to Erebor, the other to the Iron Hills. As the eldest, Thrór is both King of Durin's Folk and King under the Mountain and brings prosperity to his domain and his people. But once again, the Dwarves' fortune brings disaster upon them: this time it is the dragon Smaug who causes the Sack of Erebor and the renewed exile of the House of Durin. Many survivors make their way to the Iron Hills, but Thrór and those close to him wander south and settle in Dunland. When Thrór sets off towards Moria in 2790 T.A., the Orc Azog executes him and claims Moria as his own.

Thráin II, the son and successor of Thrór, summons all the Dwarves scattered around the world to take part in a great war of vengeance: the War of the Dwarves and Orcs. After the victory in 2799 T.A., each of the Dwarven armies returns home – Durin's Folk disperse among the troops from the Iron Hills led by Dáin, grandson of Grór, and the followers of Thráin. Thráin returns to Dunland, then moves on to the Blue Mountains. It is from there that he sets off to see Erebor again in 2841, but he is captured by the Necromancer's Orcs, who imprison him in Dol Guldur so that they can take from him the last of the Dwarves' Seven Rings of Power, which his family has held since the time of Durin III.

After his father's death at Dol Guldur, Thorin Oakenshield becomes King of Durin's Folk. He prospers in the Blue Mountains, but remains true to his duty to take revenge on Smaug, a duty he inherited from Thrór and from Thráin. He organizes the Quest of Erebor which sees the return of the Lonely Mountain to the Line of Durin, though he dies of the wounds he receives at the Battle of the Five Armies. As his nephews Fili and Kili die protecting him, Thrór's bloodline is broken and it is Dáin II Ironfoot who receives the title of King under the Mountain and that of Lord of Durin's Folk in 2941 T.A. His reign lasts until his death in battle in 3019. His son Thorin III Stonehelm then succeeds him and his heirs in turn, up to Durin VII, the last to bear this name, who finally returns to Moria, the cradle of his ancestors. Indeed, it is tradition among the Longbeards that Durin should be the name of a king so much resembling Durin I that he is named after him and considered to be his reincarnation. Thorin's Company includes many members of the Line of Durin, in addition to Thorin and his two nephews. The brothers Balin and Dwalin are first cousins of Óin and Glóin, and all four are descended from Borin, the younger brother of Dáin I. Similarly, Ori, Dori and Nori belong to the House of Durin, but are distantly related to Thorin.

Line of Durin
Family Tree (extract)

Náin II

Dáin I — Borin

Thrór — Grór   Farin

Thráin II   Náin   Fundin   Gróin

Thorin II   Dís   Dáin II   Balin   Dwalin   Óin   Glóin
Oakenshield   Ironfoot

Fili   Kili   Thorin III   Gimli
              Stonehelm   Elf-friend

The Necromancer

'[...], you would get into the land of the Necromancer; and even you, Bilbo, won't need me to tell you tales of that black sorcerer. I don't advise you to go anywhere near the places overlooked by his dark tower!' *(The Hobbit, Ch. 7)*.

The Necromancer does not appear in the adventures of Bilbo Baggins but nevertheless plays an important role in how they unfold. It is, in fact, his presence in the south of Mirkwood that forces Gandalf to depart, leaving Bilbo and the Dwarves to manage without him on their journey to Erebor and in their attempt to drive away the dragon Smaug. Thus, from a narrative point of view, it is the Necromancer who turns Bilbo's adventure into a true coming-of-age tale.

In the more general context of Middle-earth, this terrible sorcerer, who has been at Dol Guldur since 1050 T.A., is none other than Sauron, the Lord of the Rings, an incarnation of the evil spirit at work in the Second and Third Ages. Sauron's very negative image has been acquired through a history of repeated villainy that turns his personal story into one long Fall: a descent that leads one of the noblest, most angelic spirits to reach the miserable end we see recounted at the culmination of the War of the Ring. Sauron, despised by all and the source of so much destruction and death, was, in fact, originally a Maia or angelic spirit of great renown. Placed in the service of the Vala Aulë, the Blacksmith god, he was once known as Mairon the Admirable and it was said that, even after his Fall, the recollection of his greatness remained long in the memories of his former peers.

But whatever memories Mairon the Admirable may have left behind, he betrayed his people at the dawn of history, leaving Aulë to join Melkor, the disgraced Vala who brought war and ruin to the world. Mairon the Admirable then became Sauron the Abhorred and became known in the history of Middle-earth as the most zealous of the followers of Morgoth (the name by which Melkor was known in Middle-earth). Sauron

played an active part in all the treachery perpetrated by his master during the First Age, before succeeding him in the later ages: once Morgoth was defeated and thrown by the Valar outside the Gates of the World, Sauron escaped the wrath of the gods by denying, from fear, his former allegiance. But he did not dare ask his conquerors for forgiveness or come before them, preferring instead, in a cowardly fashion, to remain in Middle-earth, and there to embark on a second betrayal.

During the Second Age, he settles in the kingdom of Mordor, where he builds his monumental fortress of Barad-dûr. Then, secretly, he takes up the torch of his former master, seeking through cunning and lies to dominate the Free Peoples. Conscious of his immense power of persuasion, his pride knows no bounds and Sauron commits the ultimate treachery: with the secret aim of competing with the land of the Valar, he manages to persuade a number of Elves to work with him to heal Middle-earth, despite the extreme reservations of some of them, namely Galadriel, Elrond and Gil-galad. Making full use of his talents and knowledge, Sauron embarks on the creation of the Rings

of Power, which will allow him to slow down and hold back the decline of the world, as evidenced by the preservation of Lórien. However, in the heart of his kingdom of Mordor, the Enemy secretly forges the instrument that will enable him to control Middle-earth: in the fires of Orodruin, breathing nearly all his power into his new creation, he fashions the One Ring, capable of controlling and corrupting the Rings of Power. When Sauron slips the Ring on to his finger, the Elves realize his treachery and finally determine to resist, but are defeated. The Enemy seizes the Rings of Power, except for the Three Elven Rings, which are hidden from him. The Men of Numénor then come to the aid of Middle-earth and defeat the forces of Sauron, who is forced to flee.

In the face of this setback, he changes tack and pursues his plan to challenge the Valar through the agency of Men. By his machinations he provokes the wrath (and response) of the gods against the civilization of Númenor. Himself weakened by the Valar's reprisals, Sauron is eventually attacked by the Elves and the surviving Númenoreans and, gathered together in the Last Alliance, his enemies are able to defeat him. Many heroes, Men and Elves, perish in this war, but Sauron is defeated and his Ring is torn from him. Deprived of this object in which most of his power was contained, even his physical form is lost and his spirit is forced to go into hiding for many years in the lands of the East. During the Third Age, Sauron recovers enough of his power to take

on a new bodily form. He then summons the Nazgûl, the Ringwraiths or Dark Riders, and sets about restoring his power: in the guise of the Necromancer he settles at Dol Guldur, southwest of Mirkwood, and begins his quest for the One Ring. Quickly, however, as soon as the first effects of his dark power are felt, the Valar send emissaries to Middle-earth to combat him, including the Wizards. Some of them join forces with the Elven lords in the White Council to organize the fight against the return of Sauron. The most vigilant of them, Gandalf the Grey, enters the Necromancer's fortress several times and is convinced that this sinister character is none other than Sauron.

In 2941 T.A., the White Council decides to confront the sorcerer of Dol Guldur in order to protect Lórien and Rivendell, both of which are vulnerable to attack. Gandalf then finds himself obliged to leave Thorin and Company for a time. The Necromancer allows his enemies an apparent victory and decides to retreat in order better to organize his response: abandoning Dol Guldur, he returns to his kingdom of Mordor, where he reveals his true self and openly prepares for a military war against

Thus, from a narrative point of view, it is the Necromancer who turns Bilbo's adventure into a true coming-of-age tale.

the kingdom of Gondor. He also dispatches his most fearsome servants, the Nazgûl, to search for the One Ring, in order to thwart any hint of resistance. But his enemies who, thanks to Bilbo, have found the One Ring are preparing a two-fold response to this double strategy: they will engage in military combat only to assure the success of the secret mission to destroy the Ring by throwing it into the flames of Orodruin, where it was originally forged, in the heart of Sauron's kingdom. The operation's success puts an end once and for all to Sauron's evil power and to his physical existence.

While the story of Sauron the Necromancer may go far beyond Bilbo's adventure and seems far removed from it, it has a profound impact on the tale of *The Hobbit*. In 'The Quest of Erebor' we see that Gandalf is especially keen for Thorin and Company to succeed, as their success, depending as it does on the elimination of Smaug, will weaken Sauron by depriving him of a potential ally. The intervention of the White Council forces Gandalf to part from Thorin and Company, and the tale thus takes another turn. The ring that Bilbo finds during his crossing of the Misty Mountains is the One Ring itself. In the end, and despite the passive role he plays in *The Hobbit*, the Necromancer turns out to be an important player in the story, from the beginning of the Quest to its end.

Radagast

'Radagast is, of course, a worthy Wizard, a master of shapes and changes of hue; and he has much lore of herbs and beasts, and birds are especially his friends.' (The Lord of the Rings, II, 2).

Around 1000 T.A., the Valar send the Wizards to Middle-earth to guide the Free Peoples in their fight against Sauron. Of the five leaders of the Order of Wizards, Radagast is the third in importance. When choosing these emissaries, the Valië Yavanna, whose follower he was, interceded with Saruman to take him with him.

Like the other Istari, Radagast's appearance is that of a vigorous and wise old man, and the colour of his garments has earned him the nickname 'Radagast the Brown'. He is a master of herbs and also of shapes and changes of hues. Rhosgobel, his home, is located on the edges of Mirkwood. From time to time, Radagast meets with Beorn, the skin-changer, who lives further north, not far from the Carrock. He does not travel much outside this region, only when strictly necessary.

The origin of the name Radagast is uncertain. It could derive from the language of the Men of Dale or perhaps come from the ancient language of Numénor and mean 'animal lover'. The Wizard is attached to animals, and birds in particular, as his real name – Aiwendil, 'bird friend' – indicates.

In 3018 T.A., when Gandalf recounts his discovery of Saruman's treachery to the Council of Elrond, he explains that he met Radagast on the outskirts of the village of Bree. At Saruman's request, Radagast has been travelling these lands, which were unfamiliar to him, in order to find Gandalf. He has been sent to tell him that the nine Nazgûl have been searching for the Shire and to ask him to join him at Orthanc. Gandalf, trusting in Radagast's loyalty, travels there and falls into the trap orchestrated by Saruman, who imprisons him. Saruman, who holds the Brown Wizard in contempt as simple and a half-wit, has used Radagast to lure Gandalf there. Luckily, Gandalf has asked Radagast to have his

animal friends report any information about the Nazgûls' activities to Saruman or to him. This is how Gwaihir the Eagle, the Windlord, discovers Gandalf imprisoned at the top of the Orthanc tower, and frees him. After this, Radagast disappears: Elrond's messengers, sent to warn him of Frodo's mission, find Rhosgobel deserted, and the Wizard does not come to the Grey Havens to board the ship on which Gandalf sets sail.

Tolkien may have taken inspiration from two sources for the name Radagast: a Slavic god called Radegast, the equivalent of the god Odin in Germanic mythology, or the Goth king Radagaisus or Radogast, who attacked Italy at the head of a coalition of Germanic and Scythian peoples at the time of the Western Emperor Honorius. Any similarity, however, is purely in the names.

In his first drafts, Tolkien imagines that Radagast is in league with Saruman and traps Gandalf deliberately. In another abandoned version, he foresees that once Saruman is driven out, Isengard will be left in the care of Radagast.

The Wizard was attached to animals, and birds in particular, as his real name – Aiwendil, 'bird friend' – indicates.

Saruman

He has a mind of metal and wheels; and he does not care for growing things, except as far as they serve him for the moment.
(The Lord of the Rings, III, 4).

The name Saruman comes from the Old English *searu*, meaning 'art, skill', but also 'cunning, deception', and his character is marked as much by his predilection for craftsmanship as it is for his ability to scheme. Saruman is a Wizard, like Gandalf and Radagast. But while Gandalf embodies wisdom, Saruman symbolizes knowledge; and while Radagast is devoted to unspoilt nature, Saruman seeks to control nature and surrounds himself with machines.

Saruman the White, also known as Curunír or Curumo, is a Maia, a servant of the Vala Aulë. He is sent by the Valar to Middle-earth to assist the Free Peoples in their fight against Sauron. Once he arrives, he becomes interested in the enemy's knowledge and begins gathering writings and artefacts. His interest turns into fascination, then obsession. Saruman's investigation into the Elven Rings of Power leads him to covet the One Ring.

Saruman's knowledge is devoid of wisdom and gradually leads him to betrayal.

He nurtures a sense of resentment and competition towards Gandalf, to whom Círdan has entrusted the Elven ring Narya. Against Galadriel's advice, he is elected head of the White Council in 2463 T.A. In this position of power he is able to influence the Council's policy.

So it is under his leadership that the Council decides against attacking the Necromancer

Saruman symbolizes knowledge; and while Radagast is devoted to unspoilt nature, Saruman seeks to control nature and surrounds himself with machines.

of Mirkwood, who is actually none other than Sauron. This gives Sauron a stay of execution that allows him to assemble his forces. By doing this, Saruman hopes to learn more about the One Ring and, if possible,

find it before Sauron. When he settles in the tower of Orthanc, entrusted to him by the Steward Beren in 2759 T.A., Saruman discovers a Palantír or Seeing Stone. He believes he can use it to discover the enemy's intentions, which will ultimately lead to his downfall. The White Wizard, skilful and cunning though he is, becomes the plaything of Sauron, who stokes his craving and resentment in order to get him to fight those he should really be guiding.

Not only does he prevent the White Council from putting an end to Sauron, Saruman also lies about the fate of the Ring, claiming that as it was carried away in the waters of the Anduin, it is probably lost at sea. His treachery becomes evident during the War of the Ring: when Gandalf comes to him to ask for advice, Saruman takes him prisoner. He sends forth his hordes of Uruk-hai to search for the Guardian of the Ring, attack the kingdom of Rohan at Helm's Deep and sack part of Fangorn Forest, thus provoking the wrath of the Ents, who give battle there. Defeated and holed up in his tower, Saruman is deprived of his Wizard's staff by Gandalf. However, he still has his voice, a fearsome weapon with which he is able to persuade and bend others to his will. Though believed to be defeated, Saruman reappears in the guise of Sharkey; he enslaves the Shire, destroys the old dwellings and industrializes the land, defacing the countryside beloved by the four returning Hobbits. After the uprising in the Shire, Saruman is stabbed by his acolyte Gríma Wormtongue. His body

dissolves into smoke and his soul seems doomed to wander Middle-earth. Saruman is one of the few characters in Tolkien's work to have no burial place.

After the uprising in the Shire, Saruman is stabbed by his acolyte.

Smaug

"Smaug lay, with wings folded like an immeasurable bat, turned partly on one side, so that the Hobbit could see his underparts and his long pale belly crusted with gems and fragments of gold from his long lying on his costly bed."
(The Hobbit, Ch. 12).

Smaug the Golden, or Trágu, his true name in the language of Dale, is one of the last dragons alive at the time of the Hobbit Bilbo Baggins, and arguably one of the most powerful. It was he who, in 2770 T.A., was behind the Sack of Erebor. The Dwarven kingdom of Erebor had lived in opulence, in harmony with the Men of the town of Dale, which lay in the foothills, but Smaug, attracted by the riches the Dwarves had amassed, came down from the Withered Heath in the Grey Mountains and descended upon the Lonely Mountain region. First he set fire to Dale, killing its warriors and Lord Girion, then entered the mountain, slaughtering most of the Dwarves there before gathering all the riches into a huge pile and making it his bed. Young Thorin witnessed the attack from outside, while his father Thráin and grandfather Thrór, King of Erebor,

managed to flee through a hidden door in the side of the mountain. Smaug brought a reign of terror that lasted many years; at first the Men of Dale resisted, but eventually, with the disappearance of many young girls devoured by the dragon, they migrated south of Long Lake. After this episode, the Lonely Mountain and the area around it, now known as the Desolation of Smaug, were completely abandoned to the dragon.

For 170 years, the dragon has remained undisturbed. The Dwarves, led by Thrór, Thráin and Thorin, find refuge in the Blue Mountains, in the far west of Middle-earth. However, in 2941 T.A., Thorin, bent on revenge, hatches a plan to recover the treasure of Erebor. He meets the Wizard Gandalf the Grey on the road to the Shire and with him devises the Quest of Erebor, involving Thorin and Company and Bilbo

Baggins. For Gandalf, Smaug is a threat that must be eradicated as the dragon could potentially become Sauron's ally in the war that is brewing. In the autumn of 2941, after a journey of several months, the Company arrives in Erebor and discovers the secret door, which they are able to open thanks to Bilbo's ingenuity. Bilbo enters the tunnel and reaches the underground chamber in the heart of the Mountain. There he discovers Smaug, in all his splendour, asleep on his pile of gold. The gold-red dragon is like a bat, his wings folded over his back, his forked tail wrapped around him, and his body covered in armour made of precious stones. In the dark of the chamber, the heat of his body glows, illuminating the smoke emanating from his mouth and nostrils. Bilbo is fascinated, but takes advantage of the fact that Smaug is asleep to steal a golden cup from him and thus prove his skill as a burglar to the Dwarves. Soon Smaug awakes, discovers the theft and flies into a fierce rage. Leaving the Mountain, he perches on the summit of Erebor, looking out across the mountainside to discover the culprit. Eventually he spots the Company's tracks and sets fire to the ledge of the secret entrance just minutes after the Dwarves have taken refuge in the tunnel, though he does not spot the entrance. During the night Smaug prowls around Erebor, hoping to flush out the Dwarves. He fails to find them but captures their ponies and, in so doing, discovers that the Lakemen have helped Thorin and Company. At dawn he returns to his golden bed and falls into a half-sleep, ruminating on the theft of his cup. Meanwhile, Bilbo and the Dwarves plan a second descent of the Mountain. Around midday, the Hobbit slips on the One Ring and, now invisible, is able to enter the treasure chamber unseen. There Smaug, with his unfailing sense of smell, is able to detect the presence of the Hobbit, though he cannot see him or work out who he is, because he is unfamiliar with the smell of a Hobbit. The dragon then tries to extract as much information as possible from Bilbo by getting him to talk. But Bilbo is not fooled, and the conversation becomes an exchange of riddles in which the Hobbit takes great care to embellish his words. So rather than giving his name to Smaug, he calls himself the Ringwinner, the Luckwearer and the Barrel-rider – in reference to his adventures along the way. However, dragons too have power through words and Smaug manages to make Bilbo doubt the Dwarves' good faith. In the end, Bilbo contrives to flatter Smaug, claiming he knew that dragons were vulnerable at the chest. Smaug then reveals his belly and, importantly, his weak point: a gap under his left armpit, unprotected by his bejewelled armour. Bilbo runs back through the tunnel as Smaug spits jets of flame after him. Once outside, Bilbo shares his information with his companions and with the old thrush who had helped him find the secret entrance. During the evening, Bilbo becomes filled with a sense of foreboding and asks the Dwarves to close the entrance,

which they do just in time, before Smaug, who has surreptitiously left the heart of the Mountain, strikes the side of its slopes, totally destroying it and making the secret entrance inaccessible. Smaug then turns southwards and flies to Lake-town to take revenge on the Men who had helped the Company of Dwarves. At the behest of Bard, a descendant of Girion and heir to the throne of Dale, the Master, summons the inhabitants to take up arms and prepare to fight the dragon. Smaug flies repeatedly over the town, brushing aside the streams of arrows fired at him, which only serve to increase his fury. Overcome by anger, he swoops down on the town, spitting out flames and setting light to the dwellings. The inhabitants try to extinguish the fires but most of them flee, including the cowardly Master who leaves in his own boat. This suits Smaug perfectly as he hopes to be able to attack them when they land. But he has not reckoned on the presence of Bard, who has stayed behind with his company of bowmen. When he is about to fire his last arrow, the old thrush who had helped Bilbo tells him about Smaug's weak point. Bard then unleashes the Black Arrow passed down to him by his ancestors and said to have been forged in Erebor. It lodges in the dragon's bare chest. Smaug collapses

upon the town before disappearing under the waves. In future, the waters where the dragon's body lies will be considered as cursed, no one daring to enter them, even to retrieve the jewels of his armour. And the town will be rebuilt further along the lake. The character of Smaug takes its inspiration from the dragons of Norse mythology, largely the dragon Fáfnir from the

Smaug the Golden, or Trágu, his true name in the language of Dale, is one of the last dragons alive at the time of the Hobbit, Bilbo Baggins, and arguably one of the most powerful.

Scandinavian *Völsunga Saga*, but principally from the dragon that appears in *Beowulf*. The scene of Bilbo's theft of the cup is inspired by a similar scene in which a man steals a cup from the dragon, igniting his rage and forcing Beowulf to go and kill the creature. The name *Smaug* comes from the Old English term *smygel*, meaning 'burrow,' 'place to creep into,' from which Tolkien also derived the term smial and Gollum's original name, Sméagol.

Thorin and Company

Thorin and Company to Burglar Bilbo greeting!'
(The Hobbit, Ch. 2).

When Thorin II Oakenshield is preparing for the Quest of Erebor, Gandalf advises him to take only a small number of loyal companions. This is how he comes to choose twelve Dwarves to go to the Shire, to Bag End, and join Gandalf, who wants to introduce them to Bilbo Baggins, the Hobbit destined to be their expert treasure hunter. The majority of these Dwarves are from the Line of Durin, and some are related to Thorin.

Balin, son of Fundin, is the oldest of the Company of Dwarves, after Thorin. He appears on the doorstep of Bag End wearing a red hood and carrying his musical instrument, a large viol. Other than Thorin, he is the only one to have known Erebor. Once the Kingdom under the Mountain is restored, he mounts an expedition to liberate another lost kingdom, Moria, which he reoccupies and rules for five years before being killed by an Orc.

Dwalin, son of Fundin, is the younger brother of Balin. He was born in year 2772 of the Third Age and often takes part in his brother's adventures, although he was too young to have experienced the Sack of Erebor. It is not known if he participated in the War of the Dwarves and Orcs, though it seems likely, given his age. However, he is one of the few companions of Thráin II when he sets off from the Blue Mountains to try to reconquer Erebor in 2841. It is Balin and Dwalin who, in 2845, return to report to Thorin that Thráin has disappeared on the edge of Mirkwood. In 2941, Dwalin is the first Dwarf to reach Bag End, and wears a dark green hood. Like his brother Balin, he plays the viol at the party that follows. After the Battle of the Five Armies, Dwalin remains in Erebor until his death in 91 Fth.A. at the venerable age of 340. In Norse, his name means 'the slow one' or 'lethargic'.

Fili and Kili are the sons of Dís, Thorin's sister. They are the youngest Dwarves in the Company: Fili was born in 2859 and Kili in 2864. So the Quest of Erebor is their first big adventure. Both have blonde beards, blue hoods, and play the violin. The only difference between them seems to be that Fili has a longer nose. Because of their youth and sharp-sightedness they are regularly chosen to act as scouts, like during the crossing of the Misty Mountains. Inseparable throughout the journey, they remain so at the Battle of the Five Armies, fighting alongside their uncle Thorin Oakenshield and protecting him when he is wounded by Bolg's bodyguard. Their heroism costs them their lives, and with their deaths the bloodline of Thrór comes to an end. In Norse their names are associated with mining terms: Fili means 'file' and Kili means 'wedge' or 'key'.

Dori is one of Durin's Folk, and a distant relative of Thorin's royal line. When he arrives in Bag End, his hood is purple and he plays the flute. Thorin describes him as the strongest of the Company; indeed, he aids Bilbo Baggins by carrying him through the Goblin tunnels and helps him climb trees when threatened by the Wargs. Dori is still alive at the start of the War of the Ring, but it is not known what happens to him afterwards. In Norse, his name means 'twister' or 'borer'.

Nori, Dori's brother, is also from the Line of Durin and a distant cousin of Thorin. He is one of the quieter Dwarves in the Company.

He too wears a purple hood and plays the flute. Little is known about him, except that he is still alive at the start of the War of the Ring. In Norse, his name means 'tiny', 'little lad'.

Ori, the cousin of Dori and Nori, has a grey hood and also plays the flute. He is from the Line of Durin, and survives the Battle of the Five Armies but does not remain in Erebor. In 2989, he accompanies Balin in his attempt to reconquer the mines of Moria. After five years, the colony finds itself surrounded by Orcs and spends its final hours in the Chamber of Mazarbul. Ori records the events in a register in the archives, the *Book of Mazarbul*, which will not be discovered until 3019 by the Fellowship of the Ring as they pass through Moria at the start of the War of the Ring. Gandalf then gives the book to Gimli, son of Glóin, so that he can take it to Dáin II Ironfoot. In Norse his name means 'furious', 'violent'.

Óin, one of the Line of Durin, is descended from Borin, uncle of Thrór and brother of Glóin, and was born in 2774 T.A.. He wears a brown hood and, unlike the other Dwarves, appears not to be a musician. As part of the Company, he demonstrates particular skill in lighting fires. He accompanies Balin when he leaves for Moria in 2989. When Balin is killed, Óin attempts to exit by Moria's west gate but is carried away by the Watcher in the Water, an aquatic creature that later attacks Frodo Baggins. His death is recorded by Ori in the Book of Mazarbul. In Norse, his name means 'shy'.

Glóin, of the House of Durin, is the brother of Óin. He wears a white hood and shares his brother's skill at fire lighting; he too has no musical instrument when the Dwarves gather at Bilbo's house. Born in 2783 T.A., he is one of the companions of Thorin and Thráin after the War of the Dwarves and Orcs. Following the success of the Quest of Erebor, Glóin remains with Dáin II. He is his envoy to Elrond in 3018 and takes part in the Council held in Rivendell. His son Gimli, who at the time of the Quest of Erebor was too young, accompanies him to Rivendell, then joins the Fellowship of the Ring, facing many perils as a result, including the Battles of Helm's Deep, Pelargir, Pelennor Fields and Morannon. Glóin lives until 15 Fth.A., while Gimli establishes a Dwarven colony at Aglarond before setting sail for Valinor with Legolas in 100 Fth.A. In Norse, Glóin means 'burning' or 'shining' – a fitting name for an expert at lighting fires in the wild.

Bifur, although descended from the Dwarves of Moria, is not of the House of Durin. He is the cousin of Bofur and Bombur. In Bag End, his hood is yellow and he plays the clarinet. With his cousin Bombur he puts up fierce but futile resistance against the three Trolls when they capture the Dwarves at the start of the Quest. He too survives the Quest of Erebor and the Battle of the Five Armies and is still alive at the start of the War of the Ring. In Norse, his name can mean 'hard worker' or 'trembler', depending on the etymology chosen.

Bofur is a descendant of the Dwarves of Moria, unrelated to the Line of Durin. He too has a yellow hood and plays the clarinet. He settles in Erebor with his share of the treasure, like his cousin Bifur. In Norse, his name can mean 'grumpy' or 'fearless'. He is the second biggest of the Company after his brother Bombur.

The majority of these Dwarves are from the Line of Durin, and some are related to Thorin.

Bombur is the brother of Bofur and cousin of Bifur. He is the biggest of the Dwarves in the Company. At Bag End, he wears a pale green hood and plays the drum. He is one of the Dwarves who puts up greatest resistance against the three Trolls when they capture the Dwarves. During the crossing of Mirkwood, Bombur falls into the Enchanted River and sleeps for six days; the other Dwarves take turns to carry him in groups of four. A big eater, during the crossing of Mirkwood he keeps complaining that he is starving and eventually persuades the Dwarves to venture into the depths of the undergrowth and join the feast being held by Thranduil's Elves.

This recklessness costs him dearly when the Dwarves are captured by the forest spiders, because it is poor Bombur whom they find the largest and most appetizing. They pinch

him mercilessly until Bilbo comes to the rescue of his companions.

When they reach the foot of the Lonely Mountain, Bombur argues that his weight makes it too difficult for him to climb up to the secret door of Erebor, so he gets a great fright when the dragon awakes and sets off in pursuit of them. At the end of their adventures, Bombur remains in Erebor and continues to gain weight, so much so that in 3018 Glóin claims that he can no longer move unaided and six young Dwarves have to carry him between his bed and the dining room. In Norse his name means 'bloated,' which is obviously fitting.

Thorin II Oakenshield

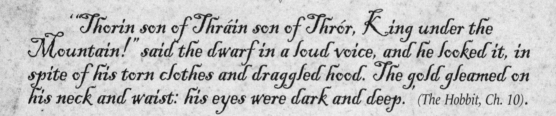

"Thorin son of Thráin son of Thrór, King under the Mountain!" said the dwarf in a loud voice, and he looked it, in spite of his torn clothes and draggled hood. The gold gleamed on his neck and waist: his eyes were dark and deep. (The Hobbit, Ch. 10).

Thorin II Oakenshield, son of Thráin II, who was son of Thrór, is the legitimate heir of Durin, the first Dwarf. King without a kingdom, he has set himself the goal of recovering the treasure of the Kingdom under the Mountain and taking revenge on the dragon Smaug, who has robbed him of his inheritance. Unable to mount a military expedition, he takes the Wizard Gandalf's advice to try burglary. Proud and calculating, he enjoys giving long speeches on solemn occasions. He is a confirmed smoker, able to control his smoke rings from a distance. Thorin was born in 2746 T.A. in the kingdom of Erebor and is the eldest of three children. Keen on exploring, he is far away from Erebor when Smaug attacks

and can only stand by as the Dwarves and Men of Dale are defeated. A small group of survivors gathers around him, soon joined by Thrór and Thráin, who escape through a secret door. The Dwarves head south and settle for a time in Dunland. After Thrór's assassination in 2790, Thráin becomes King of the People of Durin and swears to avenge his father: this is the start of the War of the Dwarves and Orcs, which culminates in the Battle of Azanulbizar, at which Thorin distinguishes himself and earns his nickname Oakenshield. After their victory, Thráin and Thorin travel around Eriador before settling south of the Blue Mountains in 2802. But Thráin is not satisfied by their modest existence and mounts a first expedition to

Erebor in 2841. After four years of hapless wandering, he is captured, then imprisoned in the dungeons of the Necromancer, where he dies, but not before giving Gandalf Thrór's map and the key to the secret door of Erebor. For many years, Thorin works hard and becomes rich, attracting more Dwarves to join him as a prosperous colony develops. As he grows old, Thorin thinks again about his duty of vengeance against the dragon. On 15 March 2941, returning home from a trip, he meets Gandalf on the road to Bree. Thorin asks for his advice and invites him to his home, where he tells him his story. Gandalf hesitates, makes a detour to the Shire and devises the idea of a burglary with the help of a Hobbit: Bilbo Baggins. Reluctant at first, Thorin is eventually persuaded. However, Bilbo makes a fool of himself, and it is only the key and the map that manage to persuade Thorin to follow Gandalf's plan, on the express condition that the Wizard join the Quest.

The first mission Thorin gives Bilbo is a failure: Bilbo is discovered by the Trolls and all the Dwarves are captured, despite Thorin's fierce resistance. After being rescued by Gandalf, Thorin and Company discover the Trolls' riches and Thorin acquires an Elven sword that will soon be revealed as Orcrist, the Goblin-cleaver. Crossing the Misty Mountains, the small troop is ambushed and their throats nearly cut because of the sword. Gandalf again rescues the Dwarves and Thorin fights valiantly to help them extricate themselves from the caves.

When Gandalf leaves the Dwarves at the edge of Mirkwood, Thorin takes command. He proves to be a talented hunter, though an unsuccessful negotiator: he is captured

King without a kingdom, he has set himself the goal of recovering the treasure of the Kingdom under the Mountain and taking revenge on the dragon Smaug,

by the Elves while begging them for food. He refuses to reveal the purpose of the expedition to Thranduil and is locked in a dungeon. Losing hope, he is surprised when Bilbo finds him and hatches an escape plan. On arriving at Lake-town, Thorin introduces himself openly as the heir to the Kings under the Mountain. Welcomed with great ceremony, he takes advantage of the enthusiasm of the Lakemen to gain support for his expedition and is eventually crowned with success.

However, the sight of the treasure brings out a certain concealed greed in Thorin, made stronger by the power of enchantment bestowed on it by the dragon. He calls his cousin Dáin to the rescue, ready to go to war rather than share his hoard with the people of Lake-town and Thranduil's Elves. Bilbo hands over the Arkenstone that Thorin so passionately desires to the enemy camp so that Men and Elves can see their rights

Thorin II Oakenshield

fulfilled. Thorin insults Bilbo and casts him out. Fortunately, however, the unexpected arrival of the Orcs and Wargs unites the Men, Elves and Dwarves. In the Battle of the Five Armies that follows, Thorin intervenes at a crucial moment with his companions, armed from head to toe. He drives back the Wargs and their horsemen and endeavours to reach Bolg, leader of the enemy troops. He is mortally wounded and his two nephews, Fili and Kili, die protecting him. After the battle, on his deathbed he forgives Bilbo and makes amends for his mistakes. He is buried in the heart of the Mountain with Orcrist and the Arkenstone placed on his chest.

As with the majority of Tolkien's Dwarves, the name Thorin is taken from the *Poetic Edda*. *Thorinn* means 'bold' in Norse. His nickname, Oakenshield, is a translation of *Eikinskjaldi*, 'with oak shield'.

Thráin II

'And Thráin your father went away on the twenty-first of April, a hundred years ago last Thursday, and has never been seen by you since...' (The Hobbit, Ch. 1).

Thráin II is a Dwarf of the Line of Durin and the father of Thorin II Oakenshield. He was born in Erebor in 2644 of the Third Age. During the Sack of Erebor, he manages to flee the Mountain with his father Thrór, King under the Mountain and Lord of Durin's Folk. Exile takes them south of the Misty Mountains, to Dunland. In 2790, Thrór gives Thráin his magic ring, the map of the Lonely Mountain and the key to the secret entrance, then sets off on an adventure. He is captured and killed at the gates of Moria by the Orc Azog. When Thráin learns the news of the event, by which he becomes King of Durin's Folk, he is distraught, pulls out his beard and remains silent for seven days; after this he decides to call upon all the Dwarven kingdoms to wage a war of vengeance. It takes three years to gather their forces, but then the Dwarves storm every Orc stronghold in the Misty Mountains. This War of the Dwarves and the Orcs lasts six years, until the Battle of Azanulbizar in

Rivendell Valley in front of the East-gate of Moria. Thráin fights alongside Thorin, but both are wounded and his younger brother Frerin is killed. Once victory is theirs, Thráin, blinded in one eye and limping, rejoices at having wreaked vengeance and determines to reoccupy the mines of Moria. However, Dáin Ironfoot, who has slain Azog on the very threshold of the ancient kingdom, prophetically announces that Durin's Bane, a Balrog, is still present and that the time has not yet arrived for Durin's Folk to return to the home of their ancestors. The Dwarves disperse, and Thráin and those close to him return to Dunland, and then to the Blue Mountains in 2802 T.A. Thráin's people gradually prosper, and their population slowly grows.

Thráin has his son Thorin with him, his daughter Dís, and Balin, Dwalin and Glóin, his cousins. But in 2841, under the power of his father's magic ring, he is driven by a lust for gold and a sense of nostalgia, and sets off

to see Erebor again, accompanied by Balin and Dwalin. The Necromancer, eager to possess Thráin's Ring, has him followed all the way to Mirkwood and there, one night in 2850, Thráin II, King of Durin's Folk in exile, is captured, taken to Dol Guldur, thrown in a dungeon, stripped of his ring under torture, and left for dead. This ring is one of the nineteen Rings of Power forged in the Second Age in Eregion by Elven blacksmiths with the help of Sauron, acting in disguise at the time. Three Rings, untouched by Sauron, were entrusted to the Elves, seven to the Dwarves and nine to Men, before Sauron forged for himself the One Ring to rule them all. Balin and Dwalin report Thráin's mysterious disappearance to his son and remain there in the Blue Mountains, though no news of Thráin is forthcoming.

In 2850, Gandalf investigates Dol Guldur and in the dungeons discovers an old Dwarf at the point of death who can no longer even remember his name, but who hands him a map and a key for him to give to his son. The Dwarf dies before Gandalf is able to discover that this is actually Thráin II, or to release him from his prison. It is not until 2941, at

Bag End, the night before the departure on the Quest of Erebor, that Thorin receives his inheritance and learns what happened to his father.

The name Thráin, like that of most of the Dwarves, belongs to Norse mythology and comes from the *Dvergatal*, the Catalogue of Dwarves in the *Eddas*. In Norse, the name means 'stubborn'.

Thranduil

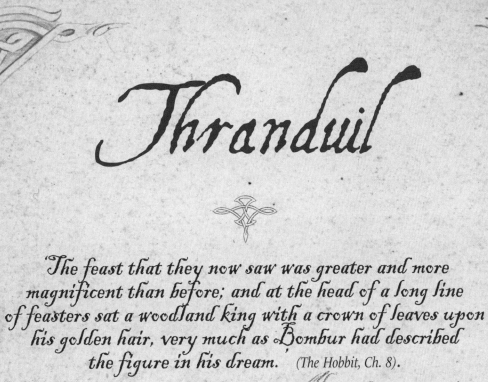

'The feast that they now saw was greater and more magnificent than before; and at the head of a long line of feasters sat a woodland king with a crown of leaves upon his golden hair, very much as Bombur had described the figure in his dream.' (The Hobbit, Ch. 8).

Thranduil is the ruler of the Woodland Elves of Mirkwood. After the death of his father Oropher in the War of the Last Alliance of Elves and Men in the Second Age, he took over and has ruled the north-east of the forest ever since.

His sceptre is made of carved oak, his throne of finely wrought wood and his crown changes with the seasons: berries and red leaves in autumn, woodland flowers in spring. He is a blond-haired Elf whose name in Sindarin, the Elven language of his people, means 'vigorous spring', and his son is Legolas 'Green Leaf', renowned for his role in the War of the Ring.

In the troubled times that follow once Sauron the Necromancer has settled at Dol Guldur, the gloomy fortress southwest of Mirkwood, Thranduil battles to retain his territory. With his warriors, he fights the evil creatures that are gradually invading the forest, including giant spiders, which are systematically slaughtered. He has an underground palace built to serve as a refuge for his people in case of war.

Like his people, Thranduil cares little for the Dwarves: the Woodland Elves and the

Thranduil is the ruler of the Woodland Elves of Mirkwood.

Dwarves were at war in the First Age over a priceless treasure, and that enmity has endured ever since. Furthermore, during their journey to Erebor, when the Dwarves of Thorin and Company become lost in the forest and are captured and brought before King Thranduil, Thorin Oakenshield does not reveal the true purpose of their expedition – to recover his riches – for fear that the king might hinder them. For his part, Thranduil gives little credence to the

story told by the Dwarf and locks him and his companions up in his dungeons.

Thranduil enjoys better relations with the Lakemen, with whom he engages in river trade. Following the death of Smaug in 2941 T.A., he provides them with aid to deal with the destruction of the town by the dragon. At the head of his army, he travels to the Lonely Mountain with Bard, the envoy of the Lakemen, to claim a share of the treasure from the Dwarves. However, when attacked there by the Orcs and Wargs, he joins forces with the Men and the Dwarves in the Battle of the Five Armies, from which he and his allies emerge victorious.

Nearly seventy years later, Thranduil is tasked with holding Gollum captive, but the creature is freed by a Goblin attack. Finally, in March 3019 T.A., Thranduil joins with Celeborn, Galadriel's husband, to drive back the forces of Dol Guldur. Once liberated from these evil beings, the forest is renamed Eryn Lasgalen and shared between Celeborn, Thranduil and the Woodmen.

Thrór

'Your grandfather Thrór was killed, you remember, in the mines of Moria by Azog the Goblin.' (The Hobbit, Ch. 1).

Thrór is a Dwarf of the Line of Durin, and is the father of Thráin II and grandfather of Thorin II Oakenshield. He was born in the Grey Mountains in 2542 of the Third Age. In 2589, when he is 47, a dragon attacks the royal palace and kills his father Dáin I and his brother Frór. The following year, Grór, his second brother leaves to found a colony in the Iron Hills and Thrór inherits the kingdom and leaves the Grey Mountains to settle in Erebor with his uncle Borin – who later becomes the great-grandfather of Balin, Dwalin, Glóin and Óin – and the rest of Durin's Folk. The Arkenstone, once found in Erebor, returns there with Thrór, and the Kingdom under the Mountain soon prospers thanks to its trade with its neighbours, the Men of Dale. But the Dwarves' fortune attracts the attention of the dragon Smaug and, in 2770 T.A., Thrór is forced to flee his kingdom via a secret door, together with his son Thráin, to escape the Sack of Erebor.

A king in exile, Thrór leads those of his people who have not already left for the Iron Hills south of the Misty Mountains, to Dunland. In 2790, at the age of 201, Thrór gives his Ring, the last of the Seven Dwarven Rings, to Thráin, along with a map of the Mountain and the key to the secret entrance. He also passes on to him a duty of vengeance against Smaug, before setting

off on an adventure with a Dwarf called Nár as his only company. Their route takes them north, across the Misty Mountains via the pass over Caradhras, and they reach the mines of Moria via the Dimrill Stair. Finding the East-gate open, and despite Nár's advice, Thrór enters the kingdom of his ancestors. Several days later, Nár, who has been waiting outside, hears screaming and sees a lifeless, decapitated body thrown on to the steps by the Orcs. Their lord, Azog, summons him and makes Nár his messenger, instructing him to let all the Dwarves know that Azog has taken possession of Moria, that he has murdered Thrór and has put his name to his crime by branding it on the victim's forehead. Before Nár is able to pick up the body, Azog tosses him a purse of coins as remuneration and drives him away. As he retreats, filled with sadness and rage, Nár sees the Orcs hacking at Thrór's body to feed it to the nearby crows. Nár then hastens to tell Thráin of the tragedy that has made him the new King of Durin's Folk. The terrible War of the Dwarves and Orcs then ensues and does not end until Azog is killed.

- The name Thrór, like most Dwarven names, belongs to Norse mythology and comes from the *Dvergatal*, the Catalogue of Dwarves in the *Eddas*. In Norse it means 'boar' and derives from the verb 'to develop, to prosper' which is appropriate for someone who enriches his kingdom and makes it grow.

Thrór is a Dwarf of the Line of Durin, the father of Thráin II and grandfather of Thorin II Oakenshield.

Tom, Bert and William

'*It was they who told me that three of them had come down from the mountains and settled in the woods not far from the road; they had frightened everyone away from the district, and they waylaid strangers.*' (The Hobbit, Ch. 2).

When Thorin and Company are caught in a thunderstorm and seek shelter, Balin sees the glow of a fire in the distance. Bilbo Baggins is tasked with going to see what the source of the glow is and discovers three Trolls sitting around a fire complaining that they have nothing but mutton to eat. These Trolls, Tom, Bert and William Huggins, have come down from the Ettendales and are the first obstacle that Thorin's Company will encounter on their Quest to regain the treasure of Erebor. Deciding to try pickpocketing them rather than return empty-handed, Bilbo attempts to do this to William but is caught in the act. The Dwarves then come to Bilbo's aid but, one by one, they are covered in a sack and taken prisoner by the Trolls, who then argue about the best way to cook them.

When Bert finally convinces his two companions to roast the Company right away and to eat them as snacks later, a voice that sounds like William's comments that the night is too far advanced to roast the Dwarves. In fact, it is Gandalf who, hidden in the woods, is imitating the Trolls' voices in turn to make them argue and buy some time. At last, the sun appears on the horizon, turning Tom, Bert and William to stone. Freed, the Company search for the hiding place the Trolls need to protect themselves from the sun and find a cave containing precious treasure they have collected while looting. There are pots filled with gold and among this booty the Company discover three swords forged at Gondolin, the famous Elven city destroyed during the First Age. Gandalf and Thorin arm themselves

– Gandalf with Glamdring and Thorin with Orcrist – while Bilbo selects a small sword which he will later name Sting. Seventy-seven years later, in 3018 T.A., when being guided by Aragorn, the Hobbits Frodo, Sam, Merry and Pippin see with their own eyes the frozen Trolls they have so often heard about in Bilbo's tales.

The chapter about the three Trolls has many similarities with certain tales by the Brothers Grimm. In the Grimm Brothers' Fairy Tales, the young hero of 'The Trained Huntsman' sees the glow of a fire in the forest and approaches it, discovering three giants busy

These Trolls, Tom, Bert and William Huggins, have come down from the Ettendales and are the first obstacle that Thorin's Company will encounter on their Quest to regain the treasure of Erebor.

roasting an ox. Similarly, 'The Brave Little Tailor' contains a scene that could have been an inspiration for the trick Gandalf plays on the Trolls. In this tale, the hero manages to get two giants to continue fighting by throwing stones at them, making each believe that it is the other who is attacking him.

Took Family

'The Took family was still, indeed, accorded a special respect, for it remained both numerous and exceedingly wealthy, and was liable to produce in every generation strong characters of peculiar habits and even adventurous temperament. (The Lord of the Rings, prologue).

The Took family is one of the most important Hobbit families in the Shire and is held in great respect, despite certain members at times behaving so extraordinarily for Hobbits that rumour has it that there was a fairy in their ancestry. Two of the Old Took's sons, for instance, have been on long journeys. The first, Hildifons, left the Shire and never returned; while the second, Isengar, went to sea, even though Hobbits are known to be wary of water. The Took descendants include some illustrious Hobbits, such as Bilbo Baggins and his cousin Frodo, as well as Merry Brandybuck and Pippin Took, all of whom are descended from the Old Took. Most of the clan settled in the West Farthing of the Shire, in the large smials of Tuckborough. This important village was where the Thain of the Shire resided when the title fell to the Took family in the person of Isumbras I in 2340 T.A. The

title then passed from father to son, and the patriarch of the family was referred to as 'the Took' or by his first name followed by the appropriate number, for example, Fortinbras I or Isumbras IV.

In 2747 T.A., Bandobras Took, a Hobbit known for his tall height (he was 1m 40 / 4ft 7in tall) and nicknamed the Bullroarer,

The Took descendants include some illustrious Hobbits, such as Bilbo Baggins and his cousin Frodo.

distinguished himself at the Battle of Greenfields. He drove back the Goblin enemy after beheading their chieftain, Golfimbul. His great nephew Gerontius Took was

known for his longevity, as he reached the age of 130, earning himself the nickname of the Old Took. He was also the father of Belladonna Took, the wife of Bungo Baggins and mother of Bilbo. In fact, Bilbo is the only Hobbit to beat the Old Took's record of longevity, reaching the age of 131 in 3021 T.A., just before leaving Middle-earth.

One of the best-known Tooks is Peregrin, known as Pippin, who joins the Fellowship of the Ring in 3018 T.A. He and his cousin Meriadoc (Merry) Brandybuck are captured by the Uruk-hai who are marauding along the Anduin river, but they manage to flee and encounter the Ents of Fangorn Forest with whom they attack Orthanc, Saruman's tower. After they meet up again with some of their companions, the Wizard Gandalf takes Pippin to Minas Tirith, where Pippin becomes a guard of the Citadel before swearing allegiance to the Steward Denethor II. Pippin takes part in the defence of Minas Tirith and the Battle of Morannon, during which he kills a Troll. He returns to the Shire with Merry, Sam Gamgee and Frodo Baggins after the coronation of King Aragorn and discovers his country sacked by Saruman. The valiant Hobbits then mobilize the population to restore order in the Shire at the Battle of Belleau Wood. From 3019 T.A. to his death in year 65 of the Fourth Age, he remains a Knight of Gondor and Messenger of the King. In year 13 of the Fourth Age, the title of Thain of the Shire passes to him, and the following year King Aragorn appoints him Councillor of the North Kingdom. In 63 Fth.A., he bequeaths his titles to his son Faramir I and leaves the Shire with Merry to go to Rohan, then to Gondor, where he dies and is buried in the necropolis of the Kings.

White Council

'It appeared that Gandalf had been to a great council
of the white wizards, masters of lore and
good magic.' (The Hobbit, Ch. 19).

It is only at the very end of Bilbo Baggins' adventure that we learn of the event that removes Gandalf from the plot from when Thorin and Company enter Mirkwood until Bilbo's attempt to find a solution to the inextricable conflict into which Dwarves, Men and Elves have strayed. Gandalf has been forced to leave his companions to take part in a council of white wizards, described to us as a council of war. This White Council is responsible for remaining alert to the expected return of Sauron, the Dark Lord. It is composed of Elven nobility, foremost among them Elrond, Galadriel and Círdan, along with Gandalf and Saruman, his superior in the order of the Istari Wizards. In this year, 2941 of the Third Age, the White Council intervenes to drive away the Necromancer – none other than Sauron himself – from his sinister lair at Dol Guldur, even if they are unable to banish him from the world once and for all. Their success will prove an illusory victory, as Sauron had, for a long

time, been planning a strategic retreat. Yet it all starts with the best of omens. In 2463 of the Third Age, the most powerful Elf Lords join forces with the Istari, emissaries of Valar, who are sent to Middle-earth to thwart Sauron's predictable return. This gathering of the Wise is known as the White Council in memory of an ancient institution founded in the Second Age with the aim, even back then, of fighting the enemy of the Free Peoples.

Yet, despite the purity of its name and its glorious patronage, the Council is tarnished from its outset by power struggles; the decision as to who should lead the Council provokes a confrontation between the pride of Saruman, the shadowy leader of the Wizards, and the Elf wisdom of Lady Galadriel. Despite Saruman's fierce opposition, Galadriel wishes to see the role of head of the Council go to Gandalf. Unwilling to take on this office, Gandalf cedes it to his superior. But this first chapter in the history of the White Council places Gandalf in a downward spiral as the

choice of Saruman proves to be disastrous. Consumed by a thirst for power, he fails in his mission and uses his position for his personal goals.

Concerned by the Necromancer's manoeuvres, Gandalf finds his way into Dol Guldur in 2850 T.A., meets with Thráin II and becomes certain that the Necromancer is none other than Sauron himself, who is gathering the Rings of Power and seeking the One Ring to finally crush the Free Peoples. At the meeting of the White Council the following year, Gandalf tries to persuade the Council members to intervene without delay. But Saruman reassures the Council, saying that his own research has led him to discover that the Ring has been lost forever and that Sauron, stripped of most of his power, no longer poses a serious threat. These machinations of its leader thus turn the White Council into the very body that allows the Enemy to continue the preparations for his return. Saruman has betrayed his noble mission and opposed Gandalf solely in order to have a better chance of finding the Ring for himself. Eventually, fearing that Sauron will overtake him in this quest, he agrees to Gandalf's request at the White Council meeting of 2941 T.A. And so it is that the Council drive Sauron out of his stronghold

at Dol Guldur, while Thorin, Bilbo and the Dwarves continue on their quest alone.

By intervening so late, the Council are only able to gain a short respite. Sauron's plans have been disrupted but his power is not reduced: he has fled from his enemies only in order to regroup and organize his counterattack. Ten years after this episode, he reveals himself blatantly, reclaims his former kingdom of Mordor and openly prepares for the War of the Ring. Faced with this threat, the White Council meets one final time, in 2953 T.A., but Saruman doggedly maintains his position. Claiming that the Ring is lost forever, he retreats to the fortress of Isengard, effectively endorsing the end of the Council.

From an intertextual point of view, it is interesting to note that this narrative element that appears only indirectly in *The Hobbit* is one of the components used by Tolkien to enrich, consolidate and harmonize the world he was fashioning over the course of his writing. To retrace the history of the Council, we must, in fact, delve into *The Silmarillion* and his *Unfinished Tales* as well as the appendices to *The Lord of the Rings*: the White Council thus creates a bridge between the different ages of Middle-earth and between Tolkien's different writings devoted to its history.

Peoples and creatures

Dragons

'Then dragon's ire more fierce than fire/
Laid low their towers and houses frail.'

(The Hobbit, Ch. 1).

According to the texts that have come down to us, it seems that the Dragons were created by Morgoth, the master of Sauron the Necromancer, in the First Age of Middle-earth, some 6,000 years before the adventures of Bilbo Baggins. The learned Elves of the First Age recorded that there were at least four types of dragons: the Urulóki, or 'Fire Drakes'; the Rámalóki, or 'Winged Dragons'; the Foalóki, or 'Spark Dragons'; and the Lingwilóki, the 'Fish Dragons' or 'Sea Serpents', but only the first two types are described in any detail in the stories now available to us.

Physically, Dragons resembled giant snakes or lizards, with or without wings, depending on their family. Their bodies were covered with scales, apart from the weak point of their breast, which they sometimes protected with armour made of gemstones from their treasure trove. Dragons spat fire through their mouth and nostrils. Their sense of smell was highly developed and their piercing stare, combined with their eloquence, enabled them to hypnotize their victims. Their intelligence made them very astute, and they loved playing riddle games that allowed them to glean considerable information from an enemy, even when the latter spoke very little. Finally, like all good guardians of treasure, they coveted wealth and were extremely avaricious. The corrupting power of their treasure meant that this avarice would also contaminate anybody else desirous of getting their hands on it.

The first Dragon in Middle-earth was an Urulókë named Glaurung, the Father of all the Dragons. He made his earliest appearance in the year 260 F.A., at the siege of Morgoth's castle laid by the Noldor Elves. Glaurung was still a youngster and was quickly repelled by Fingon, the Lord of the Elves, but he re-emerged in 455 F.A., accompanied by Balrogs and followed by many Orc soldiers. This time, the attack proved a success, as the Elven and Mannish troops were defeated in the Battle of Dagor Bragollach. Glaurung then participated in the destruction of Middle-earth by triggering the collapse of major cities on behalf of his master, before being killed in 495 F.A. by the hero Túrin Turambar (as recounted in *The Children of Húrin*). Dragons were also involved in the fall of Gondolin, one of the biggest of the Elven cities, in 510 F.A. The famous swords Glamdring, Orcrist and Sting that Bilbo and the Dwarves discovered in the treasure of the three trolls Tom, Bert and William came from Gondolin. A mere 40 years after Gondolin fell, the first winged Dragons appeared. At that time, the Valar, the divine powers, were assembling their armies to fight against Morgoth alongside Elves and Men. Morgoth chose this moment to unveil the first winged Dragons, led by the most powerful of all, Ancalagon the Black. Eärendil, the father of Elrond the Half-Elf, navigated his flying ship, the Vingilot, and, with the support of an army of birds led by the Eagle Thorondor, defeated Ancalagon in an epic aerial battle. The fall of the enormous Dragon destroyed the towers in Morgoth's castle, Thangorodrim, allowing the troops of the Valar to overcome the armies of the Dark Lord. Only a couple of winged Dragons survived this battle, and they fled eastward. We can assume that they settled in the Grey Mountains, to the north of the Forest of Great Fear and the Lonely Mountain, and that they gave rise to a new generation of Dragons, from which Smaug emerged.

Little is known about Dragons' activities during the Second Age, but they seem to have used this period to consolidate themselves. They start to be mentioned again in the middle of the Third Age, particularly on account of their frequent conflicts with Dwarves and Men. We know, for example, that the celebrated hero Fram,

The first Dragon in Middle-earth was an Urulókë named Glaurung, the Father of all the Dragons.

an ancestor of the Rohirrim, had a fight with the Dragon Scatha in 2000 T.A. After valiantly defeating him, Fram kept some of the Dragon's treasure to hand on to his descendants. The horn offered to the Hobbit Meriadoc Brandybuck by Éowyn, a warrior princess from Rohan, came from that hoard. Two hundred years after the death of Scatha, Thorin I (the ancestor of Thorin II Oakenshield) led some of his subjects into the Grey Mountains in order to exploit the local resources. They settled there and enjoyed prosperity for a while – until they found themselves confronting Dragons eager to acquire the treasures that the Dwarves were bringing to light. This war

raged for almost 380 years, until the deaths of Dáin I and his son Frór, who were killed by a large Cold-drake, a Dragon that could not breathe fire.

The Dwarves then returned to their former homes but, 200 years later, in 2770 T.A., Smaug the Golden, the last and most powerful of the great Dragons, flew from the Grey Mountains to the Lonely Mountain. He inflicted destruction on the lands of Erebor and chased the people of Thrór – the grandfather of Thorin Oakenshield – out of the Kingdom under the Mountain. Thrór and his son Thráin II, Thorin's father, escaped through a secret door in the side of the Lonely Mountain, just as Smaug was sacking the palace and installing his bed in the Great Hall. Smaug was not killed until 2941 T.A., during the Quest of Erebor, when Bard the Dragon-Slayer pierced his breast with an arrow during his attack on the lake town of Esgaroth. Smaug destroyed the town in his death throes, although it was later rebuilt further north of the Long Lake. The water into which Smaug fell was considered to be cursed and his bones were left there, in the midst of the ruins of the old town.

Tolkien mainly drew inspiration from Western mythologies and Scandinavian, Germanic and Old English literature for the creation of his Dragons. The character Glaurung was particularly influenced by the dragon Fáfnir from the legend of Sigurd, taken from *The Völsunga Saga*, a Norse text that Tolkien rewrote and published under the title *The Legend of Sigurd and Gudrún*. The circumstances of Glaurung's death, for example, are an almost identical reworking of those of Fáfnir's: Glaurung is pierced from top to bottom by Túrin's magic sword, just as Fáfnir is by Sigurd's sword, Gram. The dragon Ancalagon and his fight against Eärendil can be traced back to Nordic mythology, where the dragon Jörmungand confronts the god Thor at Ragnarök, or the end of the world, as well as St John's biblical account of the Apocalypse, in which Satan, in the guise of a dragon, enters into combat with St Michael the Archangel and is defeated. Nevertheless, Tolkien's main source of inspiration was undoubtedly the Old English text of *Beowulf*, which provided a model, for example, for Bilbo Baggins' theft of Smaug's cup and the destructive madness that ensued. In *Beowulf*, an unidentified character steals a cup from a dragon sleeping on a treasure trove, sparking such a fury in him that he lays waste the surrounding countryside until the hero arrives on the scene to confront the monster.

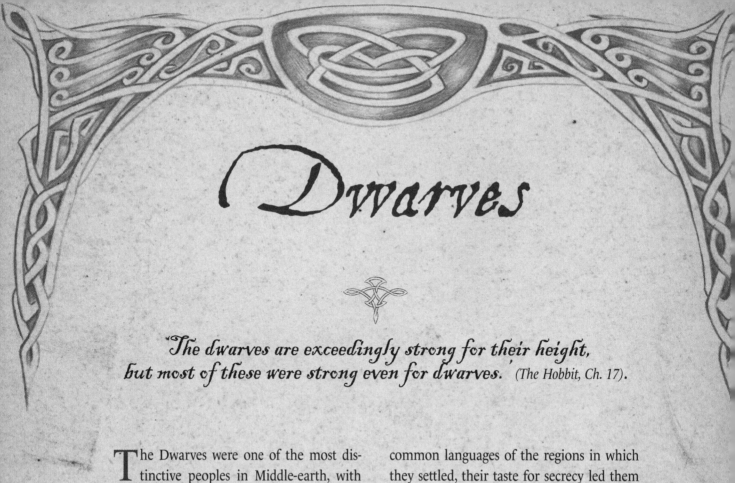

Dwarves

*'The dwarves are exceedingly strong for their height,
but most of these were strong even for dwarves.'* (The Hobbit, Ch. 17).

The Dwarves were one of the most distinctive peoples in Middle-earth, with a history that dated back to the Elder Days. Their small stature and beards made them instantly recognizable. They were fearsome warriors who were robust and resilient, as well as being goldsmiths highly skilled in working in forges and mines. Their ideal habitat was the interior of mountains, which served as their fortress, their workshop and the location for their mining operations. Their life expectancy was far longer than that of Men or Hobbits, but they were not immortal like the Elves. They were a secretive people who revealed little about their history and culture: Gandalf, for example, was kept in ignorance of even an event as decisive as the death of Thrór, the head of Durin's Folk, for a full 150 years. Despite the Dwarves' adoption of the common languages of the regions in which they settled, their taste for secrecy led them to preserve their own language, *khuzdul*, for internal use and to prevent any rare outsider who penetrated their circles from ever learning it.

The origins of the Dwarves can be traced back to the start of the First Age: the Vala Aulë, known to the Dwarves as Mahal, made the Seven Fathers of the Dwarves under a mountain in Middle-earth, out of impatience for the arrival of the Elves and the Men, which had been predicted since the beginning of the world. The Creator, Ilúvatar, forgave Aulë for his impatience but ordered him to wait for the Elves to be the Firstborn before permitting the Dwarves to awaken in their turn. Aulë then laid the Dwarves under the Blue Mountains, beneath Mount Gundabad, in the Misty Mountains, and also further

to the east. Each of the Seven Fathers gave rise to a clan, with the following names: the Longbeards, the Firebeards, the Broadbeams, the Ironfists, the Stiffbeards, the Blacklocks and the Stonefoots. Durin I founded the kingdom of the Longbeards in the mines of Moria, near Lake Kheled-zâram, while the Firebeards and the Broadbeams settled in the cities of Nogrod and Belegost under the Blue Mountains, and they were the ones who came across the Elves from Beleriand. For a long time, the Dwarves and the Elves enjoyed a relationship based on mutual aid: the Dwarves fitted out the palaces for the Elf Kings of Doriath and Nargothrond, as well as forging their weapons, gold and jewellery, while the Elves taught the Dwarves how to write runes and paid them with pearls from Balar, which they valued enormously. When the Goblins attacked the Elves of Beleriand, the two peoples joined forces in their defence. This cosy understanding would be tested, however, by a dispute over a sumptuous necklace, fashioned by Dwarves with materials provided by the Elves. This quarrel took a dramatic turn and eventually descended into outright warfare when the Elf King Elu Thingol, Lúthien's father, was murdered and Doriath was ransacked, leading to reprisals against the Dwarves of Nogrod.

Also in the First Age, the Dwarves of Moria, who had had no particular contact with the Elves, encountered the first Men, newly arrived from the East. And, when Beleriand was submerged under flood waters, many Dwarves came to the Misty Mountains to join up with the Line of Durin.

In the Second Age, the Dwarves of Moria established close links with the New Elf kingdom of Eregion, and it was probably in this period that the Elves gave them the Ring of Power of Durin's Folk. Soon, however, Sauron forged the One Ring, destroyed Eregion and set about bringing all the rings under his own power. He turned Men into his servants by distributing the Nine Rings among them. He tried the same ruse with the Dwarf Lords, but these proved harder nuts to crack: the only effect that the Rings had on them was to fan the flames of their lust for riches. After the destruction of Eregion, the Dwarves of Moria helped the surviving Elves to escape towards the North, where Elrond would soon found Rivendell. The Dwarves then took shelter in their homes under the mountains, where they would later have to fight against the advance of the Goblins.

In the Third Age, the wealth of Moria was particularly dependent on its deposits of mithril, which was becoming scarce. While they were excavating far beneath the surface, the Dwarves roused a Balrog, an ancient demon from the First Age. The Balrog killed first Durin VI and then Náin I, which led the Dwarves to abandon Moria and establish new kingdoms in the Grey Mountains, Erebor and the Iron Hills, while fighting against both Dragons and Goblins. After the death of Dáin I and his youngest son, the Dwarves abandoned the Grey Mountains too. The death of Thrór, the

Lord of the oldest branch of the seven clans, triggered the War of the Dwarves and Orcs, in which Dwarves from the other houses joined forces with Durin's Folk to exact revenge for the Goblin Azog's insult to their race. Apart from this episode, however, Durin's Folk had little contact with the other clans. After Smaug's death, Thorin Oakenshield asked Roäc to provide all the Dwarves in the region with messenger crows, in order to improve Erebor's defences.

There were considerable improvements in the relationships between Dwarves, Elves and Men after the Battle of the Five Armies, even though old suspicions and prejudices still persisted and each party kept a certain distance out of pride. The Dwarves'

Also in the First Age, the Dwarves of Moria, who had had no particular contact with the Elves, encountered the first Men, newly arrived from the East.

misfortunes made them reluctant to trust other peoples and slow to open up to outsiders, giving rise to strange misconceptions. For example, as female Dwarves were few in number, sported a beard just like the males and were rarely seen in public, rumour had it that the Dwarves did not have wives and that their females were made of stone. Similarly, mystery surrounded the circumstances of their death, as they did not form part of the original creation plan: it was sometimes thought that Dwarves returned to the stone from whence they came, while they themselves believed that they would be called upon to rebuild the world after the Last Battle. The Dwarves maintained that, as adopted children of Ilúvatar, they would finally be recognized as the equals of Elves and Men after this reconstruction, and that the Seven Fathers would return amongst them.

Practically all the names of the Dwarves in *The Hobbit* and *The Lord of the Rings* are derived from the Scandinavian *Edda*, particularly the *Dvergatal*, or 'Catalogue of Dwarves', in the great mythological poem, the *Völuspá*. Tolkien wanted to extricate his dwarf characters from fairy tales and anchor them in a mythical but historically coherent past. Accordingly, he opted to use the plural 'dwarves', instead of the then more standard 'dwarfs', in order to distance his characters, however subtly, from the debased images of these creatures in modern stories. Although the inspiration for the Dwarves clearly lay, therefore, in Northern Europe, the language that Tolkien invented for them drew, in contrast, on Semitic languages. This is also true of some of the customs that Tolkien attributed to them: shaving beards during mourning and the insistence on burying the dead (there was only one case of cremation

in the Dwarves' entire history – after the Battle of Azanulbizar). Furthermore, the history of the Dwarves is of a people in exile, and Tolkien himself stated that he had modelled the Dwarves of Middle-earth on popular depictions of Jews.

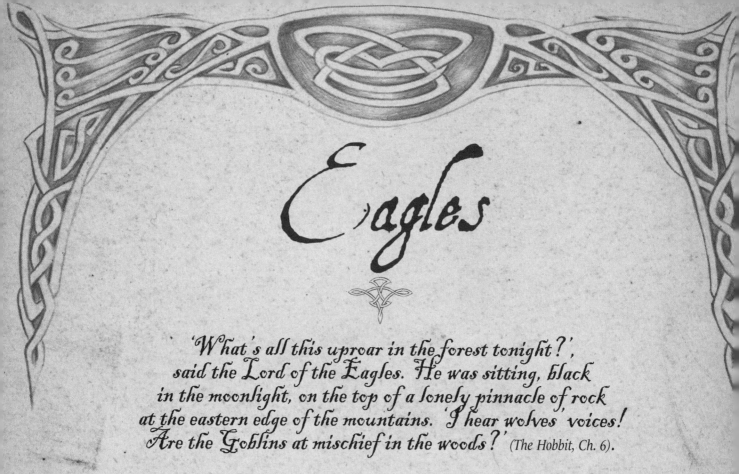

Eagles

'What's all this uproar in the forest tonight?',
said the Lord of the Eagles. He was sitting, black
in the moonlight, on the top of a lonely pinnacle of rock
at the eastern edge of the mountains. 'I hear wolves' voices!
Are the Goblins at mischief in the woods?' *(The Hobbit, Ch. 6).*

The great Eagles of the Misty Mountains made two interventions in the Quest of Erebor. The Lord of the Eagles, intrigued by the night-time screaming of the Wargs and the fire started by the Wizard Gandalf, assembled his vassals in order to find out more. He saved Gandalf at the last moment, just as the Wizard was about to jump from a treetop, and he dispatched some of his followers to disperse the Wargs and Goblins. Other Eagles went to save the Dwarves in the flaming trees. Bilbo Baggins was almost forgotten in this rescue operation and had to cling to Dori's legs during the journey to the Eagles' eyrie. Thorin and Company were then ushered onto the Great Shelf, where Bilbo discovered that the Lord of the Eagles was willing to

help them, in appreciation of the treatment that he had once received from Gandalf after being wounded by an arrow. The Eagles put the group up for the night, and the next day they took the group to the Carrock, an enormous rock in the middle of the River Anduin, but they refused to go any further because they did not want to get too close to the homes of the Woodmen.

The reader learns that the Eagles in the Misty Mountains had observed the movements of the Goblins in the Battle of the Five Armies and had assembled for the confrontation. They were spotted from afar by Bilbo, and their arrival rekindled the courage of the Elves in the Forest of Great Fear, the men in Lake-town and the Dwarves on the Iron

Hills. The Eagles dislodged the Goblins from the slopes of the Lonely Mountain and changed the course of the battle. Following the victory of the Free Peoples, Dáin II Ironfoot thanked the Lord of the Eagles by giving him a golden crown, as well as a gold necklace for each of his principal fifteen vassals. Some of the Eagles helped track down the last of the Goblins before returning home.

The origins of the Great Eagles of the Misty Mountains are obscure. Their first manifestation was the Maiar, who adopted the appearance of birds of prey to serve as messengers for Manwë, the chief of all the Valar. When Morgoth, the first Dark Lord, fled from Middle-earth, some Eagles followed to keep an eye on him and find out who was summoning him to the Valar. They initially stayed on Thangorodrim, the triple-peaked mountain that overlooked Morgoth's home. When Morgoth became too powerful, they settled in the Crissaegrim, the mountains surrounding Gondolin. The Eagles' chief, Thorondor, made an alliance with the Elf king Turgon, an ancestor of Elrond, and ensured that Morgoth's spies did not discover the location of Gondolin. During the Beleriand Wars, the Eagles kept watch over the Elves and their allies from a distance and sometimes came to their assistance, although without becoming involved in any battles between the Elves and the forces of Morgoth (the Noldor Elves having rejected the protection of the Valar). Thorondor also helped Fingon when he

ventured onto Thangorodrim to rescue his friend Maedhros, who had been taken prisoner by Morgoth. In the year 456 F.A., Thorondor witnessed the fight between Morgoth and the Great King Fingolfin and subsequently carried the latter's body to Gondolin for burial. Two years later, the Eagles saved the young Húrin and Huor, who had got lost on the arid foothills of the Crissaegrim, and took them to Gondolin. Turgon then delivered them to the family after they had sworn never to tell anybody about their adventure.

In 466 F.A., Beren and Lúthien seized one of the Silmarils from Morgoth's crown, but Beren was wounded by the wolf Carcharoth and lost the Silmaril. Thorondor and his

The reader learns that the Eagles in the Misty Mountains had observed the movements of the Goblins in the Battle of the Five Armies and had assembled for the confrontation.

two most powerful vassals, Landroval and Gwaihir, came to their rescue and took them to Lúthien's home country. In 510 F.A., Morgoth attacked and razed Gondolin. The survivors were caught in an ambush in the mountains, but the Eagles attacked the Goblins, thus enabling Tuor and the Elves to escape. Thirty-five years later, the Valar finally

came to the aid of Middle-earth, in response to the pleas of Eärendil: this was the start of the War of Wrath, which would last until 587 F.A. In desperation, Morgoth released winged dragons against the forces of the Valar. Eärendil then came to the rescue with his flying ship, aided by Thorondor, who led the great Eagles and all the birds of the sky into battle. Ancalagon the Black, the most powerful of all the dragons, was overcome after a long fight, and the Valar forces thus emerged victorious.

When Men settled on the island of Númenor, their alliance with the Valar was witnessed by the Eagles, the only birds who ventured to the sacred peak of Meneltarma. If anybody happened upon the peak, three Eagles would appear to stand guard on three rocks close to the western ridge. During the festivities in honour of Ilúvatar, however, these three Eagles, known as the Witnesses of Manwë, did not stay on their perches but instead circled above the crowd. When the last king of Númenor, Ar-Pharazôn, was persuaded by Sauron to make war against the Valar, large clouds in the form of Eagles regularly appeared from the West at nightfall, sometimes accompanied by thunder. During the evening when the forces of Ar-Pharazôn set off in the direction of Valinor, the Eagle-shaped clouds approached again, in an endless row, their wings sweeping the sky from North to South, presaging the anger of the Valar and the devastation of Númenor.

At the start of the War of the Ring, many birds were asked by the Wizard Radagast to keep watch on the movements of Sauron. The Eagles were the first to spot troop movements and the Nazgûls' ride in search of the One Ring. They also observed Gollum's escape from the prison in which he was being held by the Elves of Thranduil and passed this news on to Gandalf, who set off for Orthanc. Gwaihir was able to free Gandalf, who was being held captive by Saruman, and to take him to the Rohirrim to find a horse. Gwaihir later rescued Gandalf again on the peak of Celebdil, after the latter's victorious fight against the Balrog of Moria, and took him to Lórien to be cared for by Galadriel.

The Eagles of the Misty Mountains intervened on another occasion to assist the troops of Aragorn, who had been attacked by Goblins outside the Black Gate of Mordor. At the request of Gandalf, Gwaihir, Landroval and a young Eagle called Meneldor headed towards Mount Doom in order to rescue Frodo Baggins and Samwise Gamgee and lead them to safety. During this period, another Eagle flew towards Minas Tirith and announced the victory of the Free Peoples.

Tolkien first introduced Eagles into the early versions of *The Book of Lost Tales* and often gave them a role of *deus ex machina* at times of 'eucatastrophe'. Despite the importance of the Lord of the Eagles in *The Hobbit*, we are not told his name, although we are given to understand that he is not Gwaihir, who only transports Gandalf in the War of the Ring. The Eagle was frequently considered a royal bird in European mythologies, reputed to be able to stare into the sun without blinking (an attribute borrowed by Tolkien). To the Ancient Greeks and Romans, the Eagle was the symbol and messenger of Zeus-Jupiter, although its long-sightedness was little appreciated, as the chief of the gods was already supposed to be able to observe all things from his throne on Mount Olympus. In contrast, the Eagles' role as Manwë's eyes is directly inspired by Odin's two crows, Huginn and Muninn, in the *Eddas*, who roam the world every day so that they can bring back news to the one-eyed god. Tolkien wrote in his letters that he had refrained from involving the Eagles too often in his narrative, for fear of devaluing them and undermining their credibility.

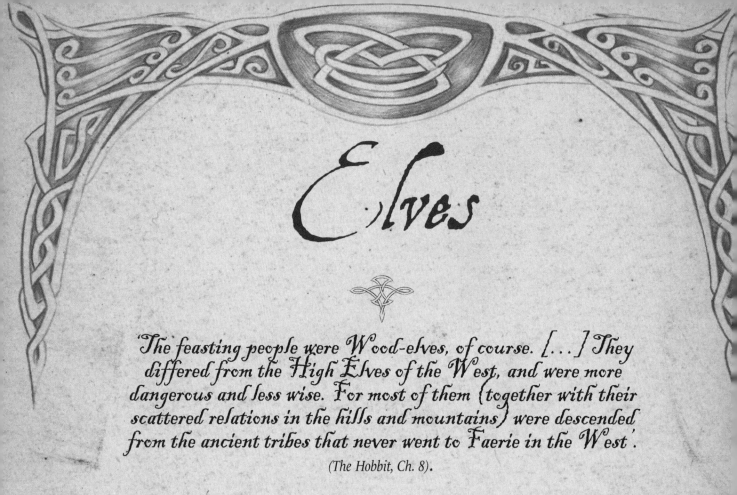

Elves

The Elves were one of the peoples inhabiting Middle-earth, distinguishable from Dwarves and Men by their exceptional longevity, verging on immortality. They were often over two metres (6ft 6in) tall and proved particularly attractive to Men (hence their popular name of the Beautiful People). Bilbo Baggins and the Dwarves of Thorin and Company encountered the Elves twice during the Quest of Erebor. The first occasion was at Elrond's house in Rivendell, where the travellers were well received, but the second, with the Elves of the Forest of Great Fear, was less agreeable, as the Dwarves were taken prisoner, under orders from King Thranduil.

Elves cannot be considered a homogeneous or unique people, as they divided into many branches over the course of their very long history. Almost at the dawn of time, before any illumination from the sun or moon, 144 Elves awoke on the shore of Lake Cuiviénen, in the far east of Middle-earth. They called themselves Quendi, meaning 'those who speak', because at that time they were the only inhabitants of Middle-earth with the power of speech. After their Awakening, they separated into three clans: the Minyar, the Tatyar and the Nelyar. When the Valar found out about this awakening, they invited the Elves to live with them in Faërie, also known as Valinor, across the sea to the West. Some Elves turned down the offer, preferring to remain below the stars: these were the

Avari. Those who agreed to follow the Valar were called the Eldar, the People of the Stars.

The Eldar maintained their division into three clans and formed three peoples: the Vanyar, or Pale-Elves; the Noldor, or Deep-Elves; and the Teleri, or Latecomers. The Vanyar went to Valinor, accompanied by some Noldor and Teleri. Some of the latter took fright in the Misty Mountains, turned back and settled in the Anduin Valley, giving rise to the Nandor people. Other Teleri crossed the mountains, but came to a halt at the shores of the Great Sea or in the forests of Beleriand; these were known as the Sindar and were ruled by Thingol, the future king of Doriath. The Teleri who did reach Valinor became expert navigators – hence their popular name of Sea-Elves. At this time, Valinor was illuminated by two extraordinary trees, one silver and one gold. The Elves who reached Valinor were then called the Calaquendi, or High-Elves, while those who remained under the stars in Middle-earth, the Avari, were grouped together, along with the Nandor and the Sindar, under the generic name of Moriquendi. The Elves in Valinor cultivated their knowledge and lived in peace. Fëanor, the eldest son of the Great King of the Noldor, created the Silmarils, three sacred jewels containing the light of the Two Trees. Centuries later, Morgoth, the first Dark Lord, the master of Sauron, stole these precious jewels, killed Fëanor's father, destroyed the Two Trees and fled to Middle-earth.

Valinor was plunged into darkness, and Fëanor and his seven sons swore to seek revenge and recover the Silmarils at any cost. A substantial portion of the Noldor rallied to their cause, but the Teleri from Alqualondë refused to come to their assistance – so Fëanor decided to steal their ships. The Teleri defended themselves, however, and the first ever fratricidal battle between Elves ensued. The Fëanorians emerged victorious, and the event would go down in history as the Alqualondë Massacre. This intervention was sternly condemned by the Valar, but Fëanor, consumed with pride, rebelled and crossed the sea, having first promised to send back ships to look for those Noldor who had been unable to obtain a place for the crossing. When Fëanor landed in Middle-earth, however, he began to doubt the loyalty of those whom he had left behind and decided to burn the ships. Those Noldor who had been abandoned on the shores of Valinor did not give in but instead embarked on a long and difficult journey across the icy North in order to return to Middle-earth.

A number of them died on the way. During this time, the Valar made the Sun and the Moon with the final fruits from the dying Trees. Their first ascent into the sky coincided with the arrival of the Noldor in Middle-earth and the start of the measurement of the Ages.

The entire First Age was marked by long and bloody battles between Morgoth and the Elves. Fëanor was killed by a Balrog in the Battle under the Stars. The Noldor then founded several kingdoms in Beleriand and laid siege to Morgoth in his castle in Angband, eventually gaining the upper hand. Nevertheless, Morgoth gradually recovered the advantage, thanks to support from Goblins, Balrogs and Dragons. He was further assisted by the impulsiveness of Fëanor's sons, who twice attacked the heirs of Beren and Lúthien, who had succeeded in winning back one of the three Silmarils. Their behaviour also led to the ultimate destruction of the kingdom of Doriath and the pillage of the harbour on the Sirion. All hope seemed lost once Morgoth had defeated the Noldor. Eärendil, recently back from a long journey, went to beg the Valar to intervene. The First Age ended with the victory of the Valar army over Morgoth and his banishment beyond the Circles of the World. The irresponsibility of Fëanor's two living sons resulted in the loss of the two remaining Silmarils in the sea and in the depths of the Earth.

Distrust between the survivors of the kingdom of Doriath and the Noldor exiles still flared up occasionally, particularly regarding Oropher and his son Thranduil, who eventually left to found their own kingdom in Greenwood-the-Great (later the Forest of Great Fear). Over the course of the Second Age, Sauron, formerly Morgoth's servant, assumed his master's lust for power. Disguised as an Elf, he insinuated himself into the entourage of Fëanor's grandson, Celebrimbor, who was leading a group of goldsmiths to the Elven kingdom of Eregion. With their help, Celebrimbor forged the Rings of Power, including the Three Rings intended to protect his people. Sauron, however, secretly forged the One Ring, destined to control the other Rings, and a new war broke out when Celebrimbor realized that he had been duped. Sauron suffered an initial defeat thanks to military assistance by Men from Númenor, but he eventually succeeded in corrupting their kings, who revolted against the Valar and were annihilated. When Sauron returned to Middle-earth, he was confronted by a huge coalition army, the result of the Last Alliance of Elves and Men. It comprised members of all the Free Peoples and was jointly commanded by Elendil and Gilgalad, the last Great King of the Noldor. This army laid siege to Mordor for many long years. The war was particularly disastrous for the Silvan Elves in Lórien and Greenwood-the-Great, who were poorly armed and reluctant to obey Gilgalad. They lost more than a third of their troops, as well as two kings, Amdír and Oropher, in the conflict. Sauron

was defeated in the final battle, however, but Gilgalad was also killed.

The Third Age was more peaceful for the Elves protected by the Rings of Power in the possession of Elrond (in Rivendell) and Galadriel (in Lórien). As for the Silvan Elves, they experienced a gradual encroachment of shadow in their forest, which was being invaded by monstrous Spiders. The Noldor realized that their time was coming to an end and that the time of Men was at hand. They trickled out of Middle-earth and headed towards Valinor, boarding ships in the Grey Havens or the port of Edhellond, although some stayed behind to take part in the War of the Ring. Elrond provided the Fellowship of the Ring with material support, while Thranduil's son, Legolas, personally participated in the great battles of Helm's Deep, the Pelennor Fields and the Morannon, where he forged a celebrated friendship with the Dwarf Gimli, the son of Glóin. Galadriel and Thranduil, meanwhile, endured attacks from Sauron's forces from Dol Guldur, but they succeeded in pushing them back. After Sauron's defeat, Galadriel destroyed Dol Guldur and the Elves purified the forest. Peace having been restored, Legolas settled for a time in Ithilien, where he nurtured the woodlands back to their former glory. Galadriel and Elrond, however, decided to leave Middle-earth, in the company of Gandalf, Bilbo and Frodo Baggins. The Elf population began to decline. Elves could sometimes be taken for

extremely good-looking Men. Although the Noldor generally had brown hair (give or take a few blondes and redheads) and great physical agility, the Vanyar were known for their blonde hair and wisdom. As for the Teleri, they had an unrivalled reputation for singing; they usually had chestnut-brown hair, although some sported silvery locks. Elves retained a smooth face for a long time, although some would end up with a beard in old age, as in the cases of Mahtan and Círdan. Elves married only once (with one known exception, which had tragic consequences) and had very few children: Fëanor and his seven sons were the exception that proved the rule. From the very first year of their existence, Elves displayed great mastery over their bodies, being capable of walking and even dancing. They then took between 50 and 100 years to grow to full size. Their ageing process was also very slow (following the same rhythm as the Earth itself, unless they were subjected to gruelling challenges). They were highly resilient, capable of recovering from wounds that would kill a Man, and they had immunity from most diseases. Although they barely experienced an ageing process, they nevertheless felt the burden of the passing years. Elves would then tire of life, as manifested in a reduction in physical strength and size. Although they remained on their earthly lands, they started to become transparent; this is why they gradually left Middle-earth and headed towards Valinor, which exerted a great attraction over them. Any Elf possessed by the desire to take to sea and go to Valinor could never be completely happy in any other circumstances. Furthermore, Elves did not die in the same way as human beings. When an Elf's body expired, their spirit left for the Halls of Mandos, the Vala responsible for the dead. There, they underwent a prolonged healing process for any wounds that they had sustained in their life.

Once their spirit had found peace, they could be resuscitated and retake their place amongst the living in Valinor. Only one Elf who died in Middle-earth ever returned there: Glorfindel, the hero of Gondolin, who died while killing a Balrog to protect Eärendil, Elrond's father. At the request of the Valar, he went back to serve Elrond when Sauron made a reappearance in the Second Age.

Tolkien devoted most of his writing to Elves. They lie at the heart of his Middle-earth, and their adventures were partly conceived as a framework for the Elven languages that he had invented. Tolkien's Legendarium was built up over time, and the definition of the nature of Elves was only gradually revealed. In his early versions, as found in *The Book of Lost Tales*, Tolkien was still heavily influenced by elves from Victorian literature: small fairies that he had already evoked in poems. He later decided that these small creatures had once been big and powerful but had degenerated when human beings took possession of the world. This notion caused him to ponder on the Elves in their peak period, and for this he turned for inspiration to the Alfar in the *Eddas* (although some of the Elven kingdoms that he invented are reminiscent of the Irish Sîdh). When Tolkien came to write *The Hobbit*, these two diverging notions were both evident: the Elves of Rivendell are singing creatures who are light and joyous, but their chief, Elrond, is wise and serious.

Family tree of the Elven peoples

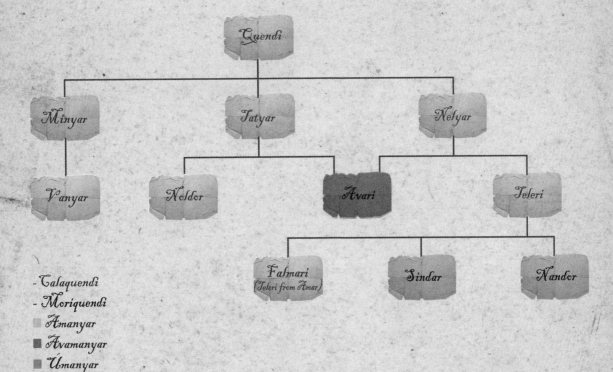

Quendi

Minyar — Tatyar — Nelyar

Vanyar — Noldor — Avari — Teleri

Falmari (Teleri from Aman) — Sindar — Nandor

- Calaquendi
- Moriquendi
  - Amanyar
  - Avamanyar
  - Úmanyar

Goblins

'There in the shadows on a large flat stone sat a tremendous goblin with a huge head, and armed goblins were standing round him carrying the axes and the bent swords that they use. Now goblins are cruel, wicked, and bad-hearted'. (The Hobbit, Ch. 4).

The Goblins (also referred to as Orcs by the Hobbits) were depraved, unnatural creatures bred by the fallen Vala Melkor out of Elves, Men and corrupted Maiar. They were small and stocky, with yellowish skin, long arms, arched legs, a flat nose, a big mouth and slanting eyes. They stayed away from sunlight. They were often fearful by nature, but they were always rude, spiteful and bloodthirsty. Any obedience on their part was due more to fear than choice. They reproduced in the same ways as Men and Elves. Their long-standing allies, the Wargs, allowed Goblins to ride them like horses.

Goblins made their initial appearance in the First Battle of Beleriand, in the First Age, before human beings found the Eldar. Melkor subsequently used them regularly in his army, but when he was expelled from the Circles of the World, the leaderless Goblins dispersed, although they continued to multiply. Some Goblins established independent colonies in the Misty Mountains, where they entered into conflicts with the Dwarves and took over some of their cities. Others were eventually reassembled in Mordor by Melkor's former servant, Sauron. In the Second Age, Goblins took part in the invasion of the Elven kingdom of Eregion and faced up to the troops of the Last Alliance. In the Third Age, Goblins took advantage of the Dwarves' flight from the Balrog to colonize Moria. The Goblin Azog unleashed a war between the Dwarves and the Goblins by murdering Thrór, and many of the Goblins in the Misty Mountains were wiped out or escaped to Rohan.

When Thorin and Company tried to cross the Misty Mountains in 2941 T.A., the Dwarves took shelter in a cave from a storm and from the Stone Giants. Orcs from Goblin Town emerged from the depths of the cave as the Company slept and took them prisoner. Goblin Town was a network of caves and galleries underneath the Misty Mountains, near the High Pass to the northeast of Rivendell. It was ruled by the Great Goblin, a ferocious Orc with an enormous head. Thorin and Company were presented to him after their capture. While the Great Goblin was ruminating on their fate, Gandalf, who had previously escaped, reappeared and killed him with Glamdring, and the prisoners took advantage of the ensuing uproar to make their escape. Unfortunately, Bilbo Baggins was knocked out in the chaotic rush. When he regained consciousness, he found the One Ring, although he did not yet realize its importance. He then came across the sinister Gollum, who was paddling a boat across an expanse of water. Gollum reluctantly took Bilbo to the exit, allowing him to rejoin his companions. So, Thorin and Company crossed the Misty Mountains via Goblin Town, from the main door on the western side to the rear door over to the east. The enraged Goblins pursued the Company and eventually trapped them in treetops, where they had already been detained by the Wargs. Gandalf started a fire in an attempt to disperse the attackers, and the Goblins were saved from the resulting conflagration by Giant Eagles.

The Orc Azog's son, Bolg, recruited an army of Goblins and Wargs, spurred by a desire to avenge the death of the Great Goblin and by news of the death of Smaug, the dragon who had guarded the treasure of Erebor. These troops headed for the Lonely Mountain. Their arrival was presaged by a swarm

They were small and stocky, with yellowish skin, long arms, arched legs, a flat nose, a big mouth and slanting eyes.

of black bats. At that time, a war over the treasure between Dwarves, Elves and Men seemed imminent, but the Free Peoples put their differences aside to defend themselves. The result was the Battle of the Five Armies, which ended with the decimation of the Goblins of the Misty Mountains, thanks to the arrival of the Eagles and the intervention of the skin-changer Beorn, who killed Bolg. The Woodmen, who had long endured the threat of attacks by Goblins, would thus be free of their presence for many years.

Around 2475 T.A., Sauron made improvements to the Goblin race, creating bigger and stronger Orcs with black skin who first appeared in Ithilien, on the edge of Mordor. They were known as Uruk-hai. These Uruks were led by the Nazgûl or by the Mouth of Sauron. They were most notably involved in the Battles of the Pelennor Fields and the Morannon. Saruman, for his part, was driven

by his lust for the One Ring to recruit these large Mordor Orcs and make them couple with Men, resulting in Half-Orcs. They had a more Mannish appearance, albeit with a sallow complexion and squinty eyes, and they did not shy away from sunlight. Saruman used the Half-Orcs to build the Ring of Isengard fortification and to form the army that he sent to invade Rohan in 3019 T.A. After its defeat, Saruman turned on the Shire, with the help of some of his Half-Orcs, and plunged the land of the Hobbits into turmoil. He was eventually stopped by Frodo Baggins and his companions, after their return from the Battle of Bywater.

The origins of the Goblins are unclear, as Tolkien drew up several different versions that left him unsatisfied. They initially came from stone, but Melkor, like Aulë, the creator of the Dwarves, is not supposed to have the power to give life. Tolkien then imagined them as corrupted Elves, but that option came up against the immortality of the Elves, which would also have to apply to Orcs. He then saw them as corrupted humans, but this was unviable because Tolkien's chronology showed Orcs appearing before Men, and he had not made sufficient changes to render this version totally compatible with the rest of the Legendarium.

In *The Hobbit*, Tolkien preferred the terms 'Goblin' and 'Hobgoblin' over 'Orc', which appears only a few times. Tolkien's Goblins are heavily indebted to the goblins of Victorian literature, particularly those in George MacDonald's novel *The Princess and the Goblin*, published in 1872. In 1915, Tolkien wrote a poem *Goblin Feet*, about fairy-like goblins resembling those of MacDonald, far closer to leprechauns than the future Uruk-hai. Tolkien himself ended up hating

> *The origins of the Goblins are unclear, as Tolkien drew up several different versions that left him unsatisfied.*

this concept of goblins. Accordingly, in *The Lord of the Rings*, Tolkien almost completely suppressed the word 'Goblin' in favour of 'Orc', derived from the Old English *orcneas*, meaning 'demon', most notably found in the phrase from Beowulf of *eotenas ond ylfe ond orcneas* (trolls and elves and orcs). Going further back in time, it also echoes Orcus, a god of the Underworld in the religion of ancient Rome.

The physical appearance of Tolkien's orcs was inspired by the false but enduring conception of Mongols that had become deeply rooted in the popular European imagination after the attacks perpetrated by Attila the Hun and the Mongols of Genghis Khan.

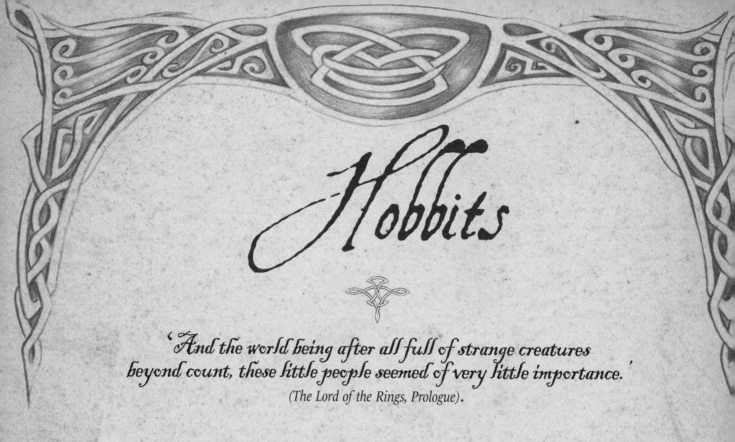

Hobbits

'And the world being after all full of strange creatures beyond count, these little people seemed of very little importance.'
(The Lord of the Rings, Prologue).

The major events of the Third Age revealed to the world the importance of a people who were usually overlooked: the Hobbits. Even wise men had considered these modest and peaceful creatures to be so insignificant that it was unimaginable that one of their number would play a crucial role in delivering the North from one of the period's greatest scourges: the dragon Smaug. It would be even harder to contemplate that the very same Hobbit, Bilbo Baggins, could discover Sauron's One Ring, or that his descendant, Frodo Baggins, could, along with three other Hobbits, help the Free Peoples of Middle-earth to emerge victorious from the terrible War of the Ring. Even Gollum, the strange creature who had possessed the Ring for over 500 years, was born from Hobbits, from another time and place (he was then called Sméagol). Gollum's great resistance to the

power of the Ring – greater than that of any human – and his affinity with Bilbo in the riddle game, during their encounter in the depths of the Misty Mountains, are striking characteristics typical of Hobbits. The Wizard Gandalf, a member of the White Council but guided more by his heart than his reason, was the only one of the Wise to show any initial curiosity about the Hobbits. Gandalf understood that, behind their insignificant exteriors, the Hobbits were a people worthy of interest. But what do we really know about them? According to the Elves and the Men of Gondor, the Hobbits were Half-Men. In effect, by the end of the Third Age, their height usually ranged between 60 and 120 cm (2ft and 3ft 11in); furthermore, their tastes and lifestyle revealed links to the human race. Physically, they barely resembled the Dwarves, who were bearded and more robust.

The Hobbits were smooth-faced, with slightly pointed ears and curly hair. As a general rule, they abhorred adventure, preferring an orderly, peaceful and sensible life. They also enjoyed food, drink, conviviality and smoking pipe-weed. They had round, cheerful faces and displayed a tendency to portliness, largely because they were accustomed to eating six meals a day. They liked clothes in bright colours, particularly yellow and green. Apart from their diminutive stature, two other features were specific to the Hobbits: their feet and their traditional dwellings. They generally went barefoot, as their soles were as tough as leather and their hands, feet and backs were covered with a brown fuzz similar to the hair on their head. They used to live in comfortable, well-equipped galleries, with varying degrees of size and luxury according to their personal affluence. These homes, which they called smials, were round, with circular doors and windows, although they also built less distinctive structures for their workshops, farms and barns. The name that they gave themselves in their own language – 'Hobbit' – meant somebody who lived in holes, and it was probably derived from the term 'Holbytla', used to describe them by the Men from Rohan. The Hobbits gradually assimilated the common language while still preserving a repository of words from their ancient tongues to identify, for example, the months and the days, as well as a host of proper names.

Hobbits were a very sociable people who loved chatting, jokes, parties, giving presents at the slightest excuse and writing letters to each other on a regular basis. They were also extremely faithful friends. They were not drawn to sophisticated technologies, but they did enjoy gardening, farming and all types of craftwork. They were very dextrous, with thin, elegant fingers. They had a taste for rumours, despite their unerring common sense, and they were fascinated by genealogies. They were also endowed with other qualities that served them outside the domestic sphere. They were

It was unimaginable that one of their number would play a crucial role in delivering the North from one of the period's greatest scourges: the dragon Smaug.

highly discreet, rendering them capable of going unnoticed. Hobbits had an acute sense of hearing, as well as exceptional eyesight, which made them formidable archers and stone slingers. They had astonishing powers of resilience against even the most difficult conditions, as they demonstrated during the Great Plague that ravaged the Shire in 1636 T.A., and in the famine resulting from the Long Winter of 2758. Although they were not aggressive, they were nevertheless capable of defending themselves and difficult to kill, as shown by their resistance against the

invasion of Goblins in 2747. These demanding tests were just distant memories for Bilbo, however, when, following encouragement by Gandalf and the thirteen Dwarves, he embarked on the Quest of Erebor, under the leadership of Thorin II Oakenshield. Bilbo lived in a particularly luxurious smial in Bag End, in the western neighbourhood of the village of Hobbiton. The Shire, in the midst of the old kingdom of Arnor, was the main territory of the Hobbits. In those times of peace, it was prosperous, lush and well-ordered, and the Hobbits took little notice of the outside world. They colonized it in 1601 T.A., after receiving authorization from the king of the Dúnedain of the North. This date thus became year 1 in the Shire's calendar.

Prior to that, the Hobbits had shown little interest in history beyond their own family trees, and they only had a few legends to evoke their distant past. These suggest that the Hobbit people originated from the upper valleys of the Anduin, between the Misty Mountains and Greenwood-the-Great. The shadow that fell over this forest, which was then renamed the Forest of Great Fear, was probably one of the reasons behind the exodus of the Hobbits. Over the course of their westward migration, the Hobbits divided into three separate branches, which were still discernible in Bilbo's time. The Harfoots were the most numerous and representative branch. They were smaller than the others, and preferred to live on highlands and hills. They were also the most attached to the tradition of smials. The Stoors, who were the last to arrive in the Shire, were bigger and gravitated towards river banks and lowlands. They were the least fearful of the Men. Finally, the Fallohides constituted the smallest branch, to the north, but they were the most adventurous of them all. They were present in the large Took and Brandybuck families. Bilbo, who was Baggins on his father's side and Took on his mother's, found two conflicting impulses within him: one more reasonable and more domestic, in keeping with the Harfoots, and another more adventurous, driven by the spirit of the Fallohides. Of these three branches, the Fallohides most often assumed a role of leadership. Thus, after the disappearance of the kings of the North, the Shire was placed under the authority of the Tháin, a title traditionally granted in Bilbo's time to the head of the Took family. In times of war, the Tháin was responsible for the armed forces, but his post was more of a formality in peacetime, less important than that of the mayor of Michel Delving, the Shire's main town, as the mayor was in charge of both the Messenger Service and the Watch. The former, responsible for postal delivery, was by far the most significant and well-resourced department. The Watch was divided into two: the Shirriffs were charged with maintaining order but essentially acted as land rangers, while the Bounders, or border guards, increased in numbers at the end of the Third Age in response to an increase in strange and unsettling incidents.

Tolkien's creation of the Hobbit people dates back to a time in the 1930s when he was immersed in the tedious task of correcting exams but was offered an unexpected moment of respite by a blank sheet of paper. He turned it over and wrote on the back: 'In a hole in the ground there lived a hobbit.' He then wondered what a hobbit was, and that was the starting point for Bilbo's story, which, years later, would lead to the account of the War of the Ring. Tolkien did not merely dream up a character, he also invented a creature and, even more, an entire people. Several sources seem to have inspired Tolkien. He stated that it had never occurred to him that there was any link between a Hobbit and a rabbit, even though the two terms rub shoulders several times in *The Hobbit*, and Hobbits traditionally lived underground. He may well have been influenced, however, by *The Marvellous Land of Snergs*, a children's story that he much admired, written by E.A. Wyke-Smith in 1927. The Snergs were small creatures who lived together off the beaten track and enjoyed drinking, eating and having fun. Tolkien went on to establish a connection between the term 'hobbit' and a hypothetical, newly minted Anglo-Saxon word 'holbytla', which would mean 'inhabitant of holes'. The name hobbit also appears in a collection of folklore published between 1846 and 1859, *The Denham Tracts*, where it signified 'a class of spirits'. Nevertheless, the Hobbit people is an invention of Tolkien's, although when he started telling Bilbo's story, he never imagined that it would occupy such a central place in his Elven Legendarium. He then considered that their great contribution would be as a means to present the ennoblement of modest, down-to-earth creatures, albeit with some heroic potential. When, in 1937, his publisher asked him to write a follow-up to *The Hobbit*, which had found great success, Tolkien did not initially think that there was any more to be said about these funny-looking, home-loving and eminently sensible little individuals. During the long years of writing *The Lord of the Rings*, however, he became fascinated by the juxtaposition of hobbits with darker and weightier far-reaching subjects. These stories from Tolkien's Legendarium thus opened up new perspectives, as they were no longer centred on Elves but rather on Hobbits, who offered a fresh vision of Faërie. So, the modern reader can now discover the Elder Days and the enchantment of the riches of Middle-earth with the same wonder as Sam, Frodo's gardener, encountering the ancient kingdom of Moria under the Misty Mountains. The invention of the Hobbit people considerably enriched Tolkien's Legendarium by allowing him to develop whole new territories and new periods of Middle-earth as habitats for Hobbits and settings for their adventures. The maps that Tolkien created for *The Hobbit* led him to dream up Middle-earth's Third Age, which permitted him to develop more fully the Elven legends of the Elder Days and delve into the new lands to the northwest of the Old World, after immersing himself in the areas in which the stories of the First Age unfurled.

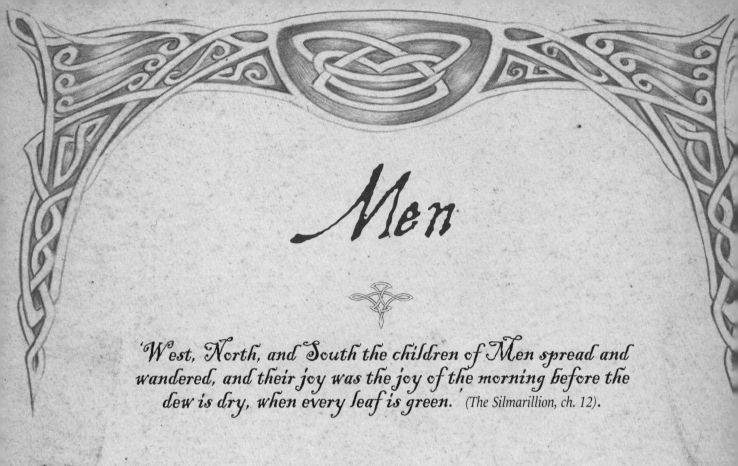

Men

'West, North, and South the children of Men spread and wandered, and their joy was the joy of the morning before the dew is dry, when every leaf is green.' (The Silmarillion, ch. 12).

The Men constituted one of the principal races inhabiting Middle-earth. The Elves referred to them as the 'Secondborn', because they were the second incarnated race to be created by the supreme deity Ilúvatar, after the Elves themselves. Physically, the Men were very similar to the Elves, to such an extent that their children could not always be told apart. They had one distinctive gift, however: the capacity to die by leaving the world for an unknown destination.

The Men's awakening occurred sometime in the First Age, to the east of Middle-earth, apparently coinciding with the first ever sunrise. Morgoth, the evil power whose foremost servant was Sauron the Necromancer, took advantage of their isolation and attempted to corrupt them. Many of the Men did choose to follow Morgoth, but others opted

to flee westward. Over the course of this migration (which lasted for centuries), some Men stopped and settled in the Wildenland or in Eriador, beyond the Misty Mountains. Three peoples of Men succeeded in crossing the Blue Mountains in 310 F.A.: those of Bëor, Haleth (the Haladin) and Marach (later to be known as the people of Hador). These three peoples formed the three Houses of Edain.

After the Elves encountered the Edain who had crossed the mountains, the Noldor gave them land and helped them settle in. An alliance was forged between Elves and Men, but the Elves became less trusting when Men professing allegiance to Morgoth began to trickle into the west of Middle-earth. After Morgoth's defeat at the end of the First Age, however, the Valar decided to reward the

Edain for their loyalty. They gave the Men a new plot of land, halfway between Middle-earth and Valinor: the island of Númenor. The Númenóreans, moreover, had a life expectancy that was three times that of an ordinary Man, but pride, envy and fear slowly corrupted their spirit. They became consumed by a desire to go to Valinor and live for ever. The kings of Númenor created colonies in Middle-earth to increase their power and showed no scruples about enslaving the local populations. The numbers of the Men who still followed the teachings of the Valar and the Elves dwindled, as they were increasingly persecuted by the King's Men. The Númenóreans tried to invade Valinor, urged on by Sauron, who had arrived at Númenor as a prisoner but managed to wheedle his way into the confidence of King Ar-Pharazôn. In response to this attack, a huge storm sent by Ilúvatar destroyed Ar-Pharazôn's fleet and flooded Númenor. The last of the Faithful had anticipated the island's submersion, however, and returned to Middle-earth, where they founded the kingdoms of Arnor and Gondor. At the end of the Second Age, under the leadership of Elendil, they formed part of the Last Alliance between Elves and Men, which resulted in the first defeat of Sauron. Over the course of the Third Age, the Elves gradually lost importance compared to the Men. Although few of the Dúnedain, Men from the West (the descendants of the Númenóreans), remained, and their numbers were continually diminishing, other

Mannish peoples were thriving, as were the Hobbits. During the Quest of Erebor, the Hobbit Bilbo Baggins and the Dwarves of Thorin and Company first came into contact with the people of Bree, the descendants of an ancient autochthonous people with links to the Haladin, and then with Beorn, a skin-changing inhabitant of the Vales of Anduin, and, finally, the residents of Lake-town, who regularly traded with the Elves of the Forest of Great Fear. On his return, Bilbo again met the Woodmen in Beorn's house, where the latter was celebrating the Mid-Winter feast. Although Tolkien introduced Men into his Legendarium very early on, his primary interest was their relationship with the Elves, because the Elven legends could only be passed on by Men once the Elves themselves start to dwindle in

The Elves referred to them as the 'Secondborn', because they were the second incarnated race to be created by the supreme deity Ilúvatar, after the Elves themselves.

numbers and then eventually are wiped out. His first texts thus focused on the great heroes of the First Age, such as Beren, Túrin and Tuor. Beren and Tuor both married Elven princesses: respectively, Lúthien, daughter of the King of Doriath, and Idril, daughter of the King of Gondolin. Elrond Half-Elven is

descended from both these unions. Tolkien's Legendarium is shot through with the idea that the Men's only true nobility comes from their Elven blood, or at the very least their familiarity with Elven teachings. Even in his writings on Men, Tolkien concentrated on the small minority of the Edain and their descendants the Dúnedain and gave limited space to 'Lesser Men' (with the notable exception of the Hobbits).

Tolkien was thus claiming a place in the lineage of the Scandinavian *Edda* and the Finnish *Kalevala*, in which men are evoked essentially for their relationships with gods and higher beings.

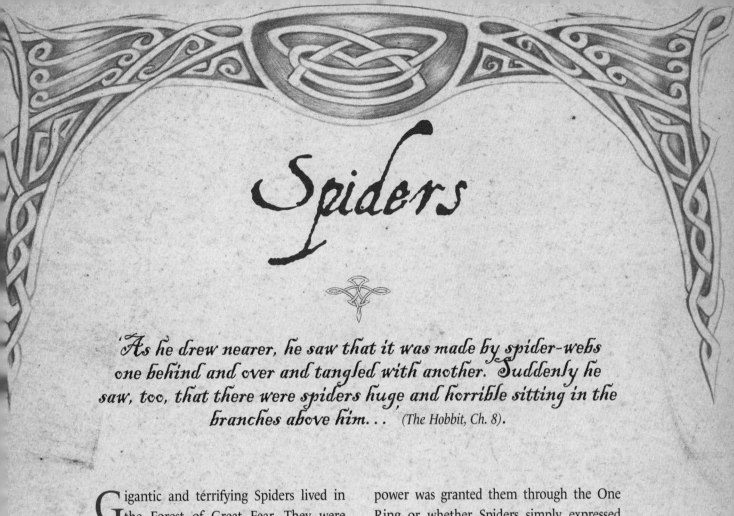

Spiders

'As he drew nearer, he saw that it was made by spider-webs one behind and over and tangled with another. Suddenly he saw, too, that there were spiders huge and horrible sitting in the branches above him...' (The Hobbit, Ch. 8).

Gigantic and terrifying Spiders lived in the Forest of Great Fear. They were endowed with a poisoned dart and produced long, sticky, silken threads. They were intelligent, with the power of speech, which was manifested in a kind of croaking or thin hissing sound and which Bilbo Baggins managed to interpret when he spied on them. Nevertheless, we do not know whether this power was granted them through the One Ring or whether Spiders simply expressed themselves in a popular dialect. There were hundreds of these Spiders, and the enormous webs that they weaved in the heart of the forest blocked out the daylight. They used these webs to trap imprudent travellers who strayed from the beaten paths. The Elves of Thranduil, who lived in the eastern part of the Forest of Great Fear, were merciless enemies of these creatures and killed them whenever they had the chance. The Spiders seemed to fear them and invariably avoided treading on the Elves' trail that passed through the forest. During Thorin and Company's journey across the Forest of Great Fear, the Dwarves were imprisoned by the spiders in their sleep and they found themselves hanging in silk

cocoons. The same misfortune almost befell Bilbo but, luckily, he woke up before being entirely enveloped and managed to stab the Spider who was trying to trap him. (He christened his small sword Sting in memory of this exploit.) Bilbo then set out in search of his companions and eventually found the Spiders' lair. Before the Spiders could devour the Dwarves, Bilbo used his ring to make himself invisible and drew the monsters away from their prey by raining down on them both insults and stones.

In Tolkien's sub-creation, the first giant Spider was Ungoliant, a malevolent evil spirit embodied as a monstrous arachnid. In the First Age, Ungoliant was an ally of Morgoth, the first Dark Lord, and she was responsible for the destruction of the Two Trees of Valinor. Ungoliant had numerous offspring in Beleriand, and one of the greatest exploits of Beren, a distant ancestor of Aragorn, was his successful crossing of their territory, the fearsome valley of Nan Dungortheb. The last of Ungoliant's children was Shelob, a giant Spider living

They were intelligent, with the power of speech, which was manifested in a kind of croaking or thin hissing sound.

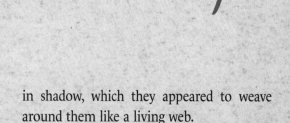

in the Mountains of Shadow, near Mordor, the land of Sauron. Gollum handed Frodo Baggins and Sam Gamgee over to Shelob, in the hope of being able to recover the One Ring once she had eaten them. Frodo was stung by Shelob, leaving him paralyzed, but Sam put up a brave fight and managed to wound her and make her run away. The countless Spiders in the Forest of Great Fear were all spawned by Shelob, and they all had the peculiarity of swathing themselves

in shadow, which they appeared to weave around them like a living web.

Legend has it that Tolkien introduced spiders into his Legendarium in the guise of monsters because he himself hated arachnids on account of a tarantula bite that he had suffered as a child. Tolkien dispelled this myth by insisting that he had no precise memory of this incident, that he had nothing against spiders and that their presence in the story simply served to make it more frightening and thus make a bigger impression on his children – particularly his second son Michael, who was afraid of spiders.

Stone Giants

'When he peeped out in the lightning-flashes, he saw that across the valley the stone-giants were out and were hurling rocks at one another for a game, and catching them, and tossing them down into the darkness.' (The Hobbit, Ch. 4).

The Stone Giants appear only in The Hobbit. They constitute an oddity, and it remains unclear as to whether Tolkien saw them as real, living creatures inhabiting Middle-earth or as poetic licence to add colour to the story of Bilbo Baggins' journey. They are barely seen again after Thorin and Company leave Rivendell. The Dwarves hoped to reach the Wild quickly, but Gandalf knew that the journey was fraught with difficulties and was not convinced that the Misty Mountains could be crossed without a serious challenge. And, indeed, this did not take long in materializing: one night, when they had stopped on a high corniche, they were surprised by a storm, or rather a duel of storms. All the surrounding peaks were shaken by awe-inspiring thunderbolts, and flashes of lightning enabled Bilbo to see Stone Giants in the valley gleefully hurling down boulders. The ponies whinnied with fear, terrified by the noise and the lashing rain. Thorin II Oakenshield, afraid of being struck by lightning or blown away by a gust of wind, dispatched his nephews Kili and Fili to look for shelter. They soon returned, having found a cave big enough to hold them all. This turned out to be one of the gateways into the kingdom of the Goblins, and the Company ended up being captured there and led underground.

There are two possible hypotheses for the somewhat surrealistic appearance of these Giants in the story. In view of their total absence elsewhere in the Legendarium, the first is that the Giants could be the hallucination of a Hobbit scared out of his wits, metaphors invoked by Bilbo to personify the two competing storms, which result in enormous rocks plummeting into the abyss. The other theory would be that Bilbo's eyes do not betray him and that there really are Giants made of bone and stone. They could thus be a variety of trolls, related to the ones found petrified a few chapters earlier. In fact, Bilbo is not alone in mentioning Giants. When Thorin insists on the urgent need to find shelter, he points out that, even if they weren't swept away by the wind, Giants could grab them and kick them into the air. Gandalf himself mentions the Giants three times. After Bilbo rejoins the Dwarves at the exit from the mountains, he asks Gandalf to explain how he saved them from the Goblins. The Wizard replies that, although he knew that this part of the mountains was infested with Goblins, he was unaware that they had opened a new entrance on the path that the Company were following. He finishes by promising to find a Giant to block it off. Gandalf refers to the Giants again when he speculates about the origin of Beorn, who could have been a descendant of the ancient mountain bears who used to live there before the arrival of the Giants. Gandalf mentions the Giants for a third and last time when he tells Beorn about the Company's eventful crossing of the Misty Mountains. The fact that even Gandalf seems to confirm the existence of the Giants leads us to doubt that that these creatures are merely figments of the imagination of an impressionable Hobbit.

Finally, the narrator himself mentions them, while describing the Carrock as an enormous fragment of a mountain flung on to the plain 'by some giant'. Is this an explicit reference to the Stone Giants from the start of the story, or is it just a rhetorical device designed to make the Carrock seem more imposing? That is for each reader to decide but, before forming an opinion, it is worth noting that Tolkien himself illustrated the storm in the mountains with an Indian ink drawing that was published in the first edition of the book. It showed the mountains under assault from bolts of lightning, but there are no Giants. This illustration was probably inspired by Tolkien's trip to Switzerland in 1911. In a letter addressed to Joyce Reeves, he described a hike on the Aletsch Glacier: 'It was while approaching the Aletsch that we were nearly destroyed by boulders loosened in the sun rolling down a snow-slope. [...] That and the "thunder-battle" – a bad night in which we lost our way and slept in a cattle-shed – appear in "The Hobbit"'. No mention of any Giants here either, although the duel between the storms is definitely present.

Are the Giants real? We shall probably never know for sure, for it is possible, as Gandalf tells us in Book III of *The Lord of the Rings*, that 'far, far below the deepest delvings of the Dwarves, the world is gnawed by nameless things. Even Sauron knows them not. They are older than he.'

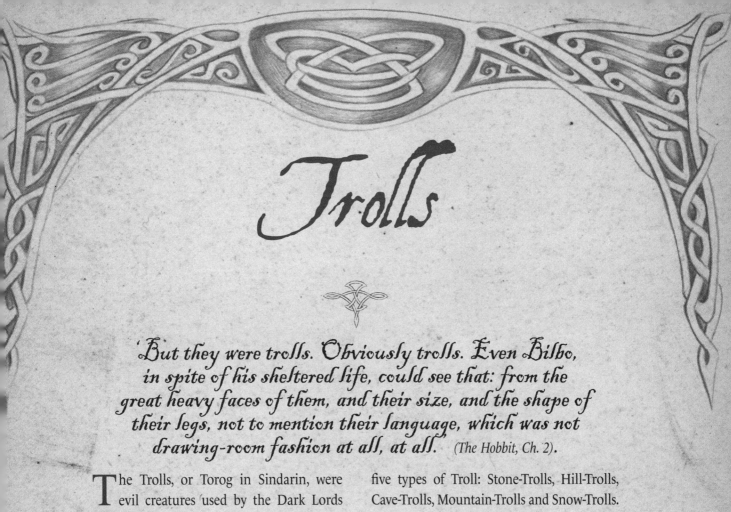

Trolls

'*But they were trolls. Obviously trolls. Even Bilbo, in spite of his sheltered life, could see that: from the great heavy faces of them, and their size, and the shape of their legs, not to mention their language, which was not drawing-room fashion at all, at all.*' (The Hobbit, Ch. 2).

The Trolls, or Torog in Sindarin, were evil creatures used by the Dark Lords Morgoth and Sauron during their wars in Middle-earth. The Ent Treebeard claimed that the Trolls were created by Morgoth in the First Age to taunt the Ents, just as the Goblins had been created out of derision for the Elves. At some point in the Second or Third Age of Middle-earth, Sauron subjugated them and taught them both the Common Speech and the Black Speech. Like their models, the Ents, the Trolls were big and strong but they were also different in that they usually had only limited intelligence. They hid from daylight, out of fear of being turned into stone, and they were as ready to eat the flesh of Men or Dwarves as that of any animal. Until around the end of the Third Age, there seemed to have been

five types of Troll: Stone-Trolls, Hill-Trolls, Cave-Trolls, Mountain-Trolls and Snow-Trolls. The Stone-Trolls lived in the Ettendales, to the north of the Rivendell Valley, on the edge of the Wilderland. The three Trolls – Tom, Bert and William – that Bilbo Baggins met on the Quest of Erebor came from this branch. This trio had come down from the mountains before their encounter with Thorin and Company in order to pillage the neighbouring villages. They devoured their inhabitants and stole their food and drink – as well as their treasures, which they stored in a cave not far from their camp. It was probably during the course of this looting that the three trolls came across the Elven swords Glamdring, Orcrist and Sting, which had been forged in the First Age in Gondolin. Gandalf, Thorin II Oakenshield

and Bilbo found them in a cave after shaking the Trolls off when they turned to stone at the dawning of the day. The Hill-Trolls lived in the same area. In 2930 T.A., a year before the birth of Aragorn, the latter's grandfather, Arador, was killed by one or more Hill-Trolls who emerged from the slopes of the Misty Mountains. The Cave-Trolls lived deep within the mountains. In the War of the Ring, the Fellowship, led by the Wizard Gandalf, was confronted by a Cave-Troll in the mines of Moria as they crossed the Misty Mountains. It is not clear how they differ from the Mountain-Trolls. Sauron used these in the Battle of the Pelennor Fields, but, other than that, we know virtually nothing about them. The Snow-Trolls are mentioned only in the Chronicles of Rohan, when its landscape was covered by snow in 2758–2759 T.A. In this period, King Helm was subject to an invasion by the Dunlendings and found himself cornered in Helm's Deep, where, dressed all in white, he defended himself – earning a comparison with a hungry, cannibalistic Snow-Troll. Finally, there were creatures in Far Harad with white eyes and red tongues who seemed like Half-Trolls or Men-Trolls. They were introduced into the Battle of the Pelennor Fields by Sauron to fight against Gondor's army.

At the end of the Third Age, a new family of trolls appeared, especially created by Sauron for their strength and ferocity: the Olog-hai, who could resist sunlight and lived to the south of the Forest of Great Fear and on the borders of Mordor. They were involved in the Battle of the Black Gate of Mordor, during which one of their number was killed by Peregrin Took. The relationship between the Ents and the Trolls goes further, however, than the kinship between the two races claimed by Treebeard. In fact, the term 'ent' used by Tolkien to name his Tree-men was taken from the Old English 'eoten', which means 'troll' or 'giant'. It can be found in the text of *Beowulf*, applied to the evil monster Grendel, and in the phrase *eotenas ond ylfe ond orcneas* – 'the trolls and elves and orcs'. The word crops up again in the name 'Ettendales', to the north of Rivendell, where the Trolls in *The Hobbit* originated. Apart from the text of *Beowulf*, Tolkien was also inspired by Scandinavian sagas in which trolls are monstrous creatures who live inside mountains and turn into stone in daylight. This notion of transformation into stone at dawn is also familiar from the *Eddas*, where the dwarf Alvíss is turned into stone after Thor keeps him talking until the morning comes.

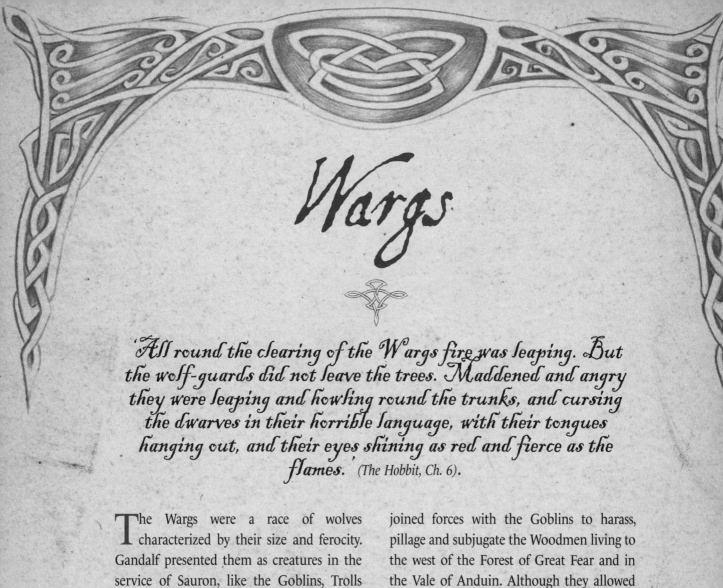

Wargs

'*All round the clearing of the Wargs fire was leaping. But the wolf-guards did not leave the trees. Maddened and angry they were leaping and howling round the trunks, and cursing the dwarves in their horrible language, with their tongues hanging out, and their eyes shining as red and fierce as the flames.*' (The Hobbit, Ch. 6).

The Wargs were a race of wolves characterized by their size and ferocity. Gandalf presented them as creatures in the service of Sauron, like the Goblins, Trolls and Werewolves. The origins of the Wargs remain unclear, but they could be related to the werewolves of the First Age – creatures with evil spirits imprisoned within them by Morgoth – or to the numerous wolves who served the Dark Lord and his vassal Sauron. In the First Age, Sauron himself had the capacity to assume the form of a wolf and was known as the master of the werewolves. By the Third Age, the Wargs seemed to form the main category of evil wolves in Middle-earth. They lived in packs, mainly to the northeast of the Misty Mountains. They joined forces with the Goblins to harass, pillage and subjugate the Woodmen living to the west of the Forest of Great Fear and in the Vale of Anduin. Although they allowed the Goblins to ride them like horses, these wolves were no ordinary animals, as they demonstrated a certain intelligence and even had their own language. Just like normal wolves, the Wargs took on specific roles within the organization of the pack, with the guards, for example, being answerable to the chief. The Wargs only began to really be described as a distinct species in the Third Age, more specifically during the Quest of Erebor and the War of the Ring. One night in the year 2941 T.A., when the Wargs were planning to pounce on the villages

of the Woodmen and kill all their inhabitants, they surprised Bilbo Baggins, Gandalf and Thorin and Company in the clearing where they had agreed to join up with their allies, the Goblins. Convinced that this small group was in cahoots with the Woodmen, the Wargs forced them to take refuge in the trees. Gandalf managed to repulse the Wargs by starting a fire with pine cones that he set alight with his stick (the Wargs were terrified of fire). The chief of the pack, a large grey wolf, had his muzzle burned by the flames, and the guards, afraid of abandoning their watch, also sustained injuries. The Goblins, however, did not share this terror of fire, and Gandalf and his companions were extremely lucky to be able to make their escape. The Wargs also intervened in the Battle of the Five Armies, both in the front lines (ridden by Goblins) and, unmounted, elsewhere in the army. This battle, which resulted in victory for the Men, the Elves and the Dwarves, temporarily put an end to the Wargs' attacks on the Woodmen and brought peace back to their villages.

At the time of the War of the Ring, the Wargs formed part of the troops serving Saruman and Sauron. Wargs attacked the members of the Fellowship of the Ring after they had failed to climb Caradhas via the Redhorn Pass. Later on, wolf-riders were among the troops chasing Théoden's army, which was heading towards Helm's Deep to confront the forces of Saruman. Although the latter are not explicitly identified as Wargs, their large size and treatment by the Goblins suggest that this is what they are, rather than a species of ordinary wolves.

The word 'warg' is supposedly derived from the language of the Men of the North. Tolkien drew on several ancient languages to create this term: Old English (*wearg*), Old High German (*warg*) and Old Norse (*vargr*). Although these words resemble one another, they do not share exactly the same meaning. The Old Norse word *vargr* does mean 'wolf' but, by extension, it also denotes an outlaw or criminal, and

The origins of the Wargs remain unclear, but they could be related to the werewolves of the First Age.

this meaning is predominant in the Old English term. Tolkien's invented word thus seeks to combine the two ideas of a wolf and antisocial activities. In the *Eddas*, the monstrous wolf Fenrir and his sons Sköll and Hati are *vargar*, destined to participate in the Ragnarök, where they fight against the Scandinavian gods. This concept could also have influenced Tolkien's Wargs. Be that as it may, their appearance in *The Hobbit* was directly inspired by an episode in the novel *The Black Douglas*, by Samuel Rutherford Crockett, which appeared in 1899, as Tolkien himself indicated in one of his letters.

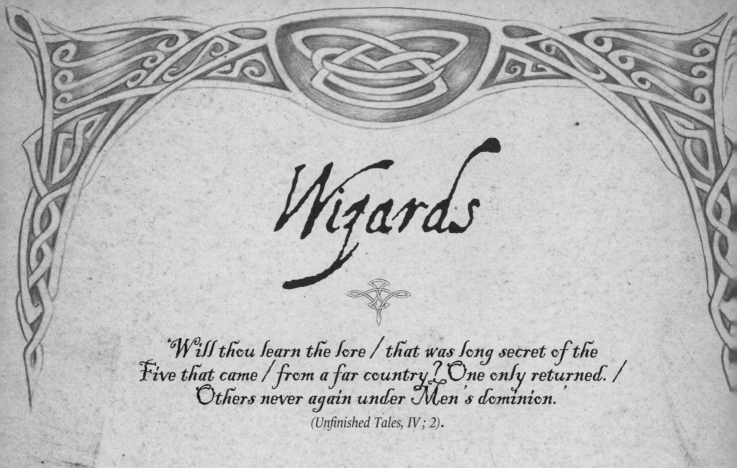

Wizards

'Will thou learn the lore / that was long secret of the Five that came / from a far country? One only returned. / Others never again under Men's dominion.'

(Unfinished Tales, IV ; 2).

The Second Age of Middle-earth finished with the victory of the Free Peoples against the Dark Lord Sauron and his supposed annihilation. When the shadow of evil began to make itself felt, however, around the year 1000 of the Third Age, the Valar dispatched mysterious emissaries charged with helping both the Men and the Elves of Middle-earth to fight against any possible return of Sauron. These envoys were known as Wizards, and they often introduced themselves as such.

Wizards were divine beings endowed with great powers, in the same way as the Valar, and they were chosen to counter Sauron, in the event that he recovered the power that he had wielded in the Second Age. Wizards were thus of the same essence as Sauron himself. When they arrived in Middle-earth

they created the Order of the Istari, 'the ones who know'.

Despite the apparent simplicity of their mission – opposing the return of an enemy who was theoretically within their grasp, the Istari had very little margin for manoeuvre. They had been forbidden to confront Sauron directly, and neither could they make way for Men or Elves to start the fighting with a preventive attack against their enemy. They had been dispatched to Middle-earth to help the Free Peoples to make enlightened decisions. They had to commit themselves to following the path of good, without abusing their power to hold sway over both Men and Elves by pushing them into war.

Moreover, the Valar were keen for their emissaries to act as guides and not as warlords, and so they agreed that the Istari

should arrive in Middle-earth in the bodies of elderly men. This appearance was inoffensive but it also conveyed wisdom. They had to learn how to gain love and respect so that, when the time came, they could serve as guides in the struggle against Sauron.

We know of five representatives of the Order of the Istari. After departing from Valinor, they landed in the Grey Havens, where they were welcomed by Círdan the Shipwright, a wise Elf who had distinguished himself over the course of the Ages in the fight against the Dark Lords – first, Morgoth, then his lieutenant, Sauron. The first of the five to set foot on Middle-earth was Curumo, who was bearded and dressed entirely in white. He would soon be nicknamed Saruman, or 'Talented (or Crafty) Man'. He was generally considered the most powerful of the Istari, and this attribute, coupled with his trailblazing arrival, led him to be naturally considered the leader of the Order.

Next came Alatar and Pallando, both dressed in blue and thus known as Ithryn Luin, or the Blue Wizards. Aiwendil then appeared, in his turn, dressed in brown. The colour of his clothes and his affinity with animals and birds earned him the name Radagast the Brown, with Radagast meaning 'animal lover' in an ancient language of the Men.

The last Wizard to arrive in Middle-earth, Olórin, initially seemed less important than his predecessors, as he was smaller in size, appeared to be older, dressed in grey, and walked with the help of a stick. Círdan, however, immediately saw that he was the most venerable of all. The Elves entrusted him with their Ring of Power (Narya, The Ring of Fire) in order to help and sustain him in his endeavours. This gentle Wizard with a long white beard is now the most familiar to us, as he is Gandalf, also known as Mithrandir, the Grey Pilgrim.

The Wizards were thus incarnated in Mannish bodies prior to their mission in Middle-earth, so, despite their divine essence, they had to accept the limits of their carnal shroud, and their wisdom was put to the test by Mannish scourges like fear, hunger, old age and the possibility of death. They were immortal by nature, but they discovered the price of life by assuming a fleshly form. This incarnation was very important because it made them into fallible beings. Of the five Istari, only Gandalf remained focused on his higher mission, while the others ended up abandoning it or betraying it.

Saruman the White was the most powerful member of the Order of the Istari, but he was also the proudest, and this would bring his downfall. He took his task extremely seriously, meticulously examining Sauron's strategies in an attempt to outmanoeuvre him, but, unfortunately, Saruman's own arrogance and lust for power caused him to deviate from the path of wisdom. Saruman ended up betraying his primary objective by manipulating the White Council and trying to impose his views, in the hope of ousting Sauron. Saruman's main purpose, however, was now not merely to defeat Sauron but rather to take over his power.

As regards the Blue Wizards, we know little about these, as they did not stay very long in the lands of the West. They soon headed eastward and disappeared from view, so it cannot be said whether they were distracted from their mission or simply failed to accomplish it effectively.

Radagast the Brown renounced the company of Elves and Men to devote himself to animals, and thus he too distanced himself from his primary mission. Beorn the skin-changer generally had little time for the Wizards but he did have a soft spot for Radagast. So, when Gandalf described Radagast as 'his good cousin' to Beorn, he managed to get into the skin-changer's good books, and Beorn subsequently agreed to play host to Gandalf, Bilbo Baggins and the Company of Dwarves. Later on, at the start of the War of the Ring, Radagast allowed himself to be manipulated by Saruman and unwittingly contributed to Gandalf's fall into the trap set for him by the leader of the Istari. Radagast immediately made amends, however, by using his friendship with the birds to set up an intervention by the Eagle Gwaihir that helped Gandalf evade Saruman's clutches.

Gandalf the Grey was thus the only member of the Order of the Istari who did not allow himself to be distracted from his mission. He spent his time travelling throughout the Westlands of Middle-earth, from Gondor to Angmar, from Lindon to Lórien, implacable in his opposition to Sauron, offering the flame of hope and healing as an antidote to the latter's cruel and brutal devastation. Gandalf was, therefore, the only one of the five Wizards who ended up returning to Valinor. The decisions taken by Gandalf perfectly illustrate the quandaries faced by the Wizards. In his desire to face up to Sauron, whose presence he could discern behind the shadowy figure of the Necromancer, Gandalf opts to support and encourage, as far as possible, the Quest of Erebor, in order to ensure the elimination of Smaug the Dragon, a potential ally of Sauron. But despite his commitment to this venture, Gandalf never neglects his principal objective, and so he later separates from his friends to address the White Council and participate in the preparations for the fight against the Necromancer.

Gandalf's narrative arc reveals the constraints to which he bound himself. Despite all his wisdom and authority, he was reluctant to

Wizards were divine beings endowed with great powers, in the same way as the Valar, and they were chosen for their capacity to strike against Sauron,

unleash his powers, and only did so when the survival of his group was threatened – whether by the misadventure with the trolls, or the capture of Bilbo and the Dwarves by the Goblins, or by the Company's encirclement by the Wargs and Goblins in the forest.

Gandalf's respect for the spirit of the mission entrusted him by the Valar led him to avoid imposing his views – or even the presence of Bilbo – on Thorin through any magical artifice: instead, he simply opted for discussion. Ultimately, Gandalf was able to enact his decisions because of the friendships that he had forged and the reputation that he had earned over the course of long centuries spent in Middle-earth, and not because of any spells or incantations. Finally, although he was fully conscious of the possibility of his own death, Gandalf was prepared to sacrifice himself for his friends: in a joint attack by the Goblins and Wargs, he was ready to jump into the fray, without any hope of victory, solely to give a chance of survival to those who had guided him thus far. The behaviour of Olórin (Gandalf in The Hobbit) thus corresponded with the expectations laid down by the Valar for the Order of the Istari, and Tolkien developed this theme more explicitly in his unfinished tales and legends. He used the formula '"I am Gandalf", said the Wizard', echoed a few lines later by '"I am a Wizard"', said Gandalf' to stress that Gandalf represents the essence of a Wizard, and of the emissaries of the Valar. Through this wordplay, Tolkien defined this key character in terms of his function, which had merged with his personality. This juxtaposition of Gandalf/Wizard and Wizard/Gandalf adds further depth to his initial introduction: 'I am Gandalf, and Gandalf means me.'

Woodmen

'This was dreadful talk to listen to, not only because of the brave woodmen and their wives and children, but also because of the danger which now threatened Gandalf and his friends.'

(The Hobbit, Ch. 6).

The Woodmen were a Mannish people who lived in villages to the west of the Forest of Great Fear and on the plains close to the River Anduin during the Third and Fourth Ages of Middle-earth. They had blood ties with the Rohan horsemen who once lived in the Anduin Valley. Although they could speak the Common Language, the Woodmen also had their own tongue.

At the end of the Third Age, the Woodmen endured hostile living conditions and harassment from various malevolent creatures that emerged from Dol Guldur's castle, to the southeast of the Forest of Great Fear. They were also subjected to raids carried out by the Goblins and their allies, the Wargs. Any survivors of these assaults would be transported to the Goblins' lairs in the Misty Mountains, where they were treated like slaves. Despite their name, the Woodmen were much more than mere lumberjacks, as they also reared livestock, particularly sheep. They thus had to cope with Eagles who enjoyed eating their animals. These neighbourly discords explain why the Woodmen, after rescuing Bilbo Baggins, Gandalf and Thorin and Company from the Goblins, refused to install this group close to their own houses and instead opted to take them to the Carrock, close to Beorn's home. However, the Woodmen were not entirely defenceless against either enemies or poachers. They were feared by both Goblins and Wargs, who only dared to attack the Woodmen in large numbers – and at night, in the hope of catching them unarmed. The Eagles, in their turn, feared the Woodmen's large wooden bows.

At the beginning of the War of the Ring, Gollum sowed terror amongst the Woodmen, after escaping from the prison of the Elf King, Thranduil. Gandalf then discovered that dark rumours were circulating in the forest, particularly among the Woodmen, who reported a new hostile presence in the forest: a blood-sucking ghost that fed on fledgling birds and snatched new-born babies from their cradles. It may well be that the Woodmen, a superstitious people, exaggerated the abuses committed by Gollum, but he undoubtedly enjoyed playing with defenceless prey. In fact, Gollum only spent a short time in the forest before heading to Moria. The Woodmen gradually found greater tranquillity at the end of the Third Age. They were defeated by an array of Wargs and Goblins in the Battle of the Five Armies. Their numbers dropped as a result, but peace returned to their lands, although they were attacked once again in the War of The Ring. The destruction of Dol Guldur's castle in 3019 T.A. dispelled the baleful aura of the forest. Following the defeat of Sauron, the Woodmen took possession of all the forest that stretched between the kingdoms of Thranduil and Celeborn.

Languages and writing systems

Elvish

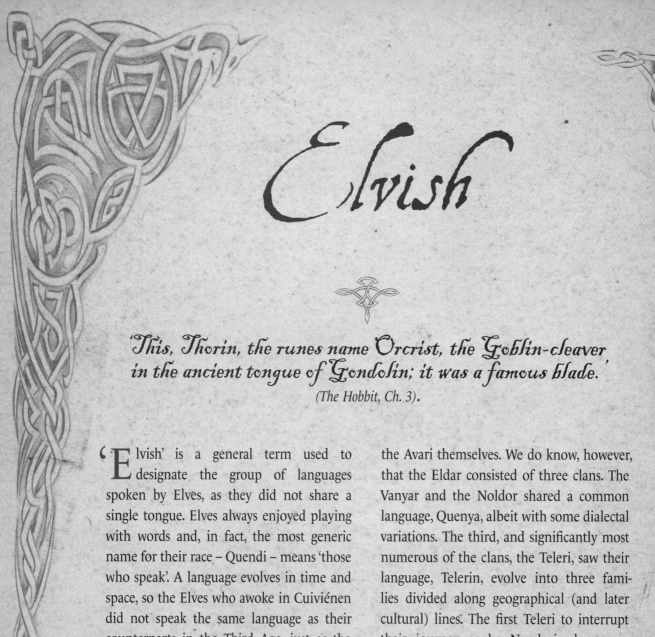

'This, Thorin, the runes name Orcrist, the Goblin-cleaver
in the ancient tongue of Gondolin; it was a famous blade.'
(The Hobbit, Ch. 3).

'Elvish' is a general term used to designate the group of languages spoken by Elves, as they did not share a single tongue. Elves always enjoyed playing with words and, in fact, the most generic name for their race – Quendi – means 'those who speak'. A language evolves in time and space, so the Elves who awoke in Cuiviénen did not speak the same language as their counterparts in the Third Age, just as the inhabitants of Valinor, beyond the Great Sea, to the West, did not talk in the same way as the residents of the forests in Middle-earth. The Elves' most ancient language was Primitive Quendian, which emerged after their first Awakening. This divided into two distinct linguistic branches when the Eldar separated from the Avari prior to the Elves' Great March to Valinor. Very little is known about the Avarin languages, or, for that matter,

the Avari themselves. We do know, however, that the Eldar consisted of three clans. The Vanyar and the Noldor shared a common language, Quenya, albeit with some dialectal variations. The third, and significantly most numerous of the clans, the Teleri, saw their language, Telerin, evolve into three families divided along geographical (and later cultural) lines. The first Teleri to interrupt their journey spoke Nandorin languages (these were the ancestors of the Silvan Elves from Mirkwood). The Sindar, or Grey Elves, who decided to stay in Middle-earth almost at the end of their journey, spoke Sindarin, and they established the kingdom of Doriath, in which they represented the majority. The Elves who did reach Valinor spoke the Telerin of Aman. When some of the Noldor went back to Middle-earth in the First Age, they brought Quenya with them

but, in the meantime, Sindarin had evolved to such an extent that the two tongues were now mutually incomprehensible. So, the Noldor adopted Sindarin as their everyday language and only preserved Quenya for ceremonial purposes.

Sindarin, initially the language of the Sindar in Beleriand, became the Elvish language that was most spoken in Middle-earth, to such an extent that it was adopted as a second language by some houses of Men. When the Edain joined forces with the Elves in the First Age to fight against Morgoth, many of them learned Sindarin and passed on this knowledge to their own descendants, the first Númenóreans. After Númenor's submersion, Sindarin became one of the official languages of the kingdoms of Arnor and Gondor. By the time of the Quest of Erebor, however, only the nobles still spoke Sindarin, as the popular language of the West of Middle-earth was now Common Speech.

Of all the Elvish languages, Quenya and Sindarin were the most fully developed by

Tolkien. His experience as a philologist had provided him with insight into the way a real language evolves, and he always sought to make the evolution of his own invented languages credible. He even declared that he created his Legendarium as a showcase for his languages. It is therefore necessary to take into account the chronology of Tolkien's life to fully understand his linguistic texts. He started to invent his Elvish languages in the 1910s and was still working on them when he died. His ideas thus had time to change, and it is difficult to view one of his texts from the 1920s in the same light as an essay from the 1970s. Moreover, Tolkien never definitively established the grammar of his different languages and many points remained unclear – and there were even changes in the meanings of words: the term *lá*, for example, means 'yes' in one text from 1959 and 'no' in the 1970s!

It seemed that Tolkien's first invented language was Quenya, spelt Qenya until the 1940s; this was heavily inflected and morphologically highly complex, with no fewer than ten declensions for nouns by the time he came to write *The Lord of the Rings*. Its grammar and vocabulary are quite well known, which is more than can be said for its syntax. According to Tolkien himself, Quenya was largely inspired by Finnish, Latin and Greek. Sindarin, meanwhile, had a very complicated development, reflecting

the various adjustments that Tolkien made to his Legendarium. The first examples that bore a resemblance to Sindarin were found in Gnomish, which he conceived in the late 1910s as the language of the Gnomes (an early name for the Noldor). At that point, Tolkien considered that Qenya would be spoken only by the Elves of the first tribe (the future Vanyar). By the 1920s, he was referring to Gnomish as Noldorin, and this language began to acquire a number of the characteristics of what would later be integrated into Sindarin. During the course of writing *The Lord of the Rings*, however, Tolkien changed his mind, as Qenya (now Quenya) was being spoken by both the Vanyar and the Noldor. Moreover, he renamed the language formerly known as Noldorin as Sindarin, and this became the language of the Grey Elves. The grammar and, above all, the phonetics of Sindarin are close to those of Welsh: it is inflected and displays both vowel alternations and consonant mutations. Tolkien did not provide enough information to make it possible to completely reconstitute, let alone speak, any of the Elvish languages. In fact, much of the pleasure that he derived from their creation came precisely from the room for manoeuvre that he allowed himself, giving him the chance to experiment and change his mind. Furthermore, several of the texts that he wrote about his invented languages have still never been published.

Khuzdul

'*But a small dark figure that none had observed sprang out of the shadows and gave a hoarse shout: Baruk Khazâd! Khazâd ai-mênu!*' (The Lord of the Rings, III, 7).

Khuzdul was the language created and taught to the Dwarves by the Vala Aulë. In comparison with the other languages of Middle-earth, Khuzdul was a conservative language that changed very little over the course of the Ages. The slight differences that did appear over time were basically due to the distance between the Seven Houses of the Dwarves. Accordingly, all the Dwarves could understand each other, whatever their lineage, even in the period of the War of the Ring. The Dwarves kept Khuzdul as a jealously guarded secret, refusing to teach it to other races. So, very few outsiders had a chance to study Khuzdul, and most Elven language teachers looked down on it. The Dwarves were particularly defensive about their real, Khuzdul name, going to great lengths to ensure that absolutely no outsider would ever find out what

it was. In public, Dwarves used names or nicknames from one of the languages of their human neighbours, while even the name engraved on their tombs was not their Khuzdul name. So, the names of Thorin and Company were derived from the Dalish language (rendered in Old Norse in Tolkien's story).

The very few Khuzdul words that we do know are confined to toponyms and war cries (mainly found in *The Lord of the Rings*). Thus, we know, for example, that the mines of Moria were called Khazad-dûm, or the Delving of the Dwarves, in Khuzdul. *Khazâd* denoted the Dwarf People, as heard in Gimli's cry in Helm's Deep: *Baruk Khazâd! Khazâd ai-mênu!* ('The Dwarves' axes! The Dwarves are upon you!'). Khuzdul was written down via a runic system known as Cirth, which the Dwarves initially borrowed from

the Grey Elves and then adapted for their own purposes, particularly when writing with a pen.

Despite the secrecy surrounding it, Khuzdul influenced other languages, particularly Mannish ones, and its presence can be felt in some Elvish words: for example, *Kasar* in Quenya and *Hadhod* in Sindarin, both meaning 'Dwarf', are directly derived from the *Khuzdul* term *Khazâd*.

Tolkien drew on Semitic languages such as Arabic and Hebrew to construct Khuzdul. In an interview with BBC Radio in 1967, Tolkien confirmed that Khuzdul words have Semitic affinities because he deliberately constructed them along these lines. Like Semitic languages, Khuzdul is based on roots made up of consonants (usually three) and words are built up by inserting vowels or adding prefixes or suffixes: the root k-b-l thus gives us the word *kibil*, meaning 'silver'. Khuzdul's vocabulary was conceived, however, to be different from that of natural languages and also to set it apart from the other languages of Middle-earth. Tolkien wanted Khuzdul to be 'cumbrous and unlovely' in comparison with the Elvish languages.

Old Norse

The still more northerly language of Dale is in this book seen only in the names of the Dwarves that came from that region and so used the language of the Men there, taking their "outer" names in that tongue. (The Lord of the Rings, App. E, II).

The stories told in *The Hobbit* and *The Lord of the Rings* are supposed to have taken place several millennia before our era, and so the languages used by the Men of Middle-earth could not be the same as our own. In the appendices to The Lord of the Rings, Tolkien stated that the language rendered in English in the books corresponds to Westron, or Common Speech. By the time of the War of the Ring, this language was understood by almost all the peoples living to the Northwest of Middle-earth, but it was not the native tongue of all the Men in the region. Some Men had preserved their own language, which occasionally resembled Westron. This was the case with the inhabitants of Dale

and Lake-town, where Tolkien explained that he had translated the corresponding languages into a Germanic language that has the same kinship with English as the language in question had with Westron. More specifically, the language of Dale was represented by Old Norse.

Historically, Old Norse constitutes a group of closely related languages spoken in Iceland, Scandinavia and Denmark. Various dialects of Old Norse started to differentiate themselves around the 7th century AD, and these would later give rise to the modern Scandinavian languages (Icelandic, Norwegian, Swedish, Danish, etc.) around the 15th century. At the time of its maximum extension, in the 10th century, Old

Norse was also spoken in Varangian towns in Northwest Russia, in East Anglia (part of the region of the Danelaw, then under Danish domination), in north Scotland, in various towns in Ireland and on the southern coast of Greenland, which had been colonized by Norwegians and Icelanders. The same was true of the northern coast of Neustria, which was conquered in 911 by the Viking chief Rollo (it would soon be renamed 'Normandy').

The first known Old Norse texts were written in a runic alphabet known as Futhark, but the progressive Christianization of Scandinavia led to the introduction of the Latin alphabet, which was adapted to the peculiarities of Old Norse and soon supplanted the runes. The best known variety of Old Norse is Old Scandinavian, the language of the *Eddas* and the Icelandic sagas. Old Norse was an inflected language with three grammatical genders (masculine, feminine and neuter) and four cases (nominative, accusative, dative and genitive), exactly like modern German. Initially there were three types of nouns (singular, dual and plural), but the dual noun disappeared in classical Old Norse. Tolkien made several nods to Old Norse: for example, Old Norse nouns ending in 'a' are generally masculine, while those ending in 'o' tend to be feminine. Appendix F to *The Lord of the Rings* indicates that the same was true of the proper names of Hobbits: Bilbo's real name would thus be 'Bilba', but Tolkien stated that he had Anglicized these names to avoid any confusion in his readers.

Tolkien's Dwarves had their own language, Khuzdul, but they did not teach it to outsiders and preferred to use local languages for trading, even going as far as taking on local names in their dealings with other races. It was therefore perfectly natural for the Dwarves originating from the Lonely Mountain to adopt Nordic names, which Tolkien represented with genuine Old Norse names. With the exception of Balin, a name whose etymology remains obscure, all the dwarves in *The Hobbit* bear names taken from the *Dvergatal*, a list of dwarves in the Völuspá, 'The Prediction of the Prophetess', a major cosmogonic poem in the *Eddas*.

All these names have a significance that Tolkien was careful to point out: Thorin means 'hardy, intrepid', while the name of his father, Thráin, means 'stubborn, obstinate' – appropriate for a character obsessed with revenge and the reconquest of the Dwarves' former homes. Similarly, Thrór, Thorin's grandfather, bore a name that reflected the major excavations that he oversaw in Erebor: *thrór* means 'boar', but it is also related to the verb *thróast*, 'to grow, to extend'. Other names refer to the tools handled by the Dwarves, as in Fili and Kili ('file' and 'wedge', respectively). Finally, some names contain humorous allusions to a character's physical characteristics: the Old Norse word *bómburr* means 'pot-bellied', and it is also related to *bumba* ('drum'), the instrument that Bombur plays at the impromptu party in Bag End.

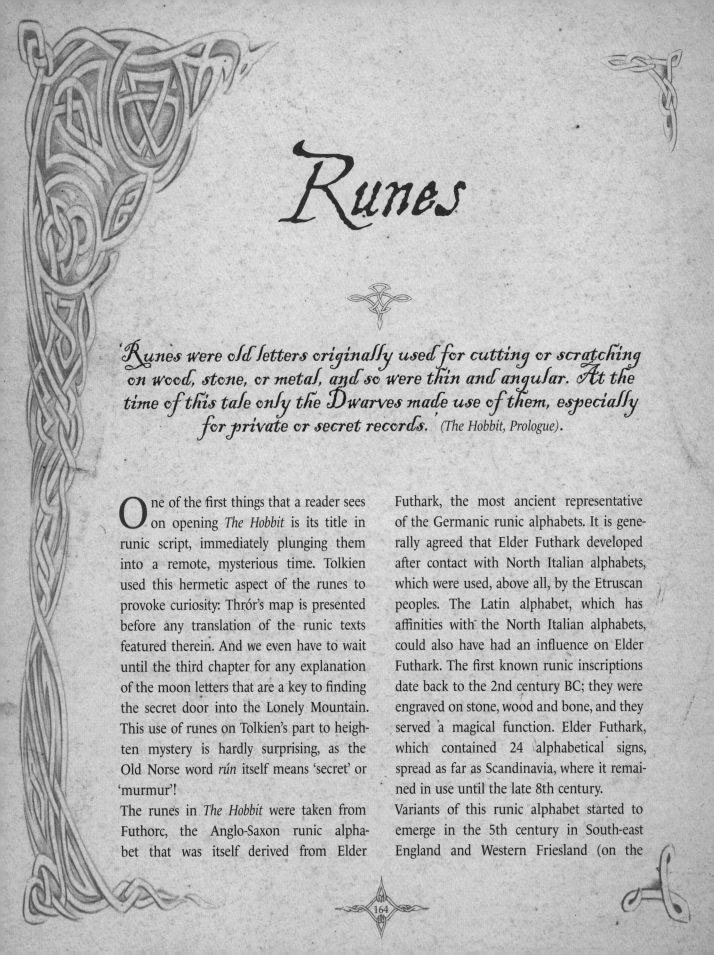

Runes

'Runes were old letters originally used for cutting or scratching on wood, stone, or metal, and so were thin and angular. At the time of this tale only the Dwarves made use of them, especially for private or secret records.' (The Hobbit, Prologue).

One of the first things that a reader sees on opening *The Hobbit* is its title in runic script, immediately plunging them into a remote, mysterious time. Tolkien used this hermetic aspect of the runes to provoke curiosity: Thrór's map is presented before any translation of the runic texts featured therein. And we even have to wait until the third chapter for any explanation of the moon letters that are a key to finding the secret door into the Lonely Mountain. This use of runes on Tolkien's part to heighten mystery is hardly surprising, as the Old Norse word *rún* itself means 'secret' or 'murmur'!

The runes in *The Hobbit* were taken from Futhorc, the Anglo-Saxon runic alphabet that was itself derived from Elder Futhark, the most ancient representative of the Germanic runic alphabets. It is generally agreed that Elder Futhark developed after contact with North Italian alphabets, which were used, above all, by the Etruscan peoples. The Latin alphabet, which has affinities with the North Italian alphabets, could also have had an influence on Elder Futhark. The first known runic inscriptions date back to the 2nd century BC; they were engraved on stone, wood and bone, and they served a magical function. Elder Futhark, which contained 24 alphabetical signs, spread as far as Scandinavia, where it remained in use until the late 8th century.

Variants of this runic alphabet started to emerge in the 5th century in South-east England and Western Friesland (on the northern coast of today's Netherlands). Futhorc adopted first 28, and then 33 runes. The literacy rates at that time were extremely low, however, contributing, along with the secrecy that surrounded the use of runes, to the sparse pickings of fewer than 200 inscriptions available to us from the entire period in which Futhorc was used. The Christianization of the Anglo-Saxons in the 7th century introduced competition from the Latin alphabet. By the time of the Norman Conquest, Futhorc had become extremely rare, and it soon faded away altogether. In Scandinavia, Elder Futhark became increasingly simplified and in the late 8th century it gave rise to Younger Futhark, whose alphabet comprised only 16 runes. This was widely used throughout the entire Viking period, although its use was constrained when the Scandinavian countries began to convert to Christianity. Nevertheless, it survived in some regions of Sweden, under the guise of medieval runes, until the early years of the 20th century.

Experts believe that all the Germanic runes must have had a name, associated with symbolic or magical properties. In *The Poetic Edda*, the runes were the preserve of Odin, the sovereign god and patron of poetry and sorcery. He gained knowledge of them by hanging himself for nine days and nights, pierced by his own spear, from Yggdrasil, the tree of the world. Another Eddic poem, the *Rígthula*, tells how the god Heimdall transmitted knowledge of the runes to humans.

In the case of Futhorc, we know the names assigned to some runes from medieval manuscripts, while others can be deduced from other Germanic runic alphabets. Twenty-nine Futhorc runes are quoted in an Anglo-Saxon runic poem in which each verse sets a puzzle for which the name of a rune is the solution. There are two other runic poems that follow a similar scheme – one Icelandic, the other Norwegian – although they both use the 16 runes of Younger Futhark. There are also several runic calendars of Scandinavian origin that use Younger Futhark to indicate days and the phases of the moon. These calendars use the metonic cycle of 19 years, after which the dates of the year again correspond to the same phases of the moon. It is hardly surprising, therefore, that some of the runes on Thrór's map can be read only in a very specific part of the metonic cycle. Furthermore, the secret gate to Erebor is endowed with a magical opening system based on a conjunction between the Moon and the Sun.

Sometimes Tolkien put a dot below a rune in order to indicate that the letter was doubled, as in the word ᚻᚩᛒ̣ᛁᛏ. It must also be pointed out Tolkien did not always use Anglo-Saxon runes along strictly historical lines in his Legendarium. For example, the rune ⁝, which he used for the sound 'oo' (as in 'book'), is not to be found in any Anglo-Saxon script. Furthermore, Futhorc contains more signs than those used by Tolkien in *The Hobbit*.

Runic texts can also be found on the title page of *The Lord of the Rings* and inside the book itself: in the inscription on Balin's

In one manuscript that long remained unpublished, Tolkien supplied details of the 'Runes used by Thorin & Company', accompanied by the English nouns that he attributed to them. These are presented below in alphabetical order, taking into account variants found in the main texts:

Letter	Sound	Rune		Letter	Sound	Rune		Letter	Sound	Rune
A	[a]	*oak*		GH	[gh]	*ghost*		Q [2]	[qu]	*quill*
A	[o]	*ox*		H	[h]	*hail*		R	[r]	*road*
A	[æ]	*ash*		I	[i]	*ice*		S	[s]	*sun*
B	[b]	*birch*		J [2]	[j]	*joy*		SH	[ch]	*shield*
C	[k]	*care*		K	[k]	*kin*		ST [3]	[st]	**stone*
CH	[tch]	*child*		L	[l]	*land*		T	[t]	*tongue*
Ð	[d]	*day*		M	[m]	*man*		TH	[þ], [ð]	*thorn*
E	[e]	*elm*		N	[n]	*need*		U	[u]	*urn*
EA	[i:]	*ear*		NG	[ŋ]	*anger*		V [2]	[v]	*vane*
EE	[i:]	*eel*		O / OO	[o]	*ox*		W	[w]	*wine*
EO, IO [1]	[o]	*ice-ox*						X [4]	[ks]	*axle*
F	[f], [v]	*fire*		OO	[u]	*ooze*		Y	[y]	*yew*
G	[g], [j]	*gift*		P	[p]	*pine*		Z [4]	[z]	*zinc*

1 – In this unpublished table, Tolkien specified that the combinations 'io' and 'eo' could be represented by the supplementary sign, which did not form part of the normal series but served as a combination of I and O.

2 – Tolkien also indicated here that, although J was usually represented by the rune for I, the special form could equally be used. There was no rune for Q, and the QU group had to be represented by the combination of runes for CW, although the form could be used for QU. Finally, V was traditionally represented by the rune for U, but the form Λ could act as a substitute. These three special signs were not considered as real letters in this runic alphabet.

3 – The rune for ST is missing from this table, but the Introduction to The Hobbit indicates that this sound was sometimes used, as in the Anglo-Saxon name 'Stan' ('Stone') that Tolkien claimed as his own.

4 – In the table, Tolkien indicates that the runes for X and Z, ' and x, denoted, respectively, 'axle' and 'zinc'. In the introduction to The Hobbit, however, the runes for X and Z are, respectively, N and z.

tomb, in extracts from *The Book of Mazarbul*, etc. Once again, Tolkien is playing a game with his reader, who can decipher more details from *The Book of Mazarbul* than from the incomplete text that Gandalf reads to his companions. The runic system of *The Lord of the Rings* is different, however, from that of *The Hobbit*, as Tolkien was now using runes that he himself invented – Cirth, supposedly created in the First Age by the Elf Daeron, minstrel to the king of Doriath, Thingol. Cirth was used for a long time by the Sindar Elves, but it was also adopted by the Dwarves, who modified it for their own purposes. They even came up with a new way of writing Cirth, with the help of a silver pen: their moon-runes could be read only by allowing moonlight to shine through them – and in some cases, the Moon had to have the same shape and season as the time at which they were written. When the Noldor returned to Beleriand, however, the Sindar Elves turned to Tengwar, and thereafter Cirth was kept alive only by Dwarves and the Men with whom they traded.

Cirth bears a superficial resemblance to Futhorc, as several letters are identical in both alphabets (although they represent completely different sounds). Unlike Futhorc, however, Cirth has a regular structure, and similar sounds, such as 'k' and 'g', have similar forms (V and $>$ instead of Λ and $<$). Tolkien explained how the several variants of Cirth work in Appendix E to *The Lord of the Rings*. In one of his letters, he stated that Cirth comprises the authentic alphabet of the Dwarves, and that the Anglo-Saxon runes are merely a representation. As the story of Middle-earth purportedly unfolds in a mythical past, it was impossible for the Dwarves to have used a system that wasn't invented until the start of our era.

Tengwar

'As Frodo did so, he now saw fine lines, finer than the finest penstrokes, running along the ring, outside and inside: lines of fire that seemed to form the letters of a flowing script.' (The Lord of the Rings, I, 2).

The *tengwar* were the letters forming part of a writing system of Elvish that was intended, unlike runes, for handwriting and calligraphy rather than engraving. Tengwar letters were used by various other peoples. The Noldor, the Deep-Elves who went Westward, beyond the sea, to Valinor, declared that these letters were created by Finwë's son, Fëanor, the greatest of all of them, responsible for both the misfortune that had befallen them and their days of glory. The word *tengwar* is the plural of *tengwa*, meaning 'letter'. The Sindar, who were in the majority in Middle-earth at the time of Bilbo Baggins, in the Third Age, used a word taken from their own language (Sindarin) to denote these letters that had come from the West: *tîw*. Tengwar comprised one of the three writing systems invented by the Elves, along with Sarati and Cirth. Sarati was

invented by Rúmil, a Noldo, and it inspired Fëanor to create Tengwar. Sarati constituted a phonographic system – in other words, every sign corresponded to a sound. They could thus be applied to various languages, on the basis of pronunciation. Sarati never seems to have left Valinor, and it was never used in Middle-earth. Fëanor decided, at an early age, to improve Rúmil's writing system. His new script was quickly adopted, and it was then taken to Middle-earth when the Noldor returned there. The Sindar who were already there initially tended to favour the Elf Daeron's Cirth but they soon forsook it in favour of Tengwar, which established itself as the Elves' main writing system. Tengwar served to transcribe all the Elvish languages, but as these contained distinct phonemes (sounds), Tengwar letters were not used in the same way in

each case and thus came to require different modes. Some modes are phonetic, while others are more alphabetical. The sound of an individual *tengwa* can also change, as its pronunciation can vary according to the mode in which it is being used.

Most of the known modes of Tengwar follow the lines of consonant alphabets, as only consonants are written in Tengwar, with tehtar (a system of diacritical dots and accents) placed above or below to indicate vowels. In Quenya, the tehtar are usually placed on the preceding consonant, while in Sindarin they are placed on the following consonant. In the mode used in Beleriand, however, vowels are written in the same way as consonants (during the War of the Ring, the Fellowship of the Ring came across this mode on the Gates of Durin, at the entrance to the mines of Moria). The Elves were not alone in taking advantage of the Tengwar. So, for instance, the One Ring found by Bilbo in the Goblins' caves,

which enabled him to win the duel of riddles against Gollum, revealed an inscription in Tengwar when it was thrown on a fire – and this same inscription would be discovered by Gandalf years after the end of the Quest of Erebor. It was not written in any Elvish language, however, but in Dark Speech, the language of Sauron the Necromancer.

Tolkien also invented several modes for writing English with Tengwar. He unveiled his first version of Tengwar to the public with the reprint of the first edition of *The Hobbit* in English, in 1937. That edition contained an illustration that has since become famous, showing the Dragon Smaug, stretched out on his pile of gold, a small silhouette of Bilbo and, in the left foreground, an earthenware jar bearing an inscription in Tengwar. This cannot be read in full, as it is partly hidden by a ladder, but its sense can be deciphered: 'gold [of] th[rór] thráin/ accursed [be] the thief'.

Objects and architecture

The Arkenstone

"'The Arkenstone! The Arkenstone!" murmured Thorin in the dark, half dreaming with his chin upon his knees. "It was like a globe with a thousand facets; it shone like silver in the firelight, like water in the sun, like snow under the stars, like rain upon the Moon!" (The Hobbit, Ch. 12).

When Thráin I settled in Erebor in 1999 T.A., a jewel of exceptional beauty was discovered: the Arkenstone, the Heart of the Mountain. This spherical stone glowed with its own inner light, although the Dwarves' intricate cutting and honing enabled it also to reflect any light that fell on it in a thousand gleams. Thorin I took the Arkenstone with him when he moved to the Grey Mountains around 2210 T.A., and it was brought back to Erebor by Thrór almost 400 years later, when it was installed in the Great Hall of Thráin's Palace. Unfortunately, the Arkenstone was left behind when the Lonely Mountain was attacked by Smaug in 2770 T.A. Towards the end of the expedition of Thorin and Company, in 2941 T.A., Bilbo Baggins found it by chance among Smaug's treasure, attracted by its irresistible glow. Although Thorin II Oakenshield was prepared to use any means necessary to obtain the Arkenstone and threatened to punish anybody who kept it from him, Bilbo did not mention his discovery to his companions and hid the stone, firstly in his biggest pocket and then in the pile of clothes that he used as a pillow.

This spherical stone glowed with its own inner light, although the Dwarves' intricate cutting and honing enabled it also to reflect any light that fell on it in a thousand gleams.

It was only after several days of the siege led by Bard and Thranduil (who were claiming their share of the booty to rebuild Lake-town, which had been devastated by Smaug) that a now extremely weary Bilbo discreetly

passed it on to them. Thorin had promised that he could choose his share of the treasure as payment for his services, and Bilbo picked the Arkenstone. He gave the stone to Bard and Thranduil in the hope of exchanging it for one fourteenth of the treasure.

The next day, Bard and Thranduil went to Thorin again. Thorin refused to listen to them, but they handed over the coveted stone in a box borne by Gandalf, and Bilbo confessed that he was responsible for giving them the Arkenstone. Thorin flew into a rage and banished Bilbo from the Mountain, although he did grudgingly agree to the proposal for an exchange. Thorin informed his cousin Dáin, who had taken to the road at the very start of the siege, that Bard was in possession of the Arkenstone. This aroused the fury of the Dwarves, who planned to attack both Elves and Men to recover the jewel, without sharing any of the treasure.

Eventually, Thorin apologized to Bilbo on his death bed, following the Battle of the Five Armies, and his heir, Dáin II Ironfoot, honoured his side of the agreement. Bard finally restored the stone to its owner by laying it on Thorin's chest in his grave.

The word 'Arkenstone' comes from the Anglo-Saxon *eorclanstán*, meaning 'precious stone', which crops up in several Old English poems, particularly *Beowulf*. Tolkien also used this term to designate the Silmarils in his translation into Old English of *The Annals of Valinor*. Moreover, Tolkien had imagined the Arkenstone to be a rediscovered Silmaril in the initial drafts of *The Hobbit*. In one unfinished version of the story, Tolkien turned the stone into the Gem of Girion, which the latter would give to the Dwarves as payment for arming his sons, since the Dwarves would have offered it to Bilbo as his share of the treasure.

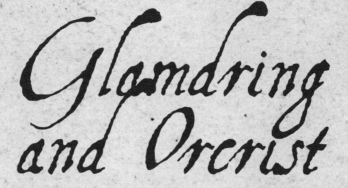

Glamdring and Orcrist

"'These look like good blades,' said the wizard, half drawing them and looking at them curiously.' (The Hobbit, Ch. 2).

Having escaped the deadly machinations of the trolls Tom, Bert and William, the participants in the Quest of Erebor found these creatures' lair, complete with a pile of objects, particularly swords of all shapes and sizes. Two stood out on account of their beautiful scabbards, their hilts studded with jewels and their blades engraved with runes. Gandalf and Thorin Oakenshield each took one of these swords. During Thorin and Company's stopover in Rivendell, they were told by Elrond that the two swords were extremely old, since they had been forged in the ancient Elven city of Gondolin by the High Elves of the West, at the time of the great wars against the Goblins. After deciphering the runes on the swords, Elrond further explained that Thorin's sword was called Orcrist and that of Gandalf, Glamdring. These names were words from the Elven language of Sindarin and they meant, respectively, 'Goblin-cleaver' and 'Foe-hammer'. According to its runic engraving, Glamdring had been borne by Elrond's great-grandfather, Turgon, the king of Gondolin. Elrond thought it likely that both swords had been looted during the sacking of Gondolin and had ended up in a Dragon's den or as part of the Goblins' booty, before the trolls managed to lay their hands on them. The Goblins had lost many of their number to these two swords and were duly terrified of them; they referred to Orcrist as 'Biter' and Glamdring as 'Beater'. Both Gandalf and Thorin (who had promised Elrond to bear Orcrist with honour) used their swords to fight Goblins during the underground crossing of the Misty Mountains. Like all the swords from Gondolin, Glamdring and Orcrist glowed with a blue light in the presence of

Goblins – Glamdring literally blazed after killing the Great Goblin. Orcrist was taken from Thorin when he was imprisoned by the Silvan Elves, before eventually being laid to rest by Thranduil on Thorin's grave, in the depths of the Lonely Mountain – where it purportedly retained its capacity to shine in the dark at the approach of an enemy. Gandalf, for his part, kept Glamdring close at hand and used it as a weapon right up to the end of the War of the Ring.

The bestowal of names on swords forms part of the legacy of heroic literature from the Middle Ages. Charlemagne's La Joyeuse and Roland's Durandal in *The Song of Roland*, King Arthur's legendary Excalibur, and the Nordic hero Sigurd's Gram are just a few examples of a sword whose special status is marked by the name allotted to it. There are other swords in Tolkien's work that bear a name: Sting, Bilbo Baggins' sword in *The Hobbit*, discovered at the same time as Glamdring and Orcrist; Narsil, the broken sword of King Elendil, which was renamed Andúril when it was forged anew and was owned by Aragorn in *The Lord of the Rings*; and Anglachel, rechristened Gurthang by its owner Túrin, the cursed hero of *The Children of Húrin*.

During Thorin and Company's stopover in Rivendell, they were told by Elrond that the two swords were extremely old, since they had been forged in the ancient Elven city of Gondolin by the High Elves of the West, at the time of the great wars against the Goblins.

Mithril

'With that he put on Bilbo a small coat of mail, wrought for some young elf-prince long ago. It was of silver-steel which the elves call mithril, and with it went a belt of pearls and crystals.'

(The Hobbit, Ch. 13).

Mithril, or True-silver, was an extremely rare precious metal that was both light and resistant. Its name in the Elvish language of Sindarin means 'grey brilliance', as it displayed a distinctive silvery gleam. The only known deposit of mithril in Middle-earth was situated under Mount Caradhras, in the Misty Mountains, and it was mined by the Dwarves of Khazad-dûm (more commonly known as Moria). This seam of mithril was the source of the enormous wealth of the Dwarves and Elves of this region in the Second Age.

Mithril had numerous properties. Its hardness made it ideal for making helmets and other pieces of armour. Similarly, the coat of mail given to Bilbo Baggins by Thorin II Oakenshield was also made of mithril. Bilbo later bequeathed it to Frodo, who was grateful for its protection when he received a fearsome strike from an Orc chief's spear after the Fellowship of the Ring entered into combat in the mines of Moria.

Mithril was also highly malleable and could be processed to produce ithildin, a material developed by the Elves of Eregion that was almost invisible, as it reflected only the light of the Moon and the stars: the moon-runes hidden in Thrór's map were made of ithildin, as were the decorations and

> *Its name in the Elvish language of Sindarin means 'grey brilliance', as it displayed a distinctive silvery gleam.*

inscriptions on Moria's Western Gate. Finally, the splendid lustre of mithril, which never tarnished, made it perfectly suited to the creation of precious jewellery. So, Nenya, one of the Elves' Three Rings (which was linked to Sauron's One Ring) was made of mithril. It was decorated with a diamond and worn by Galadriel.

The immense wealth derived from mithril proved to be the downfall of Moria. The Dwarves became increasingly greedy for mithril and thus dug ever deeper in the base of the mountain in the hope of finding larger deposits. In 1980 T.A., they unleashed a Balrog, an evil winged creature of shadow and flame which had been imprisoned under the mountain since the First Age. This monster wreaked havoc on the mines of Moria, forcing the Dwarves to abandon them. Mining of mithril ceased, making it more precious and coveted than ever. It was not until the end of the War of the Ring, in 3019 T.A., that the mines of Moria were restored and repopulated, allowing mining to be resumed.

Mithril was not mentioned in the first edition of *The Hobbit* (although there were references to steel-silver) and the term did not appear in Bilbo's story until 1966. Mithril evokes parallels with the orichalcum of Greek legends, which was also a highly prized metal used for both jewellery and elaborate armour.

According to Plato, only gold was more precious than orichalcum, which was abundant on the island of Atlantis and made its inhabitants rich – whereas in Middle-earth, the rarity of mithril made it the most coveted metal of all.

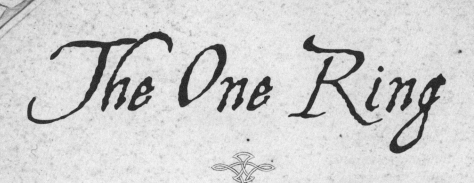

The One Ring

*'Not far away was his island, of which Bilbo knew nothing,
and there in his hiding-place he kept a few wretched oddments,
and one very beautiful thing, very beautiful, very wonderful.
He had a ring, a golden ring, a precious ring.'* (The Hobbit, Ch. 5).

When Bilbo Baggins recovered consciousness after becoming separated from Thorin and Company (who were being chased by Goblins underneath the Misty Mountains), he found himself alone, in total darkness. While trying to orientate himself, crawling across the floor of a gallery, one of his groping hands suddenly noticed a small metal ring. Bilbo slipped this object into his pocket without giving it a second thought. It was only a while later that he discovered that this gold ring belonged to Gollum, with whom he staked his own life in a game of riddles. Bilbo won the game with a question – 'What have I got in my pocket?' – that Gollum was unable to answer correctly. Gollum was enraged when he realized that his much-loved ring had disappeared and, moreover, that Bilbo had found it. Bilbo managed to evade Gollum's fury by putting the ring on his index finger – which was when he learned that the jewel bestowed invisibility on whomever was wearing it.

Even so, Bilbo still did not suspect that he had found a Ring of Power, the One Ring, which also endowed its wearer with an indefinite prolongation of their life. It was the Master Ring, forged secretly, with evil intent, by Sauron in the flames of Mount Doom in the Second Age. It governed all the rings created by

Eregion's Elven blacksmiths, with the deceitful assistance of Sauron. The One Ring was captured by King Isildur at the end of the Second Age, but the immense capacity to dominate and entrance that Sauron had instilled in it soon proved to be the downfall of Isildur, who eventually lost the Ring in the waters of the River Anduin. This was where it would be found, centuries later, by the Hobbit Déagol, who was then killed by his friend Sméagol out of eagerness to possess the Ring for himself. Sméagol became so corrupted by the Ring that he gradually transformed into a creature named Gollum, who was endowed with exceptional longevity. After escaping the clutches of Gollum and falling into the hands of Bilbo, the One Ring rendered numerous services to the Hobbit by affording him invisibility. It allowed Bilbo to leave the depths of the Misty Mountains without being seen by the Goblins; to come to the assistance of his Dwarf friends against the Spiders of the Forest of Great Fear; to escape from the Silvan Elves who had captured the Dwarves; to steal a cup from the Dragon Smaug, and to draw Smaug into a conversation in which invisibility protected him from the Dragon's murderous designs; to surrender to the besiegers of Erebor in order to entrust Bard with the Arkenstone; and, finally, to stay out of sight of the Goblins during the Battle of the Five Armies.

Once he had returned home, to Bag End, Bilbo kept the secret of the magical ring and used it primarily to avoid unwelcome visitors. In the year 3001 of the Third Age,

Bilbo became, with the help of Gandalf, the first guardian of the Ring to dispose of it voluntarily, when he entrusted it to his heir Frodo before retiring to Rivendell at an advanced age. A few years later, Gandalf discovered the properties of the Ring. Frodo then undertook a dangerous journey, from the Shire to Mordor, with the support of the Fellowship of the Ring, in order to destroy the One Ring in the place where it was forged, as this was the only possible means of preventing Sauron from subjugating Middle-earth.

The most striking characteristic of the One Ring in *The Hobbit* is its power of invisibility, echoing similar magical jewels found

Bilbo managed to evade Gollum's fury by putting the ring on his index finger – which was when he learned that the jewel bestowed invisibility on whomever was wearing it.

in ancient texts. The ring of Gyges, in Book II of *The Republic* by the Greek philosopher Plato, is the oldest known example of a ring that made its bearer invisible. A similar object crops up in medieval literature: in the story *Yvain, the Knight of the Lion* by Chrétien de Troyes, the eponymous hero is given a ring (by a woman called Lunete) that allows him to become invisible and thus evade the grim fate intended for him by his pursuers. More recently, in the 19th century,

rings of invisibility are featured in two stories, *The Enchanted Ring* and *The Dragon of the North*, contained, respectively, in *The Green Fairy Book* (1892) and *The Yellow Fairy Book* (1894), two British collections of fairy stories edited by Andrew Lang. In *The Water of the Wondrous Isles*, one of William Morris's last fantasy novels (published posthumously in 1897), the protagonist, a young girl named Birdalone, is given a ring that will make her invisible if she recites a magical formula when she puts it on her finger, thereby allowing her to prepare her escape from a witch who has held her captive. So, rings of invisibility appear in both medieval and Victorian literature, and Tolkien

was familiar with – and influenced by – both of them. Moreover, the Ring of Power in *The Lord of the Rings* and *The Silmarillion*, seen as a source of corruption and misfortune, as a revealer of the dark side of those who wear it, recalls magical rings from Scandinavian mythology, which were symbols of power, acclaim and wealth, but also of fate, or, in some cases, inevitable tragedy. This was particularly true, for example, of Andvaranaut, a ring that once belonged to the dwarf Andvari. The *Eddas* and several other Scandinavian sagas describe how Andvaranaut was stolen by the god Loki, causing Andvari to put a curse on it that would destroy anybody who possessed it.

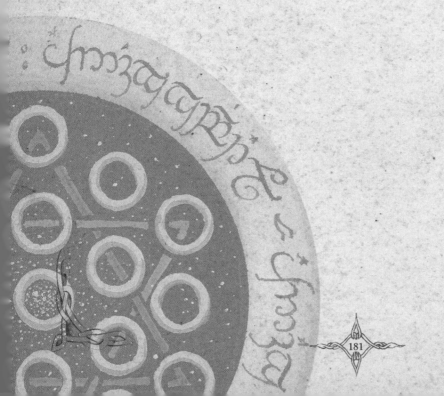

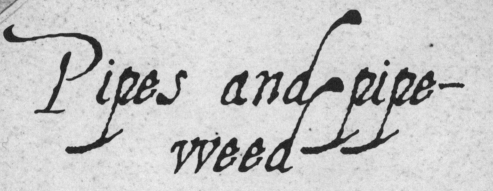

Pipes and pipe-weed

'*After some time he felt for his pipe. It was not broken, and that was something. Then he felt for his pouch, and there was some tobacco in it, and that was something more. Then he felt for matches and he could not find any at all, and that shattered his hopes completes.*' (The Hobbit, Ch. 5).

The first time we meet Bilbo Baggins, he is blowing smoke circles with his pipe in front of his smial. He invites Gandalf to smoke with him and enjoy the sunny morning, but Gandalf turns down the offer. We do not see Bilbo with a pipe again until the party in Bag End, where he is trying to outdo Thorin's smoke rings. And the very last time that we encounter Bilbo in *The Hobbit*, he again asks Gandalf if he wants to smoke. When Bilbo found himself alone and lost in Gollum's cave, his first instinct was to light up his pipe. Pipe-weed represented for Bilbo the cosiness and tranquillity of his smial; in the most agitated moments of his life, he turned to smoking as a means of consolation.

The other Hobbits also made this connection between the act of smoking and a life free of upheavals. During the War of the Ring, the young Merry and Pippin celebrated the fall of Isengard by inviting their friends to share their discovery of pipe-weed and

Pipe-weed represented for Bilbo the cosiness and tranquillity of his smial; in the most agitated moments of his life, he turned to smoking as a means of consolation.

thus attempt to return to a state of peace and serenity. Similarly, Merry and Pippin celebrated their survival after the Battle of the Pelennor Fields by lighting up a pipe. Smoking thus became a symbol for the peaceful lives of the Hobbits, and they were in fact the first peoples to experiment with it, even though the pipe-weed plant was indigenous to Númenor and was also grown in Gondor. This plant, known as Sweet Galenas or Westman's Weed, was initially used only for decoration, and the idea of smoking its dried leaves originated in Bree, a crucial hub for exchanges between the Shire and the Big Folk. So, both the Dwarves and the Men discovered pipe-weed, although the Elves, in contrast, showed no interest at all in smoking. Gandalf (and, through him, his fellow Wizard Saruman) also took up the habit. Gandalf found that, over and above blowing elaborate smoke rings, this practice helped him to reflect and it increased his patience, whether in the White Council of 2851 T.A. or during his crossing of Moria in the War of the Ring. Saruman was prompted by Gandalf's enthusiasm and bought a substantial quantity of pipe-weed, marking another step in his control over the Shire and its resources.

Tolkien used the word 'tobacco' in *The Hobbit*, but this later gave way to the term 'pipe-weed'. He added a note on smoking and Meriadoc Brandybuck's Shire Herbarium in the prologue to *The Lord of the Rings*. He also specified that pipe-weed was a variety of Nicotiana.

The Red Book of Westmarch

'There was a big book with plain red leather covers;
its tall pages were now almost filled.'

(The Lord of the Rings, VI, 9).

The Red Book was written by Bilbo Baggins, his nephew Frodo and the latter's heir, Samwise 'Sam' Gamgee, and it owed its name to its red cover. It comprised five volumes: the first contained Bilbo's account of his adventures with Thorin and Company, along with several chapters added by Frodo to tell the story of the destruction of the One Ring; the next three volumes, also written by Bilbo, were entitled *Translations from the Elvish* and recounted Elven legends and poems which Bilbo had heard in Rivendell, while the fifth and final volume collected genealogical tables and supplementary details about the main story.

Bilbo started the Red Book on his return to the Shire, following his exploits in Erebor.

His initial title was *There and Back Again, A Hobbit's Holiday*, but he eventually opted for *My Diary, My Unexpected Journey. There and Back Again*. Bilbo continued writing the book up to his retirement in Rivendell, in the home of the Half-Elf Elrond. It was there that he produced the three volumes of translations of Elven stories and legends. When Frodo arrived in Rivendell in October 3018 T.A., Bilbo asked him to note down as much as possible during his journey, in order to put on record the events surrounding the destruction of the One Ring. Frodo passed through Rivendell again a year later, when Bilbo gave him a red box containing the first four volumes of the Red Book and asked him to continue writing the text. Frodo

then took the box to Bag End, in the Shire, and recounted his own adventures, before bequeathing the book to Sam when he set off to the Grey Havens in 3021 T.A. Sam, in his turn, passed it on to his daughter Elanor when he left the Shire for good in year 61 of the Fourth Age. After her wedding, Elanor herself left to live in the Westmarch of the Shire (hence the complete title of the Red Book), and her descendants went on to add genealogies and commentaries to the original four volumes. Several copies were subsequently produced: the first, *The Tháin's Book*, was commissioned by Aragorn, the new King of Gondor. After Aragorn's death in 120 of the Fourth Age, the Red Book was supplemented by the *Tale of Aragorn and Arwen*. This version was the most exhaustive of all, containing 'much that was later omitted or lost'. A second copy saw the light of day in the reign of Eldarion, the son of Aragorn and Arwen. This was transcribed by the royal scribe Findegil and stored in the

Great Smials, the ancestral home of the Took family, in the Shire.

The main inspiration for the Red Book was undoubtedly the famous *Red Book of*

It owed its name to its red cover. It comprised five volumes: the first contained Bilbo's account of his adventures with Thorin and Company.

Hergest, a manuscript containing numerous Celtic legends, such as the Mabinogion, with which Tolkien was very familiar. This medieval manuscript with red binding was written in Welsh around 1400 and is preserved in the Bodleian Library in Oxford. Tolkien owned a copy of this text and even translated the first part, *Pwyll, Prince of Dyfed*.

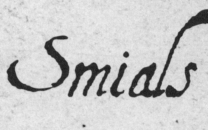

Smials

'All Hobbits had originally lived in holes in the ground, or so they believed, and in such dwellings they still felt most at home; but in the course of time they had been obliged to adopt other forms of abode.' (The Lord of the Rings, Prologue, 1).

A smial, a word purported to be the English translation of the Hobbitish *trân* and the Rohanese *trahan*, was a Hobbit's underground dwelling. It was also crucial to the etymology of the word 'Hobbit' itself, which was derived from the Old English translation, *holbytla*, of the Rohanese *kûd-dûkan*, which meant 'digger' or 'underground builder'. Smials were holes that were usually burrowed into hills, with a tunnel on a single level that opened onto various rooms. They were snug and comfortable, in keeping with the Hobbits' tastes. The main rooms were placed on the sides of a hill, so that windows could be installed to take advantage of the natural light. These windows, like the doors, were made of wood and were round, like portholes, while the walls were convex. These features were typical of the Hobbits' domestic architecture.

In the early days, all the Hobbits lived in holes of this type. According to King Théoden, the legends of the Rohirrim spoke of Half-Men dwelling in holes in the sand dunes when they still lived in the northeastern part of Middle-earth, to the west of the Forest of Great Fear. They continued this practice after their migration to the source of the River Anduin, sometime before 2510 T.A., as was confirmed by Gandalf. He described how, in around 2440 T.A., Gollum's family used to live in a smial on the banks of the Anduin,

A smial, a word purported to be the English translation of the Hobbitish trân *and the Rohanese* trahan, *was a Hobbit's underground dwelling.*

alongside the Gladden Fields. In Bilbo's time, however, this tradition was mainly perpetuated by the poorest and the richest Hobbits, and most especially by the Harfoots. The poorest Hobbits dug rudimentary holes with only basic comforts (there was sometimes no window). In contrast, the richest could afford luxurious smials with numerous offshoots. These were capable of housing a large family spanning several generations, as inthe Great Smials of the Tooks and Brandy Hall, which belonging to the Brandybucks and provided accommodation for over 200 Hobbits. Bag End, home to Bilbo and, later on, his heir Frodo, was another example of a plush smial. Most smials were concentrated in the Shire, but there were others in Staddle, next to Bree. Smials therefore required a particular topography, but some Hobbits were obliged to build above ground level, giving rise to houses that imitated smials and were equally as comfortable: these would be long and low, with no upper storeys, and they would invariably display the rounded forms typical of a smial. Their roofs would be made of dried grass, straw or peat. One example of this trend was the new house that Frodo bought in Crickhollow, built by the Brandybucks, which had a roof covered in grass. Tolkien invented the word smial from the Old English *smygel* (also the root for the names Smaug and Sméagol). These underground homes recall the burrows of Beatrix Potter's Peter Rabbit and, above all, of Badger and Mole in Kenneth Grahame's *The Wind in the Willows* (a favourite of Tolkien).

Sting

'Things were looking pretty bad again, when suddenly Bilbo appeared and charged into the astonished spiders unexpectedly from the side. 'Go on! Go on!' he shouted. 'I will do the stinging!' (The Hobbit, Ch. 8).

After the trolls Tom, Bert and William were turned to stone by the rising sun, thanks to a trick played on them by Gandalf, the participants in the Quest of Erebor discovered an array of objects in the trolls' underground den, including swords of various shapes and sizes. Gandalf and Thorin Oakenshield took possession of two of these swords (Elrond would later tell them, in Rivendell, that they were called Glamdring and Orcrist). Bilbo Baggins, for his part, took a knife protected by a leather sheath that was big enough for him to use as a short sword. This knife shared the same origins as Glamdring and Orcrist, which were forged in Gondolin by the High Elves of the West at the time of the great wars against the Goblins, many years, or even centuries, before the start of the Quest of Erebor.

After Gandalf saved Thorin and Company once again by freeing them from the Goblins, Bilbo got lost in the underground galleries of the Misty Mountains. He had the chance to verify the Elven origins of his weapon, as the blade shone in response to the presence of an enemy – just like those of Glamdring and Orcrist. The light of the sword helped Bilbo move around inside the galleries and, above all, keep Gollum at bay when Bilbo finally found him by the lake that served as his home. Later on, this weapon proved invaluable when Bilbo was confronted by Spiders in the Forest of Great Fear. After killing only one of these creatures, Bilbo suddenly felt changed, imbued with renewed courage and combativeness. He christened his sword Sting, as it had enabled him to pierce his adversary with deadly jabs. He wielded his weapon with enormous energy and – with the additional help of the One Ring – managed to release his Dwarf friends from their entrapment in the Spiders' cocoons. After the Battle of the Five Armies, which marked the end of the Quest of

Erebor, Bilbo returned to Bag End, where he kept Sting with him (even hanging it above the fireplace in his home). When, in his old age, Bilbo left the Shire after his farewell party to retire in Rivendell, he packed Sting in his luggage.

Seventeen years later, Bilbo entrusted his sword to his heir Frodo, who had agreed to set off on a mission to destroy the One Ring by throwing it into the depths of Mount Doom. Sting proved extremely useful to Frodo and his servant and companion Samwise Gamgee.

He had the chance to verify the Elven origins of his weapon, as the blade shone in reaction to the presence of an enemy – just like those of Glamdring and Orcrist.

The sword enabled Samwise to rescue Frodo by overcoming a terrifying giant Spider called Shelob, the monstrous guard at the western entrance to Sauron's realm in Mordor. Shelob was the mother of the Spiders that Bilbo himself had once fought in the Forest of Great Fear,

so Sting was a weapon inextricably linked to the Hobbits' struggles against the Spiders of Middle-earth. Once the War of the Ring had ended and Frodo had set off on a final journey towards the West, Samwise took care of Sting in the Shire.

Bilbo's naming of his sword brings to mind the weapons used by the great warriors of heroic medieval literature, whose swords acquired a special and prestigious status when they received a name, as in the case of Excalibur (King Arthur) and Durandal (Roland, a paladin of Charlemagne). Despite the modest social standing of its owner – a simple Hobbit venturing into dangerous territories far from home – Sting acquired the same aura in the hands of Bilbo when he faced an enemy as Orcrist and Glamdring did in the respective hands of Thorin and Gandalf. Thanks to the renown attached to the name of Bilbo's sword, he was able to acquire the status of an epic hero himself, even though it was his possession of the One Ring that ultimately gave him a major role in the adventure of the Quest of Erebor.

Thrór's map

'On the table in the light of a big lamp with a red shade he spread a piece of parchment rather like a map.' (The Hobbit, Ch. 1).

Thrór's map represents the Lonely Mountain and the region known in Bilbo's time as the Desolation of Smaug. As its name suggests, it was drawn by Thrór, Thorin Oakenshield's grandfather, after escaping from the attack on Erebor by the Dragon Smaug in 2770 T.A. When Thrór left for Moria in 2790, he handed the map on to his son, Thráin. In 2850 T.A., when Gandalf explored Dol Guldur in search of the identity of the Necromancer, he found a dying Thráin in the dungeon. Thráin gave the map to Gandalf, along with a small key, and asked the Wizard to bequeath it to his son, without any further explanation. Ninety-one years later, at the impromptu party organized in Bilbo's home, Gandalf returned the objects to their legitimate owner: Thorin. During Thorin and Company's stay in Rivendell, Elrond worked out that the map hid a series of moon-runes which indicated that the secret door was connected to Durin's Day: 'Stand by the grey stone when the thrush knocks and the setting sun with the last light of Durin's Day will shine upon the keyhole.' (*The Hobbit*, Ch. 3) Durin's Day was an astronomical phenomenon that could occur on the first day of the autumn Moon, at the Dwarves' New Year, when the Moon and Sun are simultaneously visible in the sky. This mysterious instruction enabled Bilbo to open the secret door of Erebor and enter inside without the Dragon Smaug's knowledge.

Like all the Dwarves' maps, Thrór's has the East at the top. On the eastern edge, an arrow shows the direction to the Iron Hills, which was ruled by Thorin's cousin, Dáin. Just below, there is a drawing of the Lonely Mountain, with a red dragon flying above it and the secret entrance, facing the viewer, indicated by a rune. The southern slope plays host to the great gate, from which the Running River flows in a long meander that weaves its way around Dale before flowing towards the Long Lake, further to the south.

At the bottom of the map, two arrows pointing west indicate the site of the Forest of Great Fear and Thranduil's kingdom. To the north, the presence of dragons is noted in the Grey Mountains. Finally, on the left of the map, a claw-like hand points to the secret door, accompanied by the runic text 'Five feet high the door and three may walk abreast. Th. Th.' (the 'Th.' and 'Th.' stand for Thrór and Thráin).

Tolkien placed the map in the novel's opening chapter, facing the passage in which Gandalf returned it to the Dwarves, so that the reader would discover it at the same time as the characters themselves. Tolkien had also wanted to print the moon-runes revealed to Elrond on the other side of the map, so that the reader could make them out if the map was placed in front of a source of light. The

Thrór's map represents the Lonely Mountain and the region known in Bilbo's time as the Desolation of Smaug.

original publisher turned down this request, on the grounds of cost, but some later editions have published the map in accordance with Tolkien's wishes.

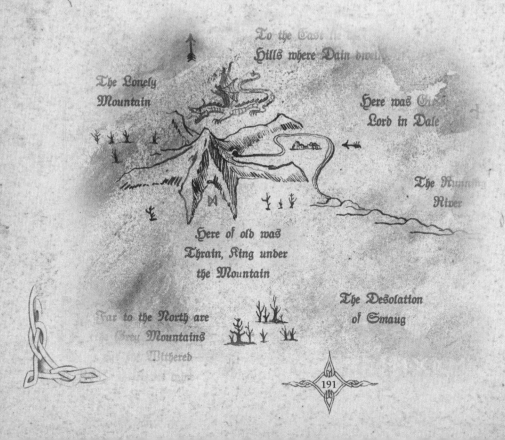

To the East in Hills where Dain dwelt

The Lonely Mountain

Here was Girion Lord in Dale

Here was of old was Thrain, King under the Mountain

The Running River

The Desolation of Smaug

Far to the North are the Grey Mountains Withered

ᚠᛁᚢᛖ
ᚠᛟᛏ·ᚢᛁᚷᚺ
ᚦᛖ·ᛞᚢᚨᚱ·ᛗ
ᛗ·ᚦᚱᛟ·ᛗᚫᚨ
ᛈᚹᛖᚾ·ᚨᛒᚱᛖ
ᛚᛁᛏ·ᚦᚦ

The Lonely
Mountain

Far to the North
the Grey Mounta
and the Withere
Heath whence cam

the Great Worms

To the East lie the Iron
Hills where Dain dwells

Here was Girion
Lord in Dale

The Running
River

Here is the
gateway of
the Long
Lake

old was
King under
untain

The Desolation
of Smaug

In Esgaroth
upon the Long Lake
dwell Men

To the West lies Mirkwood the Great.
There are Spiders

Here flows the
Forest River

The Elvenking

Places

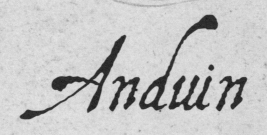

Anduin

'It is easy enough, as you remember, to get from this bank to the Carrock by the ford, but on the other side is a cliff standing up from a swirling channel.' (The Hobbit, Ch. 7).

The Anduin, a Sindarin name meaning 'great river,' is a watercourse that rises north-east of the Misty Mountains before flowing south as a raging torrent. It is relatively difficult to cross because of its depth and there are few fords. Consequently, Gandalf has to make a large detour to follow Beorn, who is investigating the Goblin and Warg attack on Thorin and Company.

Meandering past the entrances to the wooded valleys of the Brown Lands, it leads on to the Sarn Gebir rapids as it flows between the Emyn Muil hills and, after passing through the Argonath pillars, empties into the Nen Hithoel lake, and from there it gushes into the mighty Rauros waterfall. The river then widens and becomes perfectly navigable. It flows on more peacefully, encircling the island of Cair Andros, then passing between the White Mountains and the Mountains of Shadow by the ancient city of Osgiliath. After the port of Harlond, which serves the city of Minas Tirith, the Anduin reaches the large river port of Pelargir, before ending in a vast delta known as the Mouths of the Anduin in the Bay of Belfalas. The Anduin has many tributaries; first the river Rugis, then the Rhimdath, the Ninglor, the Celebrant, the Limlight, the Entwash, then the rivers of the White Mountains, the Erui and the Sirith, along with the Poros, which rises in the Mountains of Shadow. Since ancient times, the Anduin has been known for its size. During the Great March of the Elves led by the Vala Oromë, the Anduin was the largest of all the rivers the Elves came across. Faced with the impressive scale of the mountains behind it,

some of them, the Nandor, decided to stay for a time on the banks of the Anduin and then follow it south. It is from the Nandor that those known as the Silvan Elves are descended, even though they like water as much as trees and other living creatures. At the time of the Quest of Erebor, the Silvan Elves of Mirkwood were living under the authority of King Thranduil.

It is in the waters of the Anduin that Isildur, son of Elendil and bearer of the One Ring, perishes. Pursued by Goblins from the Misty Mountains, he is eventually swept away by the river to the Gladden Fields where the precious ring slips from his finger and is lost. The Ring is found many years later by Déagol and his friend Sméagol, who kills Déagol to take possession of the Ring and who, over time, gradually turns into the strange creature known as Gollum. During the War of the Ring, the Fellowship of the Ring descend the river between Lórien and the Rauros falls. The Corsairs of Umbar decide to sail up the Anduin to the port of Harlond to rally Sauron's forces for the Battle of Pelennor. However, Aragorn and his horsemen from Arnor capture and use their ships after their victory at Pelargir.

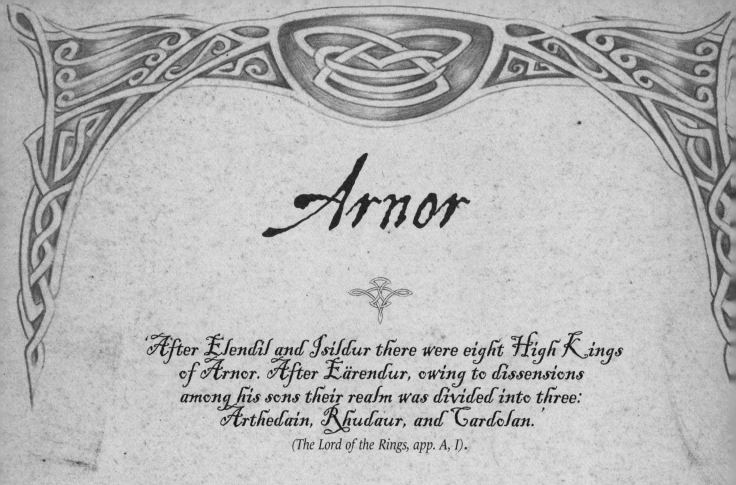

Arnor

'After Elendil and Isildur there were eight High Kings
of Arnor. After Eärendur, owing to dissensions
among his sons their realm was divided into three:
Arthedain, Rhudaur, and Cardolan.'

(The Lord of the Rings, app. A, I).

Arnor is the North-kingdom of Eriador founded by Elendil at the end of the Second Age. The name is a Sindarin word meaning literally 'land of kings'. In Quenya it is Arnarórë. Its borders extend from the river Lhûn, the Tower Hills and the Blue Mountains in the west, to the Bruinen river to the east, and from Forochel Bay in the north to the Gwathló river in the south. Arnor's most ancient city is the great port of Lond Daer, founded by the kings of Númenor. After fleeing the Drowning of Númenor, Elendil established his capital, Annúminas, on the shores of Lake Nenuial. The other important cities of the kingdom are Fornost and Tharbad, located along the Gwathló river. Two major roads cross Arnor from one side to the other: from west to east is the

Great East Road connecting the Grey Havens – the main Elven port – with the High Pass of the Misty Mountains, and passing through the Shire, where the Hobbits live. Beyond the mountains, this road crosses through Mirkwood and continues as far as Long Lake. From north to south, the Greenway connects Fornost with Tharbad and eventually reaches Gondor, the South-kingdom, founded by Isildur and Anárion, the sons of Elendil. At the point these two roads cross is the town of Bree, where Gandalf and Thorin Oakenshield meet before the Quest of Erebor.

The history of Arnor is somewhat chaotic. Upon the death of Elendil – killed by Sauron during the Last Alliance of Elves and Men – it is his eldest son, Isildur, who inherits the sceptre of the North-kingdom, leaving his nephew Meneldil to govern the South-kingdom. Unfortunately, Isildur and his three eldest sons die in a Goblin ambush while travelling back to their country. Valandil, Isildur's fourth son, then inherits this kingdom heavily depopulated by the war against Sauron. The tenth king of Arnor, Eärendur, dies in 861 of the Third Age, leaving the kingdom to his three warring sons. They end up dividing it between them. The eldest, Amlaith, keeps Annúminas and the surrounding region, calling it Arthedain, but moves the capital to Fornost. The other two settle to the south and east respectively, creating Cardolan and Rhudaur. The three kingdoms meet at the hill of Amon Sûl, where one of the Palantíri, coveted by the three kingdoms, can be found. Isildur's bloodline soon dies out in Cardolan and Rhudaur. The kings of Arthedain then claim suzerainty over the entire ancient kingdom of Arnor, but their claims are strongly challenged by Rhudaur, where the throne has fallen into the hands of Men not descended from the Dúnedain. The latter eventually make a pact with the Witch-king of Angmar, whose plan is to destroy the kingdoms of the north. In 1409 T.A., he succeeds in destroying Cardolan, leaving only a handful of survivors at Tyrn Gorthad, which would later become Barrow-downs. In 1601 T.A., some Hobbits emigrate westward from Bree, beyond the Baranduin river. The king of Arthedain, Argeleb II, agrees to them occupying the lands of the Shire, between the river and Tower Hills, but without right of ownership. A few years later, the Great Plague of 1636 devastates the population, decimating the last Dúnedain of Cardolan. Of the three kingdoms, it is Arthedain that best withstands the attacks from Angmar, aided first by Cardolan, then by the Elves of Lindon and Rivendell, led by Círdan and the half-elven Elrond. In 1975 T.A., the heir of Gondor, Eärnur, arms an expedition to help his cousins in the north. Unfortunately, his help comes too late: Fornost is taken before he arrives, and the last king of Arthedain is forced to flee and perishes in the sea not far from Forochel. Nevertheless, the Battle of Fornost ends in victory and in the dissolution of the kingdoms of Angmar and Rhudaur.

At the end of this war, Arthedain is too sparsely populated to be raised from the ashes and the last Dúnedain of the North conceal themselves as the Rangers. It is not until Aragorn II and the War of the Ring that the kingdom of Arnor will be reborn. In fact, as a direct descendant of Isildur, Aragorn is the chief of the Dúnedain of the North. On his accession to the throne, he unites Arnor and Gondor under the name of the Reunited Kingdom.

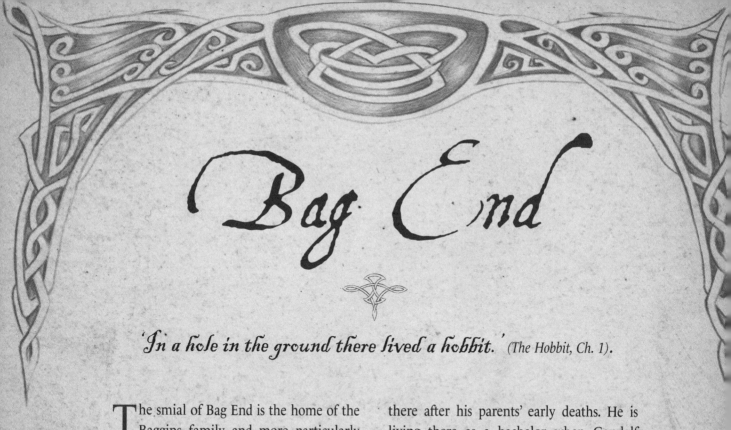

Bag End

'*In a hole in the ground there lived a hobbit.*' *(The Hobbit, Ch. 1).*

The smial of Bag End is the home of the Baggins family and more particularly of Bilbo Baggins, and later Frodo Baggins, his cousin or nephew. This rather luxurious dwelling occupies the upper part of the Hill, north of the village of Hobbiton. Three smaller smials occupy the lower part of the Hill. In keeping with traditional Hobbit architecture, this smial has round windows and doors. Its front door is painted green and opens on to a large tubular hallway giving access to the many rooms of the house: bedrooms, bathrooms, dressing rooms, as well as storerooms, pantries, kitchens and the dining room. The best rooms are those to the left of the entrance, with windows overlooking the gardens.

Bag End was built by Bungo Baggins, Bilbo's father, towards the end of the 30th century of the Third Age, as a wedding gift for his wife Belladonna Took. Bilbo Baggins was born and grew up at Bag End and remained there after his parents' early deaths. He is living there as a bachelor when Gandalf decides to introduce him as a burglar to Thorin and Company. As he does not warn anyone of his departure with the Dwarves, Bilbo is posted as missing and his property is put up for auction. At the time, Bilbo's cousin, Otho Sackville-Baggins is his heir and Lobelia, Otho's wife, dreams of living at Bag End. Bilbo's sudden reappearance when he returns from his adventure in the middle of the auction causes her great disappointment. This disappointment only grows worse when, some years later, Bilbo adopts his cousin Frodo Baggins (whom he commonly refers to as his 'nephew') and makes him his heir. Frodo and Bilbo live together at Bag End until Bilbo grows old and decides to leave for Rivendell after his birthday party.

When Frodo is forced to leave the Shire in 3018 T.A., he sells Bag End to Lobelia

Sackville-Baggins, who still wants to live there, despite the death of her husband. At the end of the War of the Ring, when the Hobbits in the Fellowship of the Ring return to the Shire, they find it laid waste by Saruman, who has set up his headquarters at Bag End itself. Lobelia's resistance to Saruman's men ends with her imprisonment. After the cleaning up of the Shire, and devastated by the death of her son Lotho, she decides to return Bag End to Frodo and go back to live with her family and enjoy a quiet old age. Bag End then has its old owner back. Frodo, who has no descendants, makes his friend Sam Gamgee his heir. When Frodo leaves Middle-earth, Sam moves to Bag End with his wife Rôsie and their many children.

The similarity between the names Baggins and Bag End was deliberate on Tolkien's part as it exists not only in English, but also in Westron, the Common Speech of western Middle-earth, in which Baggins is Labingi and Bag End is Labinnec. Bag End is the place where both *The Hobbit* and *The Lord of the Rings* begin and end. It represents a well-known and familiar place for Hobbits, who are later sent out into the wide world to live great adventures. Bag End's round, green door is the first step on the road: 'The Road goes ever on and on, down from the door where it began.'

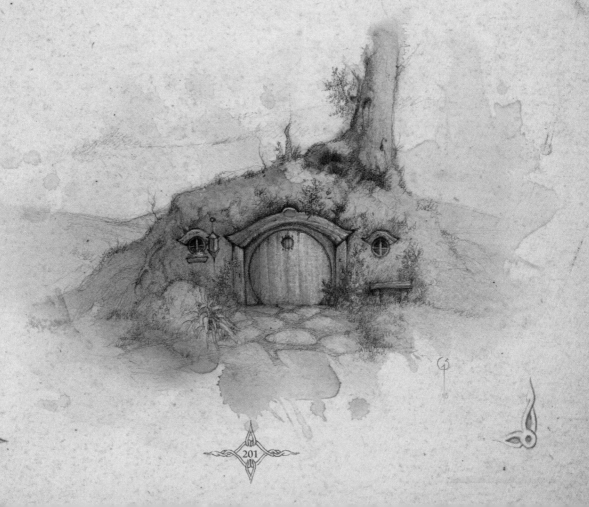

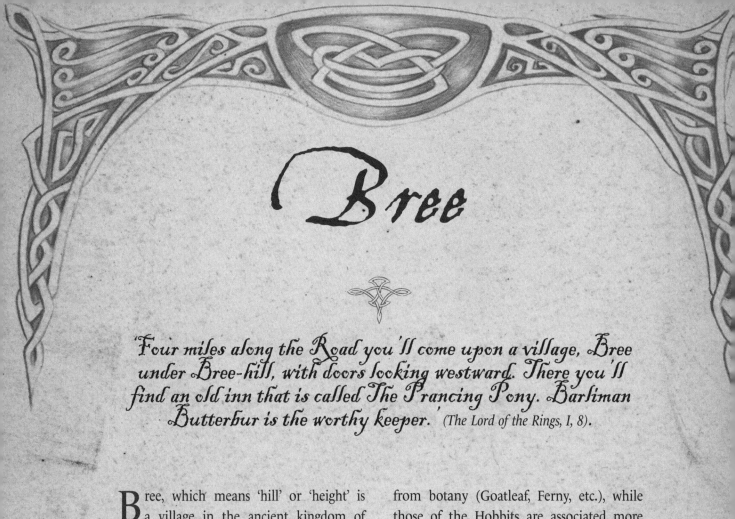

Bree

'Four miles along the Road you'll come upon a village, Bree under Bree-hill, with doors looking westward. There you'll find an old inn that is called The Prancing Pony. Barliman Butterbur is the worthy keeper.' (The Lord of the Rings, I, 8).

Bree, which means 'hill' or 'height' is a village in the ancient kingdom of Arthedain, and before that of Arnor, at the intersection of the Great East Road and the Greenway. It is built on the western slope of a hill on the edge of Chetwood. There are other villages nearby: Staddle and Combe, on other slopes of the hill, and Archet, further into the woods. Together they form what its inhabitants call Bree-land.

Nestled on the hillside below the road, the village of Bree consists of around 100 stone-built dwellings with their doors facing west. Above, on the upper slopes of the hill, are the Hobbit smials. For in Bree-land, Men and Hobbits live in harmony, and even call each other 'Big Folk' and 'Little Folk.' Interestingly, the family names of the humans are derived from botany (Goatleaf, Ferny, etc.), while those of the Hobbits are associated more with geology (Longholes, Underhill, etc.). Around the village, from north to south in a wide arc, the dwellings are protected by a deep ditch reinforced by a tall, thick hedge in which there are only three openings, with gates. At night, guards close the gates and keep watch over the comings and goings from the shelter of their gatehouses. One of the oldest buildings is a large inn with a frontage on the road and two wings connected by a large arch giving access to an inner courtyard. The three floors of the building are clearly visible at the front, but the wings are partly carved into the hill itself, so that the end windows on the second floor are at ground level. Above the arch is a sign

showing a white pony standing on its hind legs, and above is the name of the establishment: The Prancing Pony. For as long as the people of Bree can remember, the inn has always been run by the Butterbur family. A great place for conversation, its Common Room is always full of locals, with rangers and travellers exchanging stories from distant lands. 'As strange as news from Bree' is a common saying in the Shire. It is here that Gandalf and Thorin Oakenshield spend a night after meeting on the road one day in 2941 T.A. And it is this meeting that leads to the Quest of Erebor, which culminates in the retaking of the kingdom of Erebor and the death of the dragon Smaug. Doubtless, Thorin and Company must also have passed through on their journey from the Shire to Rivendell. At the start of the War of the Ring, Frodo Baggins and his companions Samwise Gamgee, Peregrine Took and Meriadoc Brandybuck also stop there, but their stay at the inn turns out to be far more eventful than they anticipate.

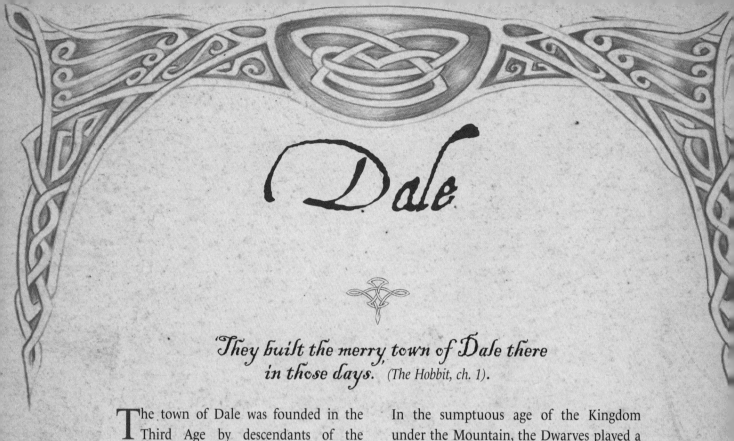

Dale

'They built the merry town of Dale there in those days.' (The Hobbit, ch. 1).

The town of Dale was founded in the Third Age by descendants of the Northmen. It was located at the foot of Erebor, east of the main mountain spur, where Ravenhill, the ancient Dwarven guard post, stood. The Running River flowed through it. The Northmen were distant descendants of the Men of the First Age, allies of the Elves against Morgoth. The Rohirrim, the Beornings and the Men of Long Lake were their main descendants. According to Thorin Oakenshield, Dale was founded back in the reign of Thrór, his grandfather, between 2590 and 2770 T.A. However, some chronicles of Gondor and Rohan mention the existence of Dale at an earlier time. In fact, some of the Northmen allied to Gondor in the Third Age are said to have taken refuge in Dale after the defeat of the Battle of the Plains, which took place south of Mirkwood in 1856.

In the sumptuous age of the Kingdom under the Mountain, the Dwarves played a large part in the construction of Dale and notably of the Running River canals which flowed through the town. The good relations between Dale and Erebor led to a flourishing trade between the two towns. In particular, the Men of Dale used Dwarven blacksmiths for many jobs and sent their sons to be apprentices in exchange for food and sometimes riches. The Men of Dale made a very nutritious biscuit-like food called 'cram'.

The contribution made by the Dwarves of the Lonely Mountain was not limited to blacksmithing and construction, they also made high-quality toys which were sold at the famous Dale toy market; Bilbo Baggins gives some to the children of the Shire at the party he organizes for his 111th birthday. The Men of Dale also had a special trading relationship with the Men

of Lake-town, who benefited for many years from Dale's prosperity.

Another special characteristic of the inhabitants of Dale was that they appeared to have used a version of Runes, the Angerthas Erebor, also adopted by the Dwarves. Certain pages of the Book of Mazarbul, found in Moria at Balin's tomb, were written in Dale Runes. Dale was also known for its bells that were rung to announce both good and bad news. They chimed gloomily during the attack on Erebor by the dragon Smaug in 2770 in the reign of Girion. Dale

was destroyed by this attack and many of the survivors took refuge at Lake-town.

The Men of Dale also knew how to communicate with the thrushes who acted as messengers for the Lakemen. This is how Bard, a descendant of King Girion, discovers Smaug's weak point and is able to shoot him down as he flies over Lake-town during the events of the Quest of Erebor. These culminate in the Battle of the Five Armies for possession of the treasure of Erebor, a battle that takes place in the ruins of Dale. Afterwards, Bard rebuilds Dale with the

help of the Dwarves and the Lakemen. Dale regains its former glory, and the kingdom extends as far as Lake-town and far to the east.

Between the Quest of Erebor and the War of the Ring, Gollum visits Dale while searching for Bilbo. And Bilbo also travels to Dale after his farewell party, before returning to Rivendell. In 3017, Sauron sends messengers to Brand, Bard's grandson, demanding the surrender of the kingdom of Dale. He is met with refusal and, while the Fellowship of the Ring and the forces of Gondor and Rohan triumph at the gates of Mordor, Dale comes under attack. For three days, a battle ensues which pits the Easterlings, who make up Sauron's army in the north, against the Men of Dale and Lake-town, allied with the Dwarves

of Erebor. Brand and the Dwarf King Dáin Ironfoot perish in the Easterling attack. The army of Dwarves and Men take refuge in Erebor. After the fall of Sauron, Thorin III Stonehelm, son of Dáin II Ironfoot, and Bard II, son of Brand, break the siege and become, respectively, King under the Mountain and King of Dale.

Dale is inspired by a fantasy novel written by William Morris: *The Roots of the Mountains: Wherein is Told Somewhat of the Lives of the Men of Burgdale, Their Friends, Their Neighbours, Their Foemen, and Their Fellows in Arms*. In this novel there is a river called the Weltering Water which flows along the bottom of a valley. Tolkien created the Running River and the town of Dale in reference to this.

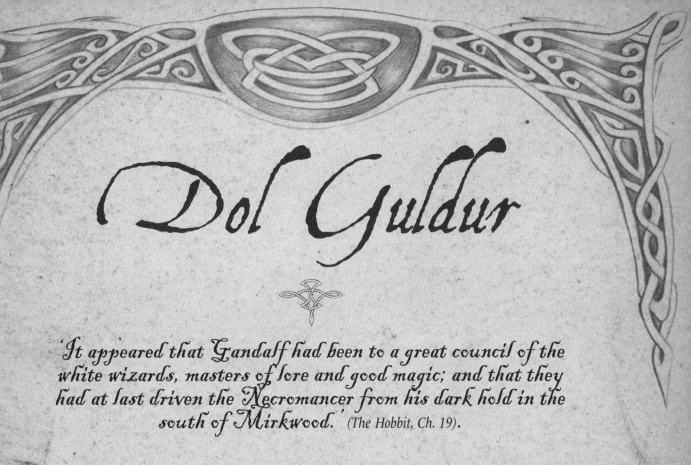

Dol Guldur

'It appeared that Gandalf had been to a great council of the white wizards, masters of lore and good magic; and that they had at last driven the Necromancer from his dark hold in the south of Mirkwood.' (The Hobbit, Ch. 19).

When the members of the Quest of Erebor reach Mirkwood, which they are preparing to cross, Bilbo Baggins asks Gandalf if there is not some way of bypassing this immense Wilderland forest. Gandalf explains that this would mean making very long detours and that even then the routes would not necessarily be safer. The Wizard mentions in particular the danger of skirting the Forest to the south, as such a route would lead straight to the lands of the Necromancer and his fortress of Dol Guldur.

In 1050 T.A., the Necromancer secretly infiltrated the Great Greenwood, where he founded Dol Guldur, the 'Hill of Sorcery' in Sindarin. His presence corrupted the forest land, and it became known as Mirkwood. The fortress was built in the south-west of the Forest, on the hill of Amon Lanc, the high point of the region, where, in the past, Oropher, King of the Silvan Elves – and father of Thranduil – had ruled before withdrawing further north with his people in the Second Age. For many years, Dol Guldur has stood on a rocky eminence surrounded by dark fir trees with rotting, dried-out branches. None of those who have entered the gates of this sinister fortress have come out, except Gandalf, who twice returns to spy on the place, in 2063 and 2850 T.A. There he finally discovers that the Necromancer is none other than Sauron who is striving to gather all the Rings of Power and, in particular, the One Ring, in order to restore his former power and to dominate Middle-earth. On his second visit to Dol Guldur, the Wizard encounters

a dying Dwarf prisoner who turns out to be Thráin II, father of Thorin Oakenshield. Captured in 2845 in Mirkwood, while on his way to the Lonely Mountain, Thráin has been locked up in the dungeons of Dol Guldur for several years after being tortured by Sauron, who is trying to recover the Ring of the House of Durin. Gandalf is there when Thráin utters his final words and he receives from him two precious objects that the Dwarf had clung on to: Thrór's map and the key to the secret entrance to the Lonely Mountain. Well aware of the danger that Sauron again poses, Gandalf tries to persuade the White Council, meeting at Rivendell in 2851, to mount an attack on Dol Guldur, but his first attempt fails as Saruman is opposed to this and wins the day. However, at another meeting of the Council in 2941, Saruman – who is now endeavouring to prevent Sauron searching the banks of the Anduin for the Ring – finally agrees to an assault on the fortress. The Necromancer then flees from Dol Guldur. However, the threat reappears sometime later, south of the Forest: in 2951, while assembling his forces in Mordor, Sauron sends the Nazgûl, his ghostly servants, to reoccupy Dol Guldur. One of them, Khamûl, the Shadow of the East, becomes his lieutenant there. During the War of the Ring, in 3019, Sauron's forces, who have assembled at Dol Guldur, attack Thandruil's Silvan Elves to the north and those of Lothlórien led by Celeborn and Galadriel to the west, but their assaults are repelled on both fronts. After Sauron's defeat, the army of the Elves of Lórien, commanded by Celeborn, cross the Anduin and take the fortress. The Forest is cleansed of all evil and ceases to be called Mirkwood. Galadriel destroys Dol Guldur, opening up its dungeons and tearing down its fortifications.

Erebor

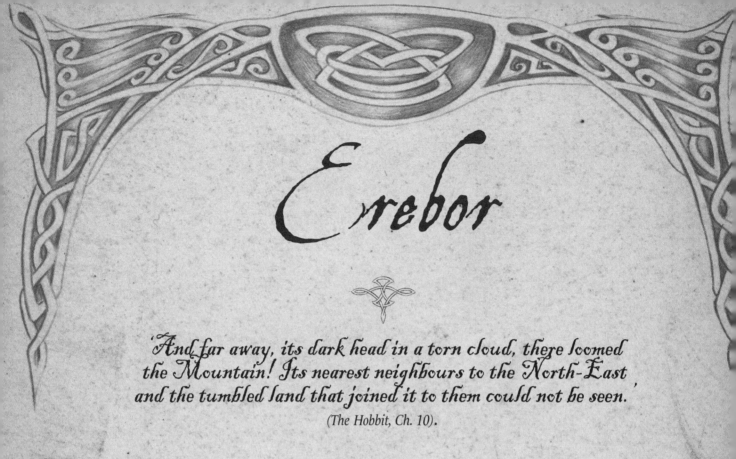

'And far away, its dark head in a torn cloud, there loomed
the Mountain! Its nearest neighbours to the North-East
and the tumbled land that joined it to them could not be seen.'

(The Hobbit, Ch. 10).

Erebor is an Elvish name in the Sindarin language meaning 'Lonely Mountain'. And indeed, this mountain rises alone in the midst of desolate heathland. Six rocky spurs spread out from its summit, giving it a star-like appearance. From its southern slope, below a large precipice, flows the source of the Running River, which continues south-west to join Long Lake. Not far from this source the town of Dale was built – in ruins at the time of the Quest of Erebor – as well as the main gate to the Kingdom under the Mountain. This kingdom was created in 1999 of the Third Age by Thráin I, King of the Dwarves of the Line of Durin, who had been forced to flee the mines of Moria after the Balrog, who had been lurking deep within the earth, was awakened. Together with many survivors, Thráin excavated the

Lonely Mountain and discovered fabulous riches within. The greatest treasure was the Arkenstone, the pride of the King under the Mountain. However, after the death of Thráin I, his son Thorin eventually left Erebor for the Grey Mountains in the north, where most of the exiles from Moria had settled. In fact, Erebor gradually became depopulated until the arrival, in 2590 T.A., of one of Thráin's descendants: Thrór, who was fleeing the Grey Mountains now laid waste by the Great Worms, the Dragons. Thrór then embarked on some major projects in the Lonely Mountain and the kingdom enjoyed a great period of prosperity which encouraged Men from the surrounding area to settle at the foot of the Mountain in order to trade. This is how the kingdom of Dale developed. Unfortunately, news of the Dwarves'

new-found wealth eventually reached the largest of the dragons – Smaug the Golden – living at the time in the Grey Mountains. His attack in 2770 T.A. caught everyone, or almost everyone, off guard: Dale was demolished, the Great Gate of Erebor was destroyed, and the Dwarves who remained prisoners in the Mountain were soon exterminated. However, Thrór, no doubt under the influence of his Ring of Power, had been cautious and managed to flee with his son Thráin through a narrow corridor and a five-foot (1.5-metre) high, trapezoidal, hidden door, concealed on the south-west flank of the Mountain. This same door much later allows Thorin and Company to penetrate Smaug's lair. To reach it from the outside, you have to climb a perilous path, skirting the rise of the great south spur, Ravenhill, where an old guardhouse stands. To open it, you must have the key and be there at the right time, on Durin's Day, the Dwarven New Year, when the setting sun shines upon the lock.

Smaug took up residence in Erebor – remaining there until the arrival of the expedition led by Thorin Oakenshield – and did as his race do, that is to say he amassed plundered riches and rested upon them to strengthen the scales protecting his body. From time to time, when necessary, the dragon reminded the Men of that region of his presence, gradually transforming the area between Long Lake and Esgaroth into

a veritable wasteland. During the Quest of Erebor, Bilbo Baggins steals a cup from the dragon; this causes him to fly into a rage and drives him to take revenge on the Men of Lake-town. Fortunately Bard, a distant descendant of Girion, manages to kill him with the Black Arrow passed down to him by his ancestors, the kings of Dale. After the death of Smaug, the Battle of the Five Armies sees the army of the Goblins and Wargs pitted against the alliance of the Free Peoples living in the Wild: Thranduil's Elves, the descendants of the Men of Dale, and the Dwarves from the Iron Hills – a three-day forced march to the south-east – whose leader, Dáin Ironfoot, is Thorin's cousin. The battle takes place between the arms of the Mountain where the ruins of Dale are located, with many feats of arms occurring on both sides on the foothills. The final victory by the Free Peoples is marred by the many deaths. After Thorin's death, Dáin assumes the title of King under the Mountain and Erebor and Dale can be reborn. The alliance of Dwarves and Men continues during the War of the Ring. Despite an initial defeat at the Battle of Dale, the two armies manage to retreat to the Lonely Mountain and successfully withstand the siege led by the Easterlings. After Sauron's defeat, the invaders are driven out and the two kingdoms come under the suzerainty of the king of Arnor and of Gondor.

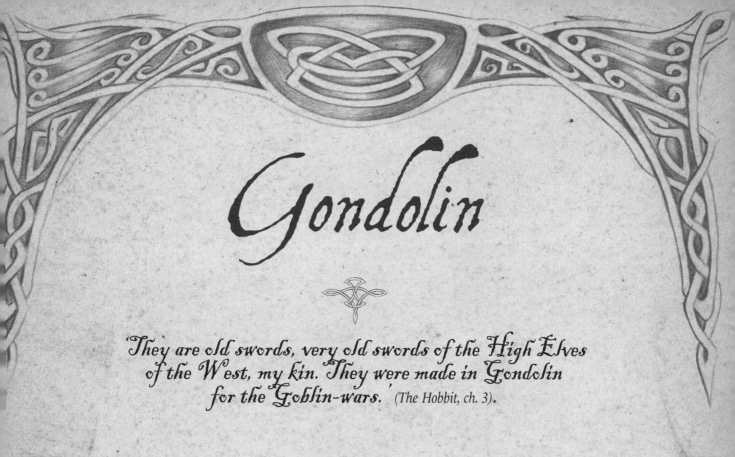

Gondolin

'They are old swords, very old swords of the High Elves of the West, my kin. They were made in Gondolin for the Goblin-wars.' (The Hobbit, ch. 3).

Gondolin is an Elven city of the First Age. At that time, Middle-earth was under threat from a powerful enemy, Morgoth, who was the cause of much destruction. In a dream, Ulmo, the Vala of the Waters, revealed to an Elf lord named Turgon the location of a valley hidden by a ring of mountains to which he could guide his people to protect them from the threat posed by Morgoth. However, Turgon was also warned that this protection would only last for a certain time and that he had to be ready for the arrival of a messenger who would come to warn him of the danger threatening his city.

In the valley of Tumladen, encircled by the Echoriath Mountains, Turgon built his city in secret over more than fifty years, before guiding his people there in 104 F.A. Gondolin was a city of great beauty and pearly whiteness: its towers and walls were white, and its steps marble. It was also known for its imposing Tower of the King, surrounded by fountains. The city, entirely concealed by the mountains, could only be reached via an underground passage barred by seven gates protected by Elven soldiers and precipitous passes, or by air with the help of the great Eagles.

In 458 F.A., two children of Men, Húrin and Huor, were flown into the city by Eagles and remained there for some time. Then, in 495 F.A., Tuor, the son of Huor, also came to Gondolin, but via the underground passage, and gave Ulmo's warning to Lord Turgon; however, Turgon refused to pay heed and condemned his people to a bitter fate. Morgoth's spies had discovered the location of the Elven city but had not yet been able to reach it. They kidnapped one of its inhabitants, Maeglin, the king's nephew, and forced him to reveal the paths leading to Gondolin. In the summer of 510 F.A., an army of Balrogs, Orcs, Wolves and Dragons attacked Gondolin. Some of the Elven people were able to flee, as the king's daughter, Idril, had foreseen the impending tragedy and had had a secret tunnel dug from the city to a path leading to a mountain pass. However, the king and many of his subjects perished in the merciless fighting and in the fires that broke out in the streets of the beautiful city. Gondolin was destroyed and abandoned, before being submerged by the sea at the end of the war against Morgoth.

During its years of protection, King Turgon's people produced many works of great beauty, some of which were stolen from the city by the Orcs and Trolls but survived for centuries, right up to the time of Bilbo Baggins in the Third Age. During the Quest of Erebor, in fact, Gandalf the Wizard and Thorin and Company discover weapons from Gondolin in the lair of the three Trolls. These weapons are: the sword Glamdring, which had belonged to Turgon himself, and which Gandalf chooses to carry; the blade Orcrist, chosen by the Dwarf Thorin II Oakenshield; and Sting, which becomes Bilbo's dagger, and which he later passes on to the Keeper of the Ring, his heir Frodo Baggins.

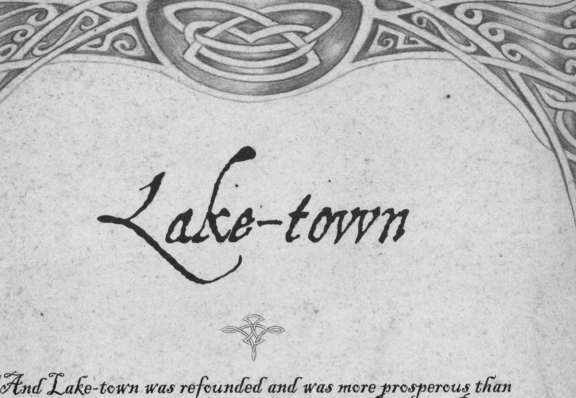

Lake-town

'And Lake-town was refounded and was more prosperous than ever, and much wealth went up and down the Running River; and there was friendship in those parts between elves and dwarves and men.' (The Hobbit, Ch. 19).

Lake-town, also known as Esgaroth in Sindarin, was a town built almost entirely on stilts. Only a few buildings and warehouses were constructed on land. Located at the western end of Long Lake, near the mouth of the Forest River, the town was protected from the currents by a rocky promontory and connected to the land by a large wooden bridge. It was populated by Men and governed by a Master elected by the oldest and wisest inhabitants. Lake-town was a trading town. It had a market that stretched from one side of a central basin to the other.

However, at the time of the Quest of Erebor, in 2931 of the Third Age, the town was in decline: the remains of old stilts, visible where the water level was low, bore witness to this. Before the arrival of Smaug in 2770 T.A., the inhabitants of Lake-town traded goods with their human neighbours in Dale, at the foot of the Lonely Mountain. However, the destruction of Dale by the dragon during the Sack of Erebor put an end to this period of prosperity. So, from 2770 T.A. to 2931 T.A., the inhabitants of Lake-town continued trading only with the winegrowers of Dorwinion and Thranduil's Silvan Elves, using rafts for part of the route and following the course of the Forest River. During this period, Lake-town also took in refugees from the former town of Dale, including the descendants of Girion, the last Lord of Dale.

In 2931 T.A., Lake-town is attacked and largely destroyed by the dragon Smaug after its people help Thorin and Company to reach the ancient kingdom of Erebor by providing them with ponies and food. The town is saved by a descendant of Girion, a bowman called Bard. Told by a thrush about a weak point in the dragon's armour, Bard shoots it down with an arrow. However, the damage done to the town is such that its inhabitants are forced to take refuge on the shores of the lake and Thranduil's Elves, originally on their way to the Lonely Mountain, stop en route to help them.

The reconstruction of the town is funded by some of the plunder the dragon amassed in the Lonely Mountain which was given to Bard by Dáin II Ironfoot, although the Master manages to escape with part of the treasure. Lake-town is eventually rebuilt slightly north of its original location.

At the time of the War of the Ring, Lake-town is part of the kingdom of Dale, governed by Brand, Bard's grandson. In March 3019 T.A., the kingdom is besieged by the Easterlings: King Brand is killed alongside Dáin Ironfoot. Brand's son, Bard II, succeeds him.

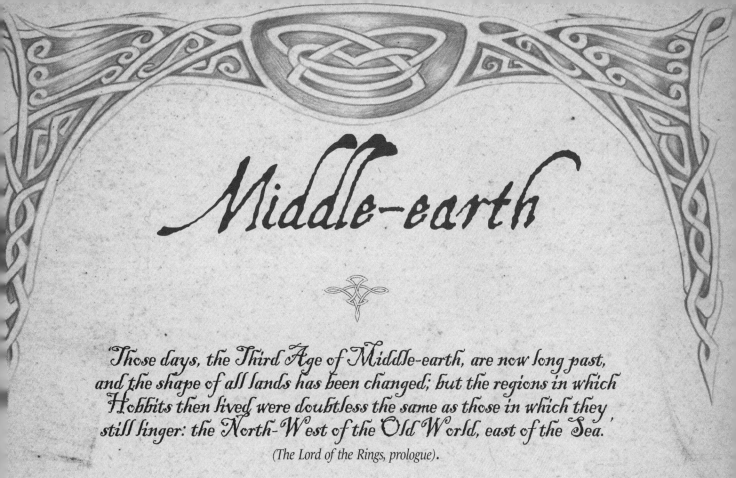

Middle-earth

'Those days, the Third Age of Middle-earth, are now long past, and the shape of all lands has been changed; but the regions in which Hobbits then lived were doubtless the same as those in which they still linger: the North-West of the Old World, east of the Sea.'

(The Lord of the Rings, prologue).

Middle-earth is the central continent of the world, separated from Valinor, the Undying Lands of the West, by Belegaer, the Great Sea, and from the distant lands of the south-east by the Eastern Sea. During the first three Ages of the world, the north-west of Middle-earth is the key site of great events involving the Elves, Dwarves and Men in their battles against the evil power of Morgoth and his servant, Sauron. Thus, in the First Age, the welcoming lands of Beleriand were the theatre of the wars against Morgoth, at the end of which Morgoth was thrown out of the world by the other divine powers he betrayed: the Valar. Following this conflict, Beleriand was submerged and disappeared from the face of the world. In the Second Age and Third Age, the fate of Middle-earth is played out in the great regions of Eriador (in the west), Wilderland (in the east), Gondor (in the south-west) and Mordor (in the south-east), from where Sauron threatens the rest of the world. Most of the land in the south and east of Middle-earth remains little known by the Free Peoples. They are generally hostile places, populated by Elves and wild Men, and produce countless enemies against the great Elven and Human realms of the north-west.

In the First Age, Beleriand was surrounded to the west and south by the shores of the Great Sea, and to the north and east by

mighty mountain ranges. In the centre of Beleriand lay the great forests that make up the kingdom of Doriath, ruled over by the Elven king Thingol, leader of the Sindar people. Across this kingdom flowed the mighty river Sirion, dividing the entire length of Beleriand from north to south. Rising in the foothills of the Shadow Mountains to the northwest, the Sirion, fed by many tributaries, continued on its course for over 600 kilometres (375 miles), before flowing into the sea. North of Doriath, first were the Mountains of Terror, home to monstrous creatures, including spiders; then came the high wooded plateau of Dorthonion, known as Taur-nu-Fuin, the 'Forest under Nightshade', when ravaged by Morgoth. Near the western foothills of the Mountains of Terror lay the encircling mountains of Echoriath, enclosing the hidden valley of Gondolin, the last Elven kingdom in Beleriand to survive the Sack of Doriath by the Dwarves in 501 F.A., then by the Noldor in 507. To the north of Dorthonion lay the vast plain of Ardgalen, renamed Anfauglith after it was destroyed by the fires of Morgoth. Morgoth lived entrenched in his fortress of Angband, in the foothills of the vast range of the Iron Hills which dominated the north. Finally, to the east of Beleriand flowed the River Gelion, running through the region of Ossiriand, and descending the Blue Mountains, which formed Beleriand's natural frontier, where

the great Dwarven cities of Nogrod and Belegost were found.

After the drowning of Beleriand at the start of the Second Age, the lands to the east became the north-west of Middle-earth, divided into four large regions by mighty mountain ranges. The longest of these, the Misty Mountains, separated the western region of Eriador from the eastern region of Rhovanion. To the north of the Misty Mountains lay a large desert area. To the extreme west of Eriador, Lindon, the last remnant of Ossiriand, extended between the coast and the Blue Mountains. Three major rivers flowed through Eriador. To the west, the Lhûn flowed along the north of the Blue Mountains before emptying into the Gulf of Lhûn, which penetrated inland, cutting the mountain range in half. Situated here was the port of Grey Havens, from which the Elves could still leave Middle-earth and set sail for Valinor and from where, around the year 1000 of the Third Age, the Wizards embarked. In the centre of Eriador, the Brandywine river rose in the Hills of Evendim, then flowed south-east through the fertile lands where, in the middle of the Third Age, the Hobbits establish the Shire. The Brandywine continued south and turned west again before flowing into the sea. In the north-east, the waters of the River Bruinen rose in the Misty Mountains and, a little further to the south, not far from Rivendell, passed by the Elven refuge where

Elrond Half-elven lived, then descended south-west to be swelled by the Hoarwell to form the mighty Greyflood river.

In the Third Age, the north of Eriador was dominated for many years by the kingdom of Arnor, before its fall in 1974 T.A. To the south, a strip of land known as the Gap of Rohan separated the end of the Misty Mountains, which stretch across the region of Gondor from east to west. In the south-east, opposite Gondor, the threatening peaks of the Shadow Mountains acted as a natural barrier to the south and west of Mordor, and then extended north, where they joined the Ash Mountains, which eventually encircled those desolate plains, only the eastern part of which remained open. To the east, beyond the Misty Mountains, flowed the mighty River Anduin, which descended southwards, dividing the Gondor mountains from the foothills of Mordor, before turning west and flowing into the sea at the Bay of Belfalas. To the east of the Anduin extended Mirkwood, the north-west of which is occupied by the Silvan Elves led by Thranduil, with Dol Guldur spreading terror from the south-east. Near Dol Guldur, between the Misty Mountains and the Anduin, was the Elven kingdom of Lórien, ruled by Galadriel. The final south section of the Misty Mountains, before the Gap of Rohan, was bounded by the Fangorn Forest, inhabited by the Ents. Lastly, to the north-east of Mirkwood lay Erebor, a great Dwarven kingdom of the Third Age which would be plundered and occupied by the dragon Smaug in 2770 T.A. This became the destination of the Quest of Erebor, on the eastward journey of the Hobbit Bilbo Baggins.

For its creator, Tolkien, Middle-earth was just another name for our world in an imaginary, distant time. The term is an updated form of the Middle English 'Middel-erde' or 'Middel-erthe', itself derived from the Old English 'Middangeard', and related to the Norse 'Miðgarðr', which refers to the common land inhabited by men, between the Valhalla of the gods and the world of giants. This origin suggests a conception of the world deeply influenced by a Nordic and Anglo-Saxon imagination. Tolkien felt intensely that he belonged to this tradition and wished, through his Elven legends, to create a mythology imbued with something of this specific ambience. Thus, the west remains the direction of the Shoreless Sea and of mythical ancestors, and the east that of infinite lands from which most enemies come. However, Middle-earth in the Third Age is larger than north-western Europe. According to one of Tolkien's letters, Rivendell and Hobbiton in the Shire are on the latitude of Oxford, which puts Minas Tirith nearly 1000 kilometres (620 miles) further south, at approximately the latitude of Florence, and the Mouth of the Anduin at that of the ancient city of Troy. Nevertheless, the shape of the world has changed, making it impossible create a perfect match between Tolkien's maps and those of the modern world. Also, while the Shire has the feel of the traditional English countryside, and the people of Rohan have a number of things in common with Anglo-Saxons, the kingdom of Gondor, especially after its restoration at the beginning of the Fourth Age, is more reminiscent of the Byzantine Empire. Be that as it may, Tolkien's fantasy geography, strongly unified by the Elven names that run through it, gives the legends of Middle-earth the unique grounding and atmosphere that make them so appealing.

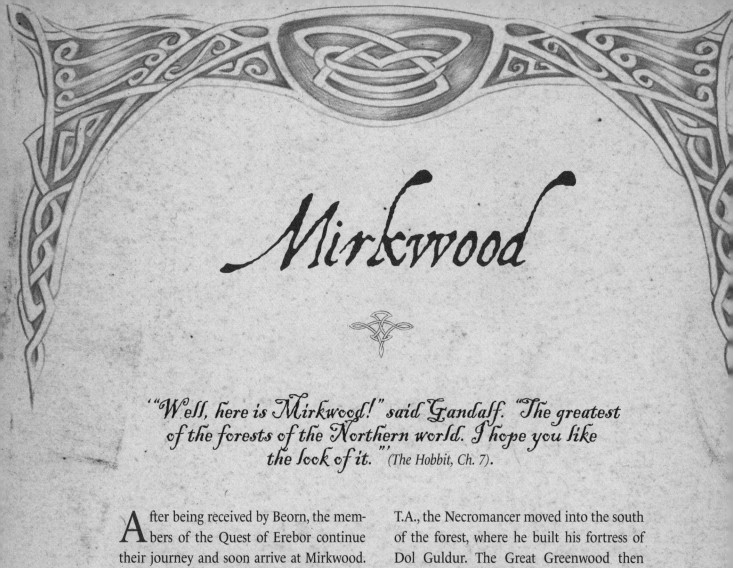

Mirkvvood

'"Well, here is Mirkwood!" said Gandalf. "The greatest of the forests of the Northern world. I hope you like the look of it. "' (The Hobbit, Ch. 7).

After being received by Beorn, the members of the Quest of Erebor continue their journey and soon arrive at Mirkwood. Gandalf points to this vast, dark and disturbing forest through which they have to pass, then takes his leave of them, advising them strongly not to leave the winding path between the trees. This forested area, which occupies much of Wilderland, to the east of the Misty Mountains and the Anduin river, has not always appeared so sinister. Originally the immense forest was known as the Great Greenwood and fauna and flora flourished there for many years, as did the Elven realm of King Thranduil, which lay in the northern part of the forest. But in 1050

T.A., the Necromancer moved into the south of the forest, where he built his fortress of Dol Guldur. The Great Greenwood then became a gloomy forest, plagued by darkness and invaded by evil creatures, so that it eventually became known as Mirkwood.

At the time of the Quest of Erebor, Mirkwood was dominated by gloominess by day, the darkness becoming almost total below its branches once night had fallen. It was a place populated by black squirrels, enormous bats and various dark-coloured butterflies. After several days of walking, the path followed by the members of the Quest led them to cross an enchanted river, a tributary of the Forest River, and thus to enter, without realizing,

the silvan kingdom of Thranduil. This Elven domain, less overcome by darkness than the rest of the forest, was populated by deer. One of them, a black deer, bowls into the members of the Quest just after they have crossed the river, while other white deer – a doe and her fawns – are able to show themselves without being struck by the Dwarves' arrows. This part of the forest is an area where the Elves like to hunt and feast, although Thorin and Company and Bilbo can only hear the sounds of horns and hunting dogs, not see them, and the lights of the Elven banquets fade from view as soon as they come too near: Mirkwood, even in its Elven part, is also inhabited by giant spiders. The Dwarves are captured by them, but are rescued by Bilbo thanks to the power of Sting and the One Ring. To the north-east of the forest are the Halls of the Elf King, in other words the palace of Thranduil, located in a vast cavern penetrating deep into a tree-covered mound beyond a bridge over the Forest River. It is there that the Dwarves are held captive by the Elves until Bilbo helps them escape in empty barrels down the Forest River, taking them out and away from Mirkwood.

Many years later, after the defeat of Sauron puts an end to the War of the Ring, the Silvan Elves of Thranduil and those of the Forest of Lothlórien manage to drive this evil from the Forest and destroy Dol Guldur. The great forest then recovers its former beauty and tranquillity and becomes known in Sindarin as Eryn Lasgalen, the 'Wood of Green Leaves', by the common will of King Thranduil and Galadriel's husband Celeborn, who then reigns over the southern half of the forest.

In English, Tolkien calls this forest Mirkwood, a name which, by his own admission, is not of his own invention. Associated with ancient Germanic legends, the term is derived from the Old German word 'mirkiwidu' and the Norse 'myrkviðr,' meaning literally 'dark forest'. In the 20th century, the anglicized name Mirkwood, used to describe a large forest with gloomy connotations, was used by William Morris in one of his novels: *A Tale of the House of the Wolfings and All the Kindreds of the Mark*, published in 1889, was a direct influence on Tolkien in various aspects of the creation of his world of Middle-earth. As well as in Middle-earth, in the 1930s Tolkien also gave forests in other works the same name – in his medieval-inspired poems published posthumously in two books: *The Legend of Sigurd and Gudrún* and *The Fall of Arthur*.

Tolkien's decision to have deer appear in the forest – especially white deer – seems to have been inspired by Celtic mythology, where the sight of a deer is often associated with the passage into another world, the 'land of fairies'. Deer appear notably in the tale 'Pwyll, Prince of Dyved,' the first of *The Four Branches of the Mabinogi*,

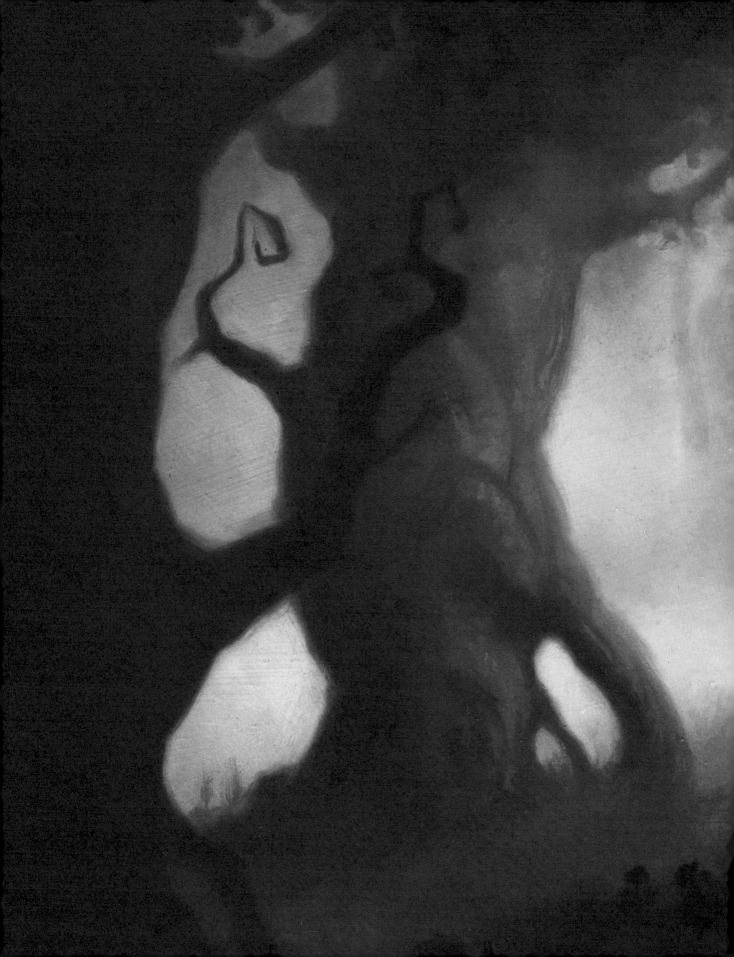

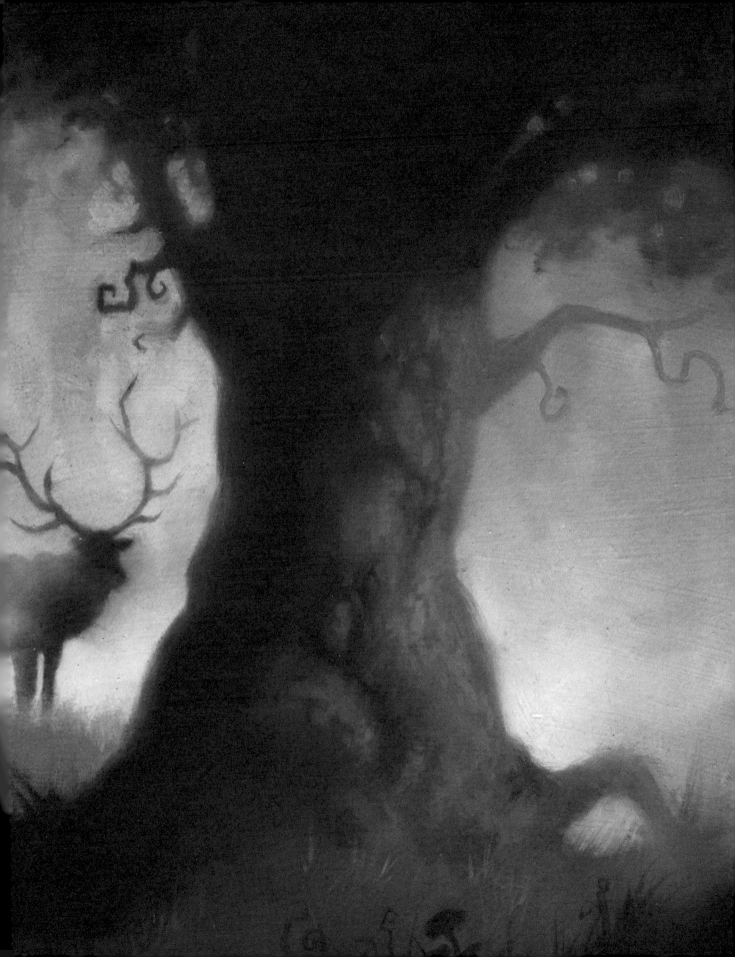

a collection of medieval Welsh tales: while out hunting deer with his dogs, Prince Pwyll meets Arawn, King of Annwn, 'The Other World'. The evocation of white deer is found in certain novels by Chrétien de Troyes: *Erec and Enide*, which refers to a white deer hunt, and *Perceval, the Story of the Grail*, in which the knight Gawain fruitlessly pursues a white doe. On the subject of hunting in a fantasy context, it seems that Tolkien was inspired by *Sir Orfeo*, a medieval English poem about a fairy king hunting in the woods with his retinue and dogs.

Finally, the difficulties the Dwarves and the Hobbit experience finding their way through and navigating the forest are reminiscent of the adventures of the characters Joe, Sylvia and Gorbo among the Twisted Trees in Edward A. Wyke-Smith's *The Marvellous Land of Snergs* (1927), a children's book much enjoyed and admired by Tolkien and his children.

Misty Mountains

'"That is only the beginning of the Misty Mountains, and we have to get through, or over, or under those somehow, before we can come into Wilderland beyond."' (The Hobbit, Ch. 3).

The Misty Mountains are a mountain range erected by Melkor in the First Age to obstruct the wandering of the Vala Oromë in Middle-earth. Named Hithaeglir or 'Misty Needles' in Sindarin, they extend along a north-south axis, bounded to the north by the Forodwaith, a great icy desert, and to the south by the Gap of Rohan and the valley of Nan Curunír, where Saruman lives in the Third Age. Thus, they separate Eriador, to the west, from Wilderland and Mirkwood in the east. The Misty Mountains are dominated by five major peaks: Mount Gundabad, in the north; the three peaks of Caradhras, which rises to an elevation of 17,500 feet (about 5,250 metres), Fanuidhol and Celebdil above the mines of Moria; and Methedras, which is the southernmost peak. The River Anduin, the largest river of Middle Earth, flows along the east flank of the Misty Mountains; Rivendell is the last refuge to the west of the mountains. Further south, to the west of the three peaks of Caradhras, Celebdil and Fanuidhol, the Dwarves of the First Age established their first underground city, known as Khazad-dûm in Khuzdul, and Moria by the Elves. To the west of this, in the Second Age, the Elves built the great city of Ost-in-Edhil and the realm of Eregion, which saw the creation of the Rings of Power by the Noldor brotherhood of silversmiths, led by the Elf

Celebrimbor. But the Elves were deceived by Sauron, who created the One Ring and unleashed a war against Ost-in-Edhil. The Orcs invaded the Misty Mountains and especially the cities of Khazad-dûm and Mount Gundabad. To the east of Khazad-dûm lies the Forest of Lórien, where Celeborn and Galadriel settle in the Third Age to rule their domain. Khazad-dûm is the scene of both glorious and very dark events for the Dwarves. The most disastrous was, without doubt, the Battle of Azanulbizar against the Orcs, which took place in the valley of that name to the east of Moria. The battle saw the death of Azog, leader of the Orcs of the Misty Mountains, and this was the trigger for the War of the Dwarves and the Orcs. The Dwarf Thorin, son of Thráin II, who later leads the Quest of Erebor, acquired the nickname Oakenshield following this battle, in which he distinguished himself.

It is possible to cross the Misty Mountains in several places. Externally, they can be traversed via the High Pass, east of Rivendell, the Mount Caradhras Pass and the Gap of Rohan, which permits travellers to skirt the Misty Mountains via the south. The underground accesses were via Goblin-town, the capital of the Orcs, and Moria.

The Misty Mountains are not only a natural barrier, but also an obstacle for the Children of Ilúvatar. In the First Age, during the journey of the Elves to the West, the Misty Mountains were where the Nandor Elves, afraid at the sight of the mountains, separated from the Teleri group. In the Third Age, the three branches of the Hobbits (Harfoots, Stoors and Fallohides), who had originally settled between the River Anduin and the Misty Mountains, also crossed them at the time when the Great Greenwood Forest appeared to fall under an evil spell and became Mirkwood. Later in the Third Age, crossing the mountains proves dangerous for Thorin and Company because of the Stone Giants, and also for the Fellowship of the Ring, who are caught in a snowstorm on the slopes of Caradhras on their way to Mordor, and are forced to turn back. In fact, Thorin and Company are taken prisoner by Goblins, and it is in the depths of these caves that Bilbo encounters Gollum and gains possession of the One Ring. The Misty Mountains are also where the Eagles have their nests and they save Thorin and Company when they are attacked by Wargs. In the Battle of the Five Armies that ends the Quest of Erebor, the Goblins of the Misty Mountains, led by Bolg, son of Azog, fight, but are ultimately defeated and dispersed. Bilbo and Gandalf bypass Mirkwood via the north and cross the Mountains by the High Pass, this time safely, to reach the Shire. In 3019 T.A., the Fellowship of the Ring undergo a terrible ordeal during their underground crossing of the Misty Mountains via Moria – the loss of their guide Gandalf in a clash with the Balrog.

Although for most of the peoples of Middle-earth, the Misty Mountains are only an obstacle to overcome, they are of importance to the Dwarves, both symbolically and as a

place of settlement. Mount Gundabad, for example, is the birthplace of the eldest of the Seven Fathers of the Dwarves, Durin I, who gives his name to the Line of Durin. In the First Age, Durin I founds the greatest Dwarven city of Khazad-dûm below the peaks of Caradhras, Celebdil and Fanuidhol – a city that remains heavily populated until the Third Age, when the Dwarves awaken Durin's Bane, the Balrog. Legend has it that the seventh and last incarnation of Durin I, Durin VII, a descendant of Thorin III who becomes King under the Mountain after the War of the Ring, will reconquer the underground kingdom of Moria.

The Misty Mountains are directly inspired by the Swiss Alps which Tolkien visited during the summer of 1911 as part of a trip organized by a family that employed his brother Hilary. During this trip, Tolkien had a brush with death while climbing the Aletsch Glacier, the largest glacier in the Alps. In a letter, Tolkien states that his description of Celebdil is inspired by the shape of the Silberhorn. Moreover, the oblong shape of the Kheled-zâram Lake resembles a lake of glacial origin, and the Dimrill Stair leading to the Azanulbizar Valley may also indicate glacial origin.

Rivendell

'*Bilbo never forgot the way they slithered and slipped in the dusk down the steep zig-zag path into the secret valley of Rivendell. The air grew warmer as they got lower, and the smell of the pine-trees made him drowsy...*' (The Hobbit, Ch. 3).

Imladris is the Elvish name of the home of Elrond Half-elven, the greatest Master of Knowledge of the Third Age. It is known as Karningul in Westron, the Common Tongue, and Rivendell in English. It nestles at the bottom of a steep valley through which flows a river, crossed by a single bridge, so narrow that ponies must cross it in single file. Beyond the bridge, a zigzag path climbs the slope, passing through forests of broad-leaved trees, oaks and beeches, then a pine forest, before suddenly opening on to the vast barren plateau that stretches east of the Bruinen river and climbs slowly towards the Misty Mountains. From there, a path marked occasionally by white stones runs through deep crevices and treacherous bogs to the Ford of Bruinen, at the edge of The Wild.

Rivendell was founded in 1697 S.A., more than 4700 years before the War of the Ring. At this time, war was raging between the Elves and Sauron, who wanted to take possession of the Rings of Power forged by Celebrimbor. King Gil-galad sent Elrond and an army to reinforce Eregion's troops. But even their combined forces were not enough to contain Sauron's hordes and Elrond was forced to retreat north. He chose the Rivendell Valley as the place to take refuge. He was besieged there for three years before Sauron's forces were annihilated by the armies from Númenor. The first White Council was held shortly afterwards in Rivendell, in the presence of Galadriel and Celeborn. Rivendell became the stronghold of the High Elves in Eriador. During the

War of the Last Alliance, the troops of Gil-galad and Elendil gathered there, forming the largest army ever seen in Middle-earth since the fall of Morgoth, the first Dark Lord. Isildur, son of Elendil, chose to leave his wife and his youngest child, Valandil, there and after the death of his father – ambushed by Goblins when returning from the war – Valandil is raised in Rivendell.

In the Third Age, Rivendell becomes a refuge for the oppressed and a centre of knowledge in the service of the Free Peoples, earning it the name the Last Homely House. Galadriel and Celeborn come to live there for many years. In 1409, Rivendell was again besieged during the wars between the Dúnedain of Arthedain and Angmar, the malevolent realm of the Witch-king. Elrond supported the Dúnedain but could not prevent the ruin of Arthedain in 1974. The following year, he sent a force under the command of Glorfindel to take part in the Battle of Fornost, at which the Witch-king's army was annihilated. After the ruin of Arthedain, the treasures of the Northern Dúnedain were kept in Rivendell. These included the ring of Barahir, the sword of Elendil, the sceptre and the royal diadem. Isildur's heirs were also raised there because of their distant kinship with Elrond. This is true of Aragorn, who lived in Rivendell until the age of twenty and met Elrond's daughter, Arwen Undómiel there, and fell in love with her.

In 2850, the Wizard Gandalf enters the fortress of Dol Guldur and discovers that the Necromancer who lives there is none other than Sauron. He comes to fear that Sauron may be gathering his forces to attack the Elves of Lórien and Rivendell. To get rid of Smaug, he devises the Quest of Erebor and takes Thorin and Company to Rivendell, where Elrond manages to decipher Thrór's map. After his return to the Shire, Bilbo Baggins retains such nostalgia for Rivendell that he decides to return there after holding a farewell party to celebrate his 111th birthday. Seventeen years later, after being pursued by the Nazgûl who are trying to seize the One Ring, Frodo finds his adoptive father there, spending his days composing poetry and completing the Red Book.

On 25 October 3018, the Council of Elrond takes place, attended by representatives of all the Free Peoples, and at which the destruction of the Ring is decided. The Nine Walkers leave Rivendell two months later. After Sauron's defeat, the Hobbits and Gandalf stop again at Rivendell. Two years later, Elrond, Galadriel and Gandalf decide to leave for Valinor. Bilbo and Frodo are invited to join them. Celeborn soon tires of Lórien and settles in Rivendell, where Elrond's sons still live. Merry Brandybuck, Frodo's former companion, visits them there more than once.

Rivendell is a place where the memory of the Ancient Days lives on, a place that has the virtue of restoring health and vigour to all, of removing anxiety from those who live there and instilling them with hope. In the heart of Rivendell is the Hall of Fire, a large room supported by carved pillars, and without windows, where a fire blazes all year long. It is here that legends are told, and songs sung on days of celebration.

Tolkien provides little parallel for Rivendell but, in one of his letters, indicates that it is approximately at the latitude of Oxford, underlining the kinship between these two centres of knowledge.

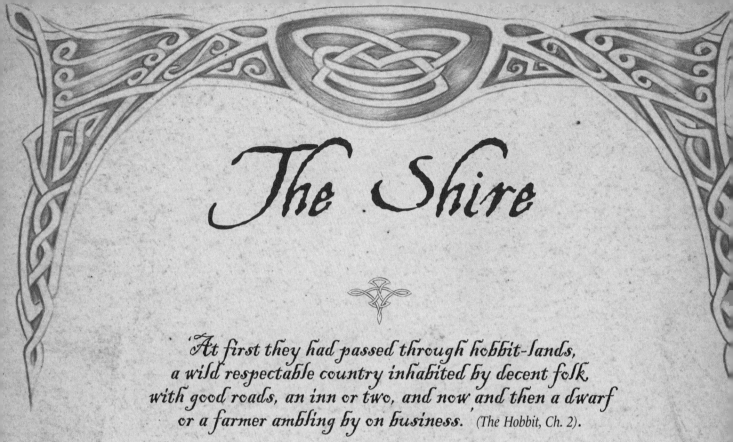

The Shire

*'At first they had passed through hobbit-lands,
a wild respectable country inhabited by decent folk,
with good roads, an inn or two, and now and then a dwarf
or a farmer ambling by on business.'* (The Hobbit, Ch. 2).

The Shire lies in the west of Middle-earth, in Eriador. It is a verdant place, allowing its inhabitants to live peacefully by cultivating their land in total tranquillity, sheltered from the world of Men. The region is divided into four Farthings, each corresponding to one of the cardinal points. The Three-farthing Stone marks the centre of the Shire and the border of the East, South and West Farthings. The Shire is crossed from east to west by the Great East Road, which connects the Grey Havens with the Wild. It is the route into the Shire for travellers and merchants and the trade route for the Dwarves from the Blue Mountains. Each of the Farthings has its own characteristics. The North Farthing is the wildest and coldest and often sees snow. It is also in this Farthing that, in 2747 of the Third Age, the Battle of Greenfields takes place. By contrast, the South Farthing, where the climate is milder, lends itself particularly well to the cultivation of pipe-weed. Its main town, Longbottom, is, in fact, known for the quality of its pipe-weed, known as Longbottom Weed, which is greatly appreciated by the Wizards Gandalf and Saruman. The West Farthing is best known for being home to Hobbiton and Bag End, where the Baggins family live. There are also several important towns there, such as Bywater, with its famous inn, The Green Dragon, and Michel Delving where the Town Hole and the Mathom-house – the Hobbit museum – are located. The East Farthing has marshland and forests, but also quarries and

farmland. This diversity makes it one of the Shire's most populous Farthings.

The Shire is a relatively young land of Middle-earth, as it was founded in 1601 T.A., which marks the start of its own calendar, the Shire Reckoning. It was on this date that the Hobbits Marcho and Blanco, originally from the village of Bree, crossed the Brandywine river and King Argeleb II of Arthedain offered them part of the land of his kingdom between the river and the Far Downs and between the Hills of Evendim and the Southern Marshes. After the destruction of the kingdom of Arthedain, the Hobbits found themselves without a ruler. It was at this time, in 1974 T.A., that the office of Thain of the Shire appeared, giving the Hobbit who holds the title the authority of a king. The Thain is Master of the Shire-Moot and Captain of Hobbitry-in-Arms. Another important office is that of Mayor of Michel Delving, who is elected every seven years and presides over banquets. He is also Postmaster and First Shirriff, in other words head of the service that acts as a police force. However, among Hobbits, the role is more that of a game warden and it is the office of Postmaster that occupies most of the mayor's time. Gradually, the office of Mayor of Michel Delving takes on greater importance and that of Thain simply becomes an honorary title, until the return of King Aragorn, who at the beginning of the Fourth Age makes the Thain a counsellor to the kingdom of Arnor.

The story of the Brandybuck and Took families is of particular interest. These two families are important land-owning clans and are therefore able to look after their own affairs. Part of the Took family, the Northern Tooks, who are descended from Bandobras Took, live in Long Cleeve. The other part of the family settled in one of the oldest and most important villages in the Shire, Tuckborough, residence of the Thain since 2340 T.A., the year in which the title of Thain passed to the Took family and was then handed down from father to son. The Brandybucks, however, are descended from Gorhendad Oldbuck, who was responsible for the growth of the Shire through the colonization of what is now called Buckland. Gorhendad founded Brandy Hall in 2340 T.A. and settled there with his family. The clan later took the name Brandybuck and its members prospered there, gaining land from the Old Forest as far as the High Hay, the hedge created to protect them from the dangers of those malevolent trees.

The Shire, the land of peaceful Hobbits, saw only two battles in its history. The Battle of Greenfields in 2747 T.A., between the Hobbits and a troop of Goblins, in which the attackers were driven back by the charge of Bandobras Took, known as the Bullroarer, a Hobbit of extraordinary size and impetuosity. The blow he struck to the head of the Goblin chieftain Golfimbul is said to have been so powerful that it flew off and landed some distance away in a rabbit hole – and that this was both how the battle was won and how the game of golf invented. The second and last battle is that of Bywater in 3019 T.A., led by the Hobbits Sam Gamgee, Pippin Took and Merry Brandybuck on their return from the War of the Ring. This battle pits them against the henchmen of Saruman who have enslaved the Hobbits and laid waste to the countryside of the Shire through industrialization. Houses were destroyed, rivers polluted, the Party Tree and many other trees were felled, Hobbiton Mill was replaced by a larger, many-wheeled building, even though there was nothing to grind, and a brick chimneystack belched black smoke from the heights of Bag End. Once Saruman is destroyed, the Hobbits set to work and begin repairing the huge damage done, notably replanting the land with trees. The following spring, a particular tree, the Mallorn – a gift to Sam from the Elf Galadriel, and the only specimen west of the Misty Mountains – adorns the Party Field where Bilbo Baggins' birthday party had once taken place. In 31Fth.A., King Aragorn gifts the Westmarch to the Hobbits. Elanor, Frodo Baggins' partner Sam Gamgee's eldest daughter, settles there and this region becomes home to the Fairbairn of the Towers family, descendants of Elanor Gamgee.

The name 'the Shire' comes from the Old English term *scir*, a word of Germanic origin meaning 'area'. The name also evokes the names of English counties which often include 'shire', as in Oxfordshire and Yorkshire. The term also refers to the initial

situation of the Shire, which was a dependent area of the kingdom of Arthedain, and underlines its rural nature, recalling the English countryside that Tolkien wished to evoke through the land of the Hobbits. Indeed, in his letters Tolkien relates that the Shire was inspired by and is a deep reflection of late 19th-century rural England – and notably the village of Sarehole near which he grew up. For this reason he was keen that the names he had chosen should be changed as little as possible in translation and, if possible, not at all. Tolkien often objected to the translations of names which, for example, Germanicized those he had so carefully chosen. For Tolkien, such translations were a betrayal as they were the reverse of what he wished to express.

Wilderland

'That is only the beginning of the Misty Mountains, and we have to get through, or over, or under those somehow, before we can come into Wilderland beyond.' (The Hobbit, Ch. 3).

Wilderland or Rhovanion in the Elvish tongue (not to be confused with the Wild, a less defined region that seems to encompass all the lands east of the Ford of Bruinen), is the name of the vast plain that extends between the Misty Mountains and the Running River. Bordered on the north by the Grey Mountains, it stretches south as far as Emyn Muil and the Ash Mountains, to the northern border of Mordor. It is crossed from north to south by the Anduin river, which flows first along the Misty Mountains, skirts around the Plateau highlands, before carving a bed through the hills of Emyn Muil at the Sarn Gebir rapids and continuing southwards. West of Rhovanion, the foothills of the Misty Mountains are well watered by the tributaries of the Anduin. Not far from the Azanulbizar Valley, near the eastern

exit of the mines of Moria, is the wooded kingdom of Lórien, ruled by Celeborn and Galadriel at the time of the War of the Ring. Further south, the Field of Celebrant extends as far as the Fangorn Forest, home to the Ents. On the left bank of the Anduin stretch vast meadows which eventually give way to Mirkwood – the Forest of Great Fear. To the south of this are the Brown Lands, the former garden of the Entwives, which by the end of the Third Age is no more than an arid and desolate land, having been ravaged by war. Between the Brown Lands and the Sea of Rhûn, into which the Running River empties, there are vast meadowlands which gradually turn to desert as they approach the Ash Mountains.

At the beginning of the Third Age, the Dwarves of the Line of Durin, the Silvan

Elves and Men lived together on good terms in Wilderland, although the people of Thranduil in the north of the forest and of Amroth in Lórien suffered terrible losses in the War of the Last Alliance, which saw the fall of Sauron. After the ambush that cost the life of King Isildur and saw the disappearance of the One Ring near the Gladden Fields, the Goblins left the other Peoples in peace. Between 490 and 541 T.A., the Easterlings attacked Gondor for the first time via the southern plains of Rhovanion. They were finally driven back by King Turambar. The power of Gondor moved eastward and reached its peak around 1050, when the kingdom extended as far as the Sea of Rhûn and the southern edge of the Forest. At this time, a shadow began to fall over the Forest, soon renamed Mirkwood. With great foresight, Thranduil built his underground palace to serve as a fortress for his people in the event of war. He was not alone in fearing a conflict: some of the Hobbits who lived in the Anduin Valley migrated eastward to Eriador. Three centuries later, Sméagol's ancestors crossed back over the mountains to settle again in Wilderland.

In the first half of the 13th century, the Easterling attacks resumed, but they were routed by the regent Minalcar in 1248, who destroyed their camps and settlements east of the Sea of Rhûn. He fortified the western banks of the Anduin and forged an alliance with Vidugavia, a king whose territories extended between Mirkwood and the Running River. His son Valacar married Vidumavi, daughter of Vidugavia. This marriage was contested, and Edalcar, son of Valacar, was driven out by a rebellion when it was his turn to ascend the throne. He took refuge in Wilderland and rallied his troops before leading a successful attack in 1447. After his restoration, he encouraged many Northmen to settle in Gondor. In 1635–36, the Great Plague ravaged Gondor and Rhovanion, considerably weakening the two kingdoms. Two centuries later, the Wainriders, manipulated by Sauron's emissaries, began attacking Gondor. In 1856, King Narmacil II was killed and Gondor lost all its eastern territories north of Emyn Muil. The Northmen were enslaved or fled. Some settled in the Anduin Valley under the command of Marhwini, a descendant of Vidugavia. In Gondor, there were alternating victories and defeats until the general and future king Eärnil won a decisive battle over the Wainriders in 1944.

After the fall of the Witch King of Angmar, some Northmen moved away towards the sources of the Anduin and renamed themselves the Éothéod. Shortly after, the Balrog awoke in Moria and killed King Náin I. The Dwarves took flight and Thráin I founded a new kingdom under the Lonely Mountain. Many of Lórien's Elves also fled and King Amroth disappeared. Celeborn and Galadriel settled in Lórien and kept watch over its people. In 2063, Gandalf ventured to Dol Guldur and the Necromancer (Sauron) went into hiding in the east, only returning from there four centuries later, with increased

strength. Goblins began to colonize the Misty Mountains.

In 2510, Goblins and Easterlings invaded the north of Gondor and were only defeated by the valour of the Éothéod, under the command of Eorl. With the agreement of the Steward Cirion, the Éothéod settled in Calenardhon, which was renamed Rohan. During this time, the dragons increased in number in the Grey Mountains and drove away the Dwarves. In 2770, Smaug attacked the Lonely Mountain and Dale was destroyed. Twenty years later, the murder of Thrór sparked the War of the Dwarves and the Orcs, which ended in 2799 with a costly victory by the Dwarves at Azanulbizar.

In 2850, Gandalf discovers that the Necromancer is none other than Sauron. However, Saruman does not agree to attack Dol Guldur until 2941. Sauron flees once again. The same year, the Quest of Erebor ends in the death of Smaug and the Battle of the Five Armies, in which the Orcs are defeated. Dáin I Ironfoot becomes King under the Mountain and Bard becomes king of the rebuilt Dale. Beorn is the new leader of the many Woodmen of the Anduin Valley. However, Sauron settles again in Mordor in 2951 and sends three Nazgûl to reoccupy Dol Guldur. In June 3018, the War of the Ring breaks out: Sauron attacks Gondor. Wilderland is also badly affected by the war:

Lórien is attacked three times in June 3019, while Thranduil, too, has to repel an attack. Dale is invaded, forcing the survivors to take refuge in the besieged Lonely Mountain. The destruction of the Ring brings victory to the Free Peoples: Celeborn seizes Dol Guldur, which is razed by Galadriel. Sauron's northern army is put to flight by the besieged forces of Erebor. After the war, Thranduil's kingdom extends across the entire north of the Forest, which is renamed the Forest of Green Leaves. Celeborn takes the southern part, renamed East Lórien, while the central region of the Forest is given to the Beornings and the Woodmen. Some years after Galadriel's departure, Celeborn moves to Rivendell, and Lórien is almost deserted.

Tolkien's Wilderland, a little-known and dangerous place, prey to many invasions from the east, to some extent evokes Central Europe at the time of the barbarian invasions. The Northmen and the Rohirrim, who ally themselves with Gondor and eventually settle on its territory, correspond quite well to the federated Germanic peoples such as the Visigoths, to whom the Western Roman Empire allocated vast territories in Gaul. The Wainriders, hereditary enemies of the Northmen and Gondor, may have been inspired by the Huns who, for many years, fought the Goths before going on to attack the Roman Empire.

Notable events

The Ages of Middle-earth

"'You are a very fine person, Mr. Baggins, and I am very fond of you; but you are only quite a little fellow in a wide world after all!'" (The Hobbit, Ch. 19).

The history of Middle-earth forms part of the far larger picture of the creation of the world by Ilúvatar, the One, as announced by the music of the Ainur, the primordial beings that he created as company. The Ainur who entered into the world were known as the Valar, while the secondary beings in their entourage were called Maiar. Melkor, the most powerful of the Valar, rebelled by trying to corrupt and dominate Ilúvatar's creation. During the long ages that preceded the appearance of the Sun, the Valar founded Valinor, to the west of the world. There they created two Trees of Light that illuminated the Undying Lands. They then made the stars as a counterpoint to the darkness of Middle-earth, where the Children of Ilúvatar – the Elves (the Firstborn) and the Men (the Successors) – were destined to awaken. One of the Valar, Aulë, created the Dwarves, and Ilúvatar agreed to give them life, on condition that they did not awaken before the Firstborn.

The Ainur who entered the world were known as the Valar, while the secondary beings in their entourage were called Maiar.

It is difficult to calculate the duration of the First (and longest) Age. When the Elves awoke under the stars, to the east of Middle-earth, Melkor was the first to discover them. He was intent on persecuting them, but when the Valar became aware of the emergence of the Elves, they imprisoned Melkor. They subsequently invited the Elves to come and join them, and those that accepted this offer were called the Eldar. Others remained in Beleriand, to the north-west of Middle-earth, alongside their king, Thingol, who married Melian, a Maia from Middle-earth, and founded the kingdom of Doriath. When Melkor was freed, after feigning repentance, he became obsessed with revenge and secretly sought to corrupt the Elves. Fëanor, the primary creator of the Elves, then made the Silmarils: three magnificent jewels energized by the light of the Two Trees. Melkor reacted by destroying the Trees and seizing the Silmarils. Fëanor then made his seven sons swear to track down whoever was in possession of the Silmarils, and he also recruited a large number of the Noldor to pursue Melkor (whom he referred to as Morgoth, the Black Foe). In the course of this expedition, the Noldor rebelled against the Valar and committed the first ever fratricides by killing other Elves to gain possession of their ships. When Morgoth returned to Beleriand, he embarked on a war against the Elves, who fought back for five whole centuries without ever gaining a decisive victory. After the first sunrise (created by the Valar), the solar years of the First Age began to be counted and the Men awoke in the Far East of Middle-earth, where they fell under the domination of Morgoth. Some of them rebelled and headed westward, and those who eventually arrived in Beleriand joined forces with the Elves and became known as the Edáin. As the years passed, the Eldar who had settled in Beleriand built up several kingdoms, which prospered until 455 P.A., when Morgoth launched a major offensive. Shortly afterwards, an Edáin called Beren met Lúthien, Thingol and Melian's daughter, who was the most beautiful of all the Elves. They fell in love and together they set out on the highly dangerous mission to steal one of the Silmarils from Morgoth. However, the Elves and their allies were eventually crushed by Morgoth at the Battle of Unnumbered Tears. In 495, Tuor, Beren's cousin, discovered the hidden kingdom of Gondolin, where he married an Elf who was the daughter of Turgon, the king of Gondolin. They had a child, Eärendil. Following a dispute, Thingol was killed by the Dwarves, who subsequently sacked Doriath in 503. Dior, the son of Beren and Lúthien, inherited both the kingdom of Doriath and the Silmaril, but he was killed by the sons of Fëanor, who also razed Doriath. Dior's daughter, Elwing, sought sanctuary in the Havens of Sirion while guarding the Silmaril, and there she married Eärendil, who was similarly taking refuge after the fall of Gondolin in 510 F.A. Eärendil then went to sea to beg the Valar to help the Elves and the Men.

Ëarendil took advantage of the Silmaril given to him by Elwing to make his way to Valinor. The Valar defeated Morgoth, who was thrown out of the world, but Beleriand was submerged as a result of the violent conflict and the two other Silmarils disappeared. Thus ended the First Age. At the start of the Second Age, the Men of Númenor (an island between Valinor and Middle-earth given to the Edáin by the Valar) consolidated their power. In Middle-earth, Sauron convinced the Elves of Eregion to create the Rings of Power and secretly forged the One Ring, which was destined to dominate all the others. Sauron's deception was exposed, however, and he devastated Eregion, before being overcome by a Númenórean intervention. Over time, the Númenóreans became extremely arrogant and began to envy the immortality of the Elves. Their last king, Ar-Pharazôn, was determined to remove any obstacles to his power and thus captured Sauron – but Sauron won him over and persuaded him to embark on the conquest of Valinor. The Valar responded furiously and mercilessly: both the Númenóreans' fleet and their island itself were engulfed by water, and only a few Faithful, headed by Elendil, managed to escape. They settled in Middle-earth, as did Sauron, who returned to Mordor. In the War of the Last Alliance (3429–3441 S.A.), the Elves and the Men succeeded in overthrowing Sauron, and Isildur, the son of Elendil, took possession of the One Ring. These events marked the close of the Second Age.

Over the course of the Third Age, the kingdom of Arnor, originally founded by Elendil, grew weak and was eventually destroyed, but Isildur's lineage was secretly perpetuated in Rivendell, which was home to Elrond. Further south, the kingdom of Gondor flourished but then fell into decline when its royal line of descent was extinguished. Around the year 1000, it became apparent that Sauron had reappeared and the Valar mobilized the Wizards in response to this threat. The White Council brought together both the Wizards and the main Eldar to tackle the shadow that was hanging over Mirkwood (the Forest of Great Fear). Saruman managed to convince the Council members that the One Ring was lost for good but, unbeknownst to all of them, it had fallen into the hands of one of the Hobbits who was still living to the east of the Misty Mountains – Sméagol, who later became the creature called Gollum. In 2940–41 T.A., the Quest of Erebor freed the North from the danger posed by the dragon Smaug and the horde of invading Goblins. The White Council decided to drive Sauron out of Mirkwood, and he secretly took refuge in Mordor. The most decisive factor in this period, however, was the discovery of the One Ring by Bilbo Baggins, although it was not until 3001 that Gandalf began to suspect the true nature of Bilbo's ring. The terrible War of the Ring erupted from 3018 to 3019, during which the One Ring was destroyed by Bilbo's heir, Frodo Baggins. Sauron was finally defeated and Isildur's

heir, Aragorn, came to the throne and restored the kingdoms of Arnor and Gondor. Bilbo and Frodo went to Valinor in the company of Gandalf, Elrond and Galadriel – bringing the Third Age to a close.

At the start of the Fourth Age, the Reunited Kingdom of Aragorn thrived, while the Shire, which enjoyed the king's protection, was also prosperous. Frodo's old friends had become important figures in the Shire and were responsible for keeping alive the stories of the major events of Middle-earth. After Aragorn's death, Legolas, Thranduil's son, set off for the Undying Lands, accompanied by his friend Gimli, who was the son of Glóin – leaving no members of the Fellowship of the Ring in Middle-earth.

Very little is known about the Fourth Age and the ones that succeeded it. In the 1950s, Tolkien started to write a story that took place after Aragorn's death but he soon abandoned it. He realized that once the Men had taken over and visible incarnations of Evil (such as Morgoth, and later Sauron) had been removed, the narrative lost much of its power and had to fall back on banal suspense. As far as he was concerned, only the Elder Days could convey the enchantment of Faërie.

Tolkien's decision to tell the story of the War of the Ring obliged him to develop the first three Ages of Middle-earth more fully. The Third Age thus threw new light on the stories of the Silmarillion, set in a low period for the world that was imbued with nostalgia, even though the First Age belonged to an extremely remote past. The Men and, above all, the Hobbits of the Third Age had a connection with the Elder Days that reflects our own yearnings for an idealized past, although Tolkien's characters are sufficiently removed from our times to allow him to weave the enchantment of Faërie. As Tolkien often pointed out, his Legendarium did not unfurl in an imaginary place, since Middle-earth is our world in an imaginary era, long before our own history began. Tolkien would suggest that a period of at least 6000 years separates the start of the Fourth Age from the opening of our historical era. Accordingly, we would now be at the end of the Sixth Age or the start of the Seventh (bearing in mind that the succession of the Ages speeded up once human domination was established). Nevertheless, as Tolkien himself insisted, there is no perfect correlation between our scientific and historical knowledge of our planet and the Ages of Middle-earth, which will always remain shrouded in the mists of time, witnesses to a Faërie wondrously revealed by Tolkien's writing.

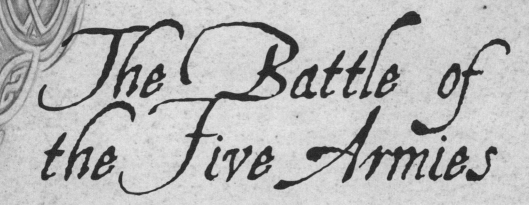

The Battle of the Five Armies

"So began a battle that none had expected; and it was called the Battle of Five Armies, and it was very terrible." (The Hobbit, Ch. 17).

The death of the Dragon Smaug transformed the lives of all the peoples living in the vicinity. The Dwarves of Thorin and Company found themselves masters of the Lonely Mountain and Thrór's treasure – this came as a great surprise, after a hiatus of three days before Roäc and the old thrush arrive with the news of Smaug's death. This unexpected fillip was tempered, however, by the announcement of an imminent influx of armed soldiers hunting for treasure.

The Elves of Thranduil left Mirkwood and headed towards the treasure, believing it to have been abandoned. They stopped en route to provide assistance to the inhabitants of Lake-town, which had endured Smaug's attack and was now in ruins. Winter was approaching and the Men comforted themselves with thoughts of the treasure and the benefits that it may bring them. As for Bard, the Dragon-slayer, he dreamed of reviving the kingdom of his ancestor, Girion, as many of the inhabitants of Esgaroth want to make him king of Dale. Once they had completed their preparations, the respective armies of the Elves and the Men set off, and the local population sought a safe haven.

Meanwhile, Thorin sent ravens with messages to the nearest Dwarf kingdoms, most notably to his cousin Dáin in the Iron Hills. He requested reinforcements in order to resist the new invaders on the treasure trail. Thorin also set about fortifying Erebor in preparation for a siege. Tension mounted

still further with the arrival of ambassadors from the Men from the Lake and the Elves of the Forest. Thorin demanded the departure of the Elves responsible for imprisoning him, while Bard and Thranduil refused to leave without taking a share of the treasure. Bilbo Baggins believed his adventures have come to an end with the death of the Dragon,

The Goblins and the Wargs had a numerical advantage and were able to encircle the Mountain. The Free Peoples repel their first attacks but the Goblins climb up the Mountain and oblige their opponents to fight on several different fronts.

but he felt obliged to fight against the gold fever that seemed to have infected the land. He devised a plan to resolve the situation and finally return home, with the help of Thráin's Arkenstone. One night, while supposedly on guard duty, Bilbo slipped into the camp of Bard and Thranduil, using the invisibility afforded by his ring. He wanted the negotiations to reach a swift conclusion, before the arrival of Dáin's army, and so he gave the Arkenstone to Bard. On the road leading to the Mountain, Gandalf congratulated and encouraged him, without giving him the chance to ask a single question. Bilbo was reunited with the Dwarves and wondered what the future held in store.

The following day, Bard, Thranduil and Gandalf had a meeting with Thorin and offered the Arkenstone as a bargaining chip. Thorin was furious with Bilbo and chased him away, even though he eventually gave into the besiegers' demands. Then came the news that Dáin and his army of Dwarves were on their way, making a battle between them and the Lake and Forest coalition seem inevitable. Furthermore, the Dragon's death had served the purposes of the Goblins and their allies, the Wargs. Their desire to avenge the death of the Great Goblin and conquer new territories had led them to secretly recruit a large army, which was heading towards Erebor under a cloud of bats that darkened the sky. Gandalf, acting as a mediator between the Dwarves, the Men and the Elves, convened a meeting to discuss the imminent threat posed by their common enemy, the Goblins. This impromptu alliance gave rise to the Battle of the Five Armies, which pitted the Elves, the Dwarves and the Men against the Wargs and the Goblins.

The Goblins and the Wargs had a numerical advantage and were able to encircle the Mountain. The Free Peoples repelled their first attacks, but the Goblins climbed up the Mountain and obliged their opponents to fight on several different fronts. Thorin mounted an attack in an attempt to kill the Goblins' military leader, Bolg (Azog's son), but he found himself cornered by a hail of spears. Thorin's nephews, Fili and Kili, fought to the death to prevent the Goblins from capturing him. At that critical moment when all seemed lost, Bilbo – removed from the battle

but still equipped with his ring – announced the arrival of the Eagles with unfettered exuberance. The birds immediately dislodged the Goblins fighting on the slopes of the Mountain, enabling the Elves and the Men to concentrate their forces in the valley – where a gigantic bear appeared, crushing wolves and Goblins underfoot and disrupting their battle lines. This was none other than Beorn, who welcomed Thorin and Company after their escape from the Misty Mountains. He rescued Thorin from the battlefield and then returned in a fearsome rage to crush Bolg, thereby causing the Goblins to scatter in total disarray. The victory was overwhelming: it was estimated that the Goblins had lost three quarters of their troops in the North. After the departure of the Necromancer from Dol Guldur and the death of Smaug, this military triumph brought peace back to the region. Thorin died after saying goodbye to Bilbo, and his closest relative, Dáin II Ironfoot, replaced him as King under the Mountain. Bard was the new king of Dale and Lake-town was rebuilt. Beorn became chief of the Men living between Mirkwood and the Misty Mountains. The Elves, the Dwarves and the Men were now united in mutual understanding.

As Gandalf pointed out to Gimli and Frodo during their stay in Minas Tirith, after the War of the Ring, things would have turned out very differently after Sauron attacked the North if there had been no resistance from Erebor, Dale and Thranduil, if the Goblins had remained numerous and powerful, and, above all, if the Dwarves, the Elves and the Men had set about killing each other on that day. The Battle of the Five Armies, the most significant military encounter to take place between the War of the Dwarves and Orcs and the War of the Ring, was the first battle to involve a Hobbit for several generations, and also the only one in that Age to bring together so many different factions. The arrival of the Eagles at such a desperate moment is an example of 'eucatastrophe', and the course of the battle itself demonstrates the effects of good fortune. If the armies of the Dwarves, the Men and the Elves had not already been on a war footing, the Goblins and the Wargs would have taken advantage of their numerical superiority and the element of surprise, or they would merely have had to kill any survivors of the Free Peoples if they had arrived after the latter's fight over the treasure.

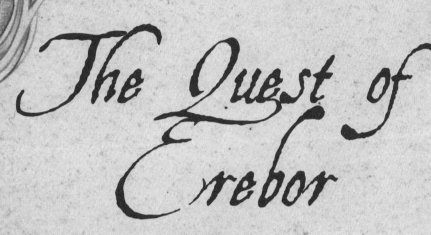

The Quest of Erebor

'Well, that is how the Quest of Erebor began; and from that day on the Dwarves and the Hobbits have been wonderfully entangled together on all the chief events of our time.'

(*The Annotated Hobbit*, Appendix A, p. 375).

The Quest of Erebor was an expedition undertaken in 2941 T.A. by Thorin and Company to recapture the treasure of the Lonely Mountain from the Dragon Smaug and wreak vengeance on him.

In March 2941, 100 years after his father's first, unsuccessful attempt to mount an expedition to Erebor, Thorin Oakenshield was planning to organize one of his own. While travelling along the Great East Road, not far from Bree, he met Gandalf the Grey. Thorin hoped to benefit from Gandalf's wisdom and so he told the Wizard about his plan and asked for help and advice, particularly with respect to killing Smaug. Gandalf himself was also extremely anxious to see

the last of the monster. To the East, Sauron had regained power, much to the concern of the Free Peoples, most particularly the Elves Galadriel and Elrond, who were in charge of Lórien and Rivendell. Gandalf feared that Smaug could join forces with Sauron and provide him with a path to the North, leading to an invasion of Eriador and an attack on Rivendell, the last bastion of the High Elves. Gandalf was willing to use his brainpower to help bring the project to fruition and he started to draw up a plan of action for Thorin. Whereas Thorin envisaged a full-scale assault on Erebor by the Dwarf armies, Gandalf advocated a secret expedition based on stealth and wile. The Wizard knew that

the Dwarves could not approach the Dragon without being discovered, as Dragons recognized the smell of Dwarves and had a perfect memory. Gandalf therefore recommended adding a Hobbit to the group. Gandalf knew the Shire and its inhabitants

The Quest of Erebor was an expedition undertaken in 2941 T.A. by Thorin and Company to recapture the treasure of the Lonely Mountain from the Dragon Smaug and wreak vengeance on him.

well, and he immediately thought of the Hobbit Bilbo Baggins. Given the Dwarves' antipathy towards Hobbits, Gandalf had to draw on all his powers of ingenuity, so to gain the Company's approval he described Bilbo as an expert burglar. On 26 April, he led the Company to Bag End and introduced them to Bilbo Baggins. Unfortunately, the Hobbit became flustered by the unexpected appearance of thirteen Dwarves and a Wizard in his home. Thorin lost his temper and was on the point of leaving the Shire and giving up on the Quest of Erebor, but Gandalf pulled out his trump card: an old map and a key, which the dying Thráin II had entrusted to him ninety-one years previously in the dungeons of Dol Guldur. Thrór's map revealed a secret entrance on the side of the Lonely Mountain that was decisive in convincing Thorin of

the wisdom of a secret expedition in the company of a master burglar.

Shortly after the group's departure, when they were unsuccessfully trying to take shelter from the rain and Gandalf was nowhere to be seen, the glow of a fire on a nearby hill attracted their attention. Bilbo was sent to reconnoitre. He approached the fire surreptitiously and discovered three trolls, Bert, Tom and William, roasting mutton. Instead of retracing his steps and warning the Dwarves of the danger, Bilbo decided to steal a bag from one of the trolls. Unfortunately, Bilbo's dexterity counted for little against the magic powers of the troll bag, which was endowed with the gift of speech and promptly warned its owner of the attempted theft. Bilbo was caught by William, causing the trolls to argue about the best way to cook a Hobbit; they eventually came to blows over this conundrum, giving Bilbo a chance to escape. The rumpus also alerted the Dwarves, who rushed to assist Bilbo, but the trolls caught them in sacks as soon as they appeared on the scene. Soon, the entire Company was trapped, apart from Thorin. He used a flaming branch to strike two of the trolls, before being captured in his turn by William. The trolls started to squabble again, this time over the best ways to cook Dwarves. Gandalf returned at this juncture. He confused the trolls by imitating their voices, causing them to forget about the approaching dawn, and they ended up petrified as a result.

The group then continued their journey, before resting in the house of the

Half-Elf Elrond on the foothills of the Misty Mountains. Elrond examined Thrór's map and identified the moon-runes that described how to open the secret entrance into the Lonely Mountain. The travellers set off again on Midsummer's Day, intent on crossing the Misty Mountains, but they were surprised by a violent thunderstorm. Then, a fight between Stone Giants forced them to take refuge in a cave. While they were sleeping, however, the back of the cave opened to make way for Goblins, who took them prisoner – except for Gandalf, who managed to evade capture after being alerted by shouts from Bilbo. The group were taken to the Great Goblin, who was about to kill them when Gandalf reappeared. He killed the Great Goblin and led his friends to safety along a series of dark tunnels. Bilbo lost his way and, while groping in the pitch blackness, his hand fell on the One Ring. Moving forward by guesswork, he came to a flooded cave, where he encountered Gollum, who challenged Bilbo to a riddle-game. Bilbo won the game, but when Gollum realized that his opponent had the ring that belonged to him, the Hobbit was forced to flee. Bilbo slid the ring on to his finger and discovered that it rendered him invisible. This power enabled him to follow Gollum to the eastern exit of the Misty Mountains, where he was reunited with the Dwarves. Unfortunately, however, the reassembled company were cornered by the Goblins and the Wargs, and when they were obliged to take refuge in the trees, the Goblins promptly set fire to them. They were

only saved at the last moment by the Lord of the Eagles and his followers, who had received assistance from Gandalf on a previous occasion. The Company spent the night in the Eagles' eyries before being deposited on the Carrock. From there, they headed towards the home of Beorn the skin-changer.

They stayed for a few days with Beorn, who provided them with food and ponies for the next stage of their journey. When they arrived at the edge of Mirkwood, Gandalf bid the rest of the group farewell as he had been summoned to the South to participate in the attack on Dol Guldur. The crossing of the Forest proved particularly arduous and the Company ran out of supplies. Despite their exhaustion, they managed to reach the border of the realm of Thranduil, the Elf King, but the Dwarves were taken prisoner by Spiders. Their captivity proved short-lived, however, as Bilbo made use of his ring and his sword, Sting, to release them. Nevertheless, the Dwarves were almost immediately captured again, this time by Thranduil's Silvan Elves. They were led before the Elf King and then thrown into dungeons. Bilbo, who had remained unnoticed thanks to his ring, hatched a plan to rescue them – one night, he took advantage of the fact that their jailer was getting drunk with the king's steward to steal his keys and free the thirteen Dwarves. He led them to a cellar, where each Dwarf hid in an empty barrel and was then swept along by the Forest River to the Long Lake. When they reach Lake-town, they were welcomed by the Lake-men, who accompanied

them to the North of the Long Lake. After walking for a few days, Thorin and Company finally reached Erebor. They found the secret door and Bilbo demonstrated his powers of ingenuity by opening it. Bilbo entered the heart of the Mountain, where he found Smaug asleep, and he stole a golden cup; then he came back again, and, under the cloak of invisibility, struck up a conversation with Smaug. The Quest of Erebor came to a fitting conclusion with the death of Smaug, who was struck down by Bard the Bowman above the Long Lake. Thorin was unable to enjoy the recovery of his kingdom, however, as he was killed by the Goblins in the Battle of the Five Armies, but Bilbo and his companions were generously rewarded by his heir, Dáin II Ironfoot, who ruled Erebor with great wisdom for many years.

The Sack of Doriath

'In ancient days they [the elves] had had wars with some of the dwarves, whom they accused of stealing their treasure. It is only fair to say that the dwarves gave a different account, and said that they only took what was their due, for the elf-king had bargained with them to shape his raw gold and silver, and had afterwards refused to give them their pay.' (The Hobbit, Ch. 8).

When the Dwarves of Thorin and Company pass through Mirkwood during the Quest of Erebor, they meet with a degree of hostility from the Silvan Elves who live there. It would be wrong to conclude, however, that such animosity was the key note in all the relationships between the Elves and the Dwarves. The Company were warmly received, for example, in Elrond's house in Rivendell. In that case, what was the source of the Silvan Elves' ill feelings? We have to look deep into the past to find the answer, for these tensions can be traced back several millennia from the time of Bilbo Baggins's adventures in 2941 T.A. to the sack of the kingdom of Doriath in 503 F.A.

Doriath was a kingdom of Sindar Elves situated in the forests of Neldoreth, in the Beleriand region. It was crossed by various rivers (particularly the Esgalduin), which all flowed into the River Sirion. Its capital was an underground palace called Menegroth, or the Thousand Caves, and it was ruled by King Thingol, who was married to Melian, a Maia. She protected the kingdom through a magic frontier that could not be breached without the king's authorization. This protection enabled the kingdom of Doriath to prosper and keep its distance from the numerous wars of the First Age. In 501 F.A., Húrin, a Man who had been cursed by Morgoth, discovered some treasure in the ruins of Nargothrond, another great Elven kingdom

of the First Age that had been devastated a short time before. Húrin took the treasure to Doriath and gave it to Thingol. The Elf king then decided to call on the expertise of the Dwarves to make a necklace, the Nauglamír, which would serve as a setting for the Silmaril, which he had received as a gift from his son-in-law, Beren. This jewel was considered the most beautiful of all the masterpieces produced by the Dwarves.

The Dragon Glaurung, who was responsible

It would be wrong to conclude, however, that such animosity was the key note in all the relationships between the Elves and the Dwarves. The Company were warmly received, for example, in Elrond's house in Rivendell.

for the fall of Nargothrond, hoarded the gold that had provided the source of the necklace, and which had now been contaminated by Glaurung's wicked intentions. The Nauglamír was the root cause of the dispute between the Dwarves and the Elves: the Dwarf blacksmiths were so spellbound by the Silmaril that they wanted to keep it for themselves, thus provoking the wrath of Thingol, who proceeded to expel them from his kingdom. In 503 F.A., Thingol was killed by the Dwarves and Doriath was subsequently sacked. The Elves of Doriath never forgave the Dwarves for this assassination, or indeed the kingdom's subsequent decline after the departure of Melian and the elimination of the magic frontier, which resulted in its total destruction three years later. Oropher, Thranduil's father, was an exile from the kingdom of Doriath, and so the old antagonisms festered in the Silvan Kingdom in Mirkwood (immortal Elves had long memories!).

In his early drafts of The Hobbit, Tolkien envisaged a more limited chronology than that of the three ages of Middle-earth that we know about from the appendices of The Lord of the Rings. He had imagined that the Quest of Erebor would take place a few hundred years after the major events of the First Age, at most. In those initial outlines, the king of the Silvan Elves seemed to have been Thingol himself (as he was not killed by the Dwarves), just as the Arkenstone was supposed to be a Silmaril. This version of the story therefore provides a better explanation of the animosity of the Silvan Elves towards Thorin and Company. It would have required substantial rewrites of the history of the First Age, however, and this seems to have been one of the reasons that led Tolkien to abandon these narrative elements.

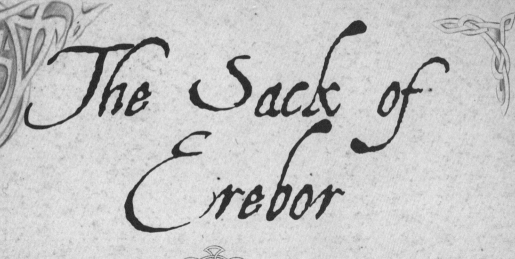

The Sack of Erebor

'*By that time all the bells were ringing in Dale and the warriors were arming. The dwarves rushed out of their great gate; but there was the dragon waiting for them. None escaped that way.*' (The Hobbit, Ch. 1).

The Sack of Erebor is the term used to denote the attack on the Lonely Mountain by Smaug the Dragon, in the year 2770 T.A. The relationship between the Dwarves of Erebor and the Dragons of the Grey Mountains had always been very bad. During the reign of Thorin I, the forefather of Thorin II Oakenshield, the Dwarf people left the Lonely Mountain to settle in the Grey Mountains, where they increased their already considerable wealth by opening up new mines. This region was also home, however, to a growing population of Dragons, who had an insatiable lust for gold. They began to pillage the fruits of the Dwarves' labour, and in 2590 T.A., Thrór, Thorin Oakenshield's grandfather, decided to flee the Grey Mountains and leave them to the Dragons. The Dwarves returned to

Erebor and reformed the Kingdom under the Mountain, thereby ushering in the country's Golden Age (in every sense of the term). Erebor and its region enjoyed prosperity for a long time by taking advantage of the resources they discovered in the Mountain (including the Arkenstone), as well as establishing commercial links with the neighbouring cities and regions. The Dwarves dug mines and tunnels in the heart of the Mountain to extract minerals and gemstones, including gold, silver and mithril, while also establishing highly profitable forges. In return both for these talents and for the instruction that the Dwarves imparted to their children, the Men provided food and other raw materials that the Dwarves did not produce for themselves. Dale, the town founded around 2600 T.A. at a bend

in the River Running, in a valley at the foot of the Mountain, also thrived and basked in the reflected glory of the Dwarf kingdom. Dale's famous toy market was a major attraction for travellers. Word about the achievements of the Dwarf kingdom soon spread to the north of Middle-earth, before reaching the Grey Mountains and the ears of the big dragons that lived there – and, most notably, the most powerful of them all: Smaug the Golden.

One day in 2770, when Thorin Oakenshield was away with some other Dwarves, Smaug came down to Erebor from the North, in

This region was also home, however, to a growing population of Dragons, who had an insatiable lust for gold. They began to pillage the fruits of the Dwarves' labour.

search of treasure. The first signal of his advance came in the form of a thunderous wind that split trees in two, soon followed by the sight of the Dragon himself standing on a mountain top. Smaug then set about burning the vegetation on the slopes of Erebor. While the Dwarves tried to escape from the Mountain by the Great Gate, the Men from Dale took up arms – but the Dragon managed to trap them. He shrouded Dale in fog by breathing fire on the River, allowing him to take the town by surprise and kill almost all the warriors (probably including the king of Dale, Girion). He then

headed to the Great Gate and penetrated the heart of the Mountain. Once inside, he chased out all the surviving Dwarves and then gathered together all the gold and jewels into one big pile in the depths of the Mountain and settled in for the next 171 years.

Thorin, for his part, could only look on, powerless, at the loss of his kingdom – but, to his astonishment, his grandfather and his father, Thráin, reappeared, having both escaped from the attack unharmed via a secret door that only they knew about. Thorin told them that the Men had still put up resistance even after the Dragon's intrusion, but his sorties to capture and devour young girls had finally led the Men to abandon the town and settle to the south of the Long Lake. The lands that had once been controlled by the Dwarves and the Men and subsequently fell under the yoke of the Dragon became known as the Desolation of Smaug.

The surviving members of Durin's Folk divided into several groups: some went back to the Iron Hills, but most followed Thrór to the far southwest of the Misty Mountains. A few years later, Thrór tried to explore Moria, which had fallen into the hands of the Goblins, but he was killed by Azog, a Goblin who had proclaimed himself master of Moria. Thráin was consumed by a desire for revenge. He gathered together all the Dwarf clans and initiated the long War of the Dwarves and the Orcs. Azog was eventually defeated by Dáin II Ironfoot at the Battle of Azanulbizar. After the war, Thráin and Thorin settled in the Blue Mountains, in the west of Middle-earth.

The War of the Ring

'We might now hope to return from the victory here only to ruin and ash. But that has been averted – because I met Thorin Oakenshield one evening on the edge of spring in Bree.' *(The Annotated Hobbit, Appendix A).*

During the Quest of Erebor, Bilbo Baggins found the One Ring that Sauron had previously lost, and he secretly took it with him to the Shire in 2942 of the Third Age. This action was the key to what would prove to be the last conflict in this Age: the War of the Ring.

Gandalf came up with a solution that Sauron was unable even to imagine: to destroy the Ring in the place where it was forged, in the heart of the land of Mordor.

The whereabouts of the Ring were actively investigated during the Third Age by both Gollum and Sauron (who had consolidated his armed forces). Saruman was also looking for the Ring; he was the White Council's specialist in the tradition of the Rings of Power but he ended up coveting their power himself. In the 2851 Council, Saruman started to suspect the Shire and Gandalf of being mixed up with the One Ring. He refused to attack Dol Guldur, the home of the Necromancer, who was now known to be Sauron, but he changed his mind in 2941, fearing that Sauron would get his hands on the Ring first. Sauron escaped, however, and even Gandalf still did not know the entire

truth about Bilbo's ring. In 3001 T.A., Bilbo organized a party to celebrate his 111th birthday, before leaving the Shire and passing on both Bag End and the Ring to his heir, Frodo Baggins.

Gollum was also anxious to find the Ring, so he left the Misty Mountains and headed to Mordor. Once there, he was captured by Sauron, who tried to make him talk, but Gollum saw Sauron as a rival and was unwilling to divulge any important information. In 3017, Sauron released Gollum, who quickly fell into the hands of Aragorn and was then led to the Elf King Thranduil in Mirkwood. On 13 April 3018, Gandalf told Frodo of his great discovery: the ring that Bilbo had taken on his journey was no vulgar magic bauble – it was the One Ring forged by Sauron thousands of years previously. If Sauron found it, he would regain all his power to enslave the peoples of Middle-earth. Gandalf decided to seek the advice of Saruman, while Frodo planned to take the Ring to Rivendell under cover of taking up residence in the Eastern Neighbourhood of the Shire. By June 3018, Sauron had grown sufficiently concerned about the Free Peoples' investigations to simultaneously attack the Men in Gondor and Thranduil's Elves. Gollum took advantage of this commotion to escape. Boromir left Gondor to ask for help in Rivendell. Saruman, who also coveted the Ring, imprisoned Gandalf, who only succeeded in breaking free in September

– at the same time as Sauron's Nine Black Riders arrived in the Shire. Frodo and his friends went ahead of the Nine, receiving help from, first, Tom Bombadil and then Aragorn, who guided the Hobbits from Bree to Rivendell to ensure that the Ring remained out of Sauron's reach. Frodo also received treatment for the injury that he had sustained in the chase, before meeting the Elf Glorfindel, who had come from Rivendell to look for him.

In Rivendell, Elrond assembled a council to decide what to do with the Ring, whose power was so great that nobody could use it without being dominated by it. Moreover, the Ring was difficult to destroy and hiding it, however astutely, would never stop Sauron winning the war. The resistance against Sauron lay in the hands of the Men from Gondor and Rohan, but they were depleted and divided. The Dwarves and the Elves were already under threat from the enemy. Gandalf came up with a solution that Sauron was unable even to imagine: to destroy the Ring in the place where it was forged, in the heart of the land of Mordor. This task was entrusted to the Hobbit Frodo Baggins, Bilbo's cousin and heir, accompanied by Peregrin Took, Meriadoc Brandybuck and Samwise Gamgee, the Wizard Gandalf, the two Men Aragorn and Boromir, the Elf Legolas (Thranduil's son) and the Dwarf Gimli (Glóin's son). This Fellowship of Nine Walkers had to take the Ring to Mordor and throw it into the depths of Mount Doom, while foiling the efforts

of Saruman, Sauron and Gollum to seize it for themselves.

They set off from Rivendell in late December of 3018 and passed through the mines of Moria, the former Dwarf kingdom that Balin had tried to recapture. The Fellowship was forced to flee the mountains, however, due to the presence of Goblins and a Balrog, although they had to leave Gandalf behind because he fell into an abyss along with the Balrog. After travelling through the Elf kingdom of Lórien, ruled by Galadriel and Celeborn, the bearer of the Ring and his companions followed the course of the Anduin towards the South. The power of the Ring exerted its influence on Boromir, who tried to grab it by force but later repented. Frodo and Sam headed to Mordor alone, as their companions were under attack from Saruman's servants. Boromir was killed and the other two Hobbits were captured by Saruman's Uruk-hai. Aragorn, Legolas and Gimli left to look for them, while Frodo and Sam met Gollum, who guided them towards Mordor (although he intended to betray them in order to steal the Ring).

Aragorn, Gimli and Legolas met up with Gandalf again and confronted Saruman's troops in Helm's Deep with the Men from Rohan, while Peregrin and Meriadoc led the attack on the Wizard's fortress with the Ents, the Tree-hosts. They then set off to assist Gondor, which was under siege from soldiers from Mordor. In mid-March 3019, Sauron simultaneously attacked Minas Tirith, the capital of Gondor, and the kingdoms of Thranduil, Galadriel, Dale and Erebor. Dáin II Ironfoot and Brand, Bard's grandson, fought to the death at the foot of the Lonely Mountain, while Gandalf and his companions succeed in repulsing the enemy in Gondor and won the Battle of the Pelennor Fields, thanks to the arrival of horsemen from Rohan and armies from South Gondor led by Aragorn, Legolas and Gimli. The latter trio had defeated the Corsairs of Umbar, doing so along with the Oathbreakers, whom Aragorn redeemed from their oath before using pirate ships to surprise the enemy from the rear. The chiefs of the Free Peoples attacked Mordor in order to distract Sauron and enable Frodo to advance unnoticed. On 25 March 3019, while the army of the Free Peoples (with Gandalf, Aragorn, Gimli, Legolas and Peregrin in its ranks) was encircled in front of the Black Gate, Frodo and Samwise reached the Cracks of Doom (Sammath Naur). The power of the Ring prevented Frodo from destroying it, but Gollum leaped towards him and snatched it away, only to fall into the fiery depths of the mountain. The destruction of the Ring sent tremors throughout the kingdom, particularly amongst Sauron's servants, as well as rekindling the fire of Mount Doom. It was at this point that the Eagles came to the rescue of the fighters and Gandalf told them to bring back the two Hobbits.

The fall of Sauron's kingdom marked the end of the fighting in both the South and the North. Brand's son became the King of Dale (as Bard II), Thorin III Stonehelm, the son of

Dáin, became the King under the Mountain and the Fellowship of the Ring went their separate ways after Aragorn's marriage to Arwen Undómiel, Elrond's daughter. On 28 August, Gandalf and the Hobbits encountered Saruman wandering along the South Road leading to Bree. On 21 September, he reached the Shire, while Gandalf and his friends were in Rivendell. Frodo and his companions arrived in the Shire in their turn on 30 October and discovered that Saruman had wreaked havoc in their land, along with the Men in his pay. The Hobbits revolted and Saruman was killed by his last servant. That day, 3 November 3019, marked the end of the War of the Ring.

The War of the Dwarves and the Orcs

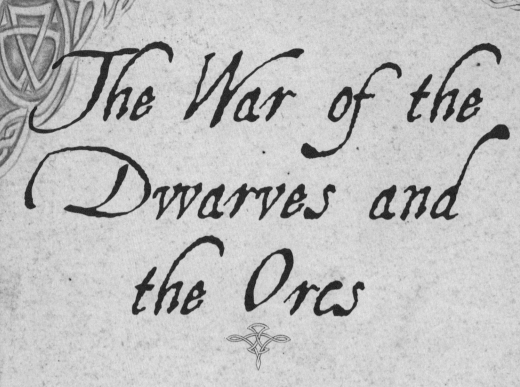

'That was the beginning of the War of the Dwarves and the Orcs, which was long and deadly, and fought for the most part in deep places beneath the earth.' (The Lord of the Rings, Appendix A, III).

The War of the Dwarves and Orcs was an armed conflict in the Third Age that lasted for less than six years (between 2793 and 2799). The war was sparked off three years prior to its start, however, by the murder and decapitation of Thrór, the chief of Durin's Folk, by Azog the Goblin, at the Eastern Gate of Moria. It was the culmination of a long period of misfortunes and exiles borne by the Dwarf people since their expulsion in 1980, in the middle of the Third Age, from Khazad-dûm. This historic kingdom had been founded in the heart of the Misty Mountains in the First Age by Durin I, the Eldest of the Seven Fathers of

the Dwarves. The Dwarves' obsession with extracting precious mithril from the mountain led them to awaken a Balrog, Durin's Bane, who chased them out of their home. Although Thráin I the Old, son of Náin I, founded the kingdom of Erebor under the Lonely Mountain (where he discovered the Arkenstone and became King under the Mountain), many exiles ended up settling in the Grey Mountains, the northeastern prolongation of the Misty Mountains, to the north of Mirkwood. The Dwarves' mining activities in these mountains eventually led them to further disaster because, after several centuries of prosperity, they stirred the greed

of the Dragons, who wrecked the Dwarves' houses and forced them to evacuate the Grey Mountains.

The Dwarf Thrór, a descendant of Thráin the Old, fled from the Grey Mountains with his people and decided to settle under Erebor, which had once been colonized by his ancestor. The Dwarves enjoyed a new period of wealth and fortune, enhanced by a close trading relationship with the Men from Dale. The splendour of this kingdom once again inflamed the greed of a Dragon from the Grey Mountains. This one was called Smaug, and he went on to ravage the Lonely Mountain and seize its riches. A period of wandering followed for Thrór, his son Thráin and their relatives. Thrór eventually grew tired of this nomadic life and, after passing on to his son a ring – one of the Dwarves' Seven Rings still in his possession – he set off with a companion named Nár with the intention of exploring Khazad-dûm. He was eventually killed and beheaded at the East Gate of Moria by the Goblin Azog, who spared Nár's life so that he could report this act of aggression to the heir of the Line of Durin, Thráin. After a long period of silent mourning, Thráin swore to avenge his father's death. The recruitment and training of soldiers from all the dispersed Dwarf houses lasted for three years. The Dwarves then attacked the various Goblin strongholds under the Misty Mountains, from Mount Gundabad in the north to the Gladden River in the south, and their superior numbers and weaponry forced the Goblins on to the defensive. The conflict came

to a head at the Battle of Azanulbizar, which took place in the valley of the same name, which was also called Dimrill Dale or, according to the Elves, Nanduhirion. Azanulbizar was situated to the east of the three peaks of Caradhras, Celebdil and Fanuidhol, which loomed over Moria and could be reached by the Dimrill Stair, which led down from the Redhorn Pass.

The valley also contained Kheled-zâram, a lake that was considered sacred by the Dwarves. A series of Dwarf attacks on the Misty Mountains obliged the Goblins to regroup in Azanulbizar. The Dwarves were

The War of the Dwarves and Orcs was an armed conflict in the Third Age that lasted for less than six years (between 2793 and 2799).

highly motivated by the sight of their former homeland but they were at a disadvantage in the first clash because the Goblins occupied the upper reaches of the valley. The Dwarves were forced to retreat into the woods around Kheled-zâram. Thráin's son, Thorin, had his shield split during this retreat and was obliged to defend himself with an oak branch, thus earning himself the nickname of Oakenshield. Many Dwarves lost their lives in the woods, including Frerin, Thorin's brother, and Fundin, the father of Balin and

Dwalin. The survivors were saved by the late arrival of Dwarves from the Iron Hills, led by Náin, who tilted the balance of the battle and brought Azog out into the open. Although Azog killed Náin in a hand-to-hand fight, his forces were routed. Furthermore, Náin's son, Dáin, was quick to take revenge on his father's killer – this was considered quite a feat, since Dáin was barely 32 years old. He cut off Azog's head and the surviving Dwarves put it on a pole, thus marking not only the end of the Battle of Azanulbizar but also the war itself.

The Goblins were dispersed and fled to the White Mountains to the south of Rohan. Although the Dwarves emerged victorious, they had lost over half their numbers and were in no condition to challenge the Balrog and reconquer Khazad-dûm. As the excessive number of Dwarf corpses made it impossible for them to practice their traditional funeral rite of burying their dead in stone, the

Dwarves carefully skinned the dead bodies and made a huge fire that could be seen even in Lórien. Their descendants thus referred to the victims of this battle as 'Burnt Dwarves', which became an honorific title. After the dispersal of the Dwarf army, Dáin went back to the Iron Hills, while Thorin and Thráin settled in the Blue Mountains. Their companions included Balin and Glóin, who would team up with Thorin and Company for the Quest of Erebor.

The Battle of the Five Armies over the ownership of the treasure of Erebor was a direct consequence of the War of the Dwarves and Orcs, as it brought together, at the foot of the Lonely Mountain, an army of Goblins led by Bolg, Azog's son, who was determined to avenge the death of his father. Bolg was eventually killed by Beorn in this battle, which brought victory to the Free Peoples.

Sources of inspiration

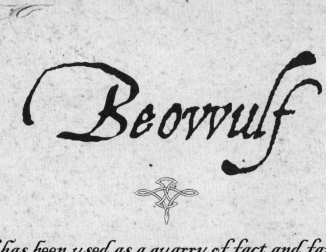

Beowulf

'Beowulf has been used as a quarry of fact and fancy far more assiduously than it has been studied as a work of art'

The Monsters and the Critics and Other Essays, 'Beowulf: the Monsters and the Critics'.

Beowulf is an epic medieval poem, a Christianized Scandinavian legend 3,182 lines long, written in Old English, the language spoken in England before the Norman conquest of 1066. It is the oldest long heroic poem known to us in a European language other than Latin and Ancient Greek. It was probably written sometime between the 7th and 9th centuries, but the only surviving manuscript dates from around the year 1000. The poem tells the story of Beowulf, a young prince who was the nephew of King Hygelac, who ruled over the Geats, a people living in the south of present-day Sweden. One day, Beowulf found out that an ogre called Grendel was making nightly attacks on Heorot, the palace of Hrothgar, the King of the Danes. Hrothgar and his subjects had been enduring these terrible and deadly visits by this gigantic monster for twelve years without being able to put up any resistance. So, Beowulf organized an expedition to go to their aid, setting off at the head of a small group of fifteen warriors in the direction of the kingdom of the Danes (or Scyldings). The prince and his companions were warmly welcomed to Heorot by Hrothgar and his wife Wealhtheow. They then awaited the arrival of Grendel. Beowulf trusted in the physical strength granted to him by providence and decided to confront the ogre with his bare hands as the Geats' swords had proved incapable of even penetrating Grendel's skin. For the first time ever, the monster had to come to grips with an enemy who was stronger than he was. There followed an extremely violent encounter, which ended with the ogre retreating to his lair, having been deprived of an arm by Beowulf.

Grendel's injury turned out to be fatal. Beowulf's victory was celebrated by the Danes, and the Prince of the Geats was richly rewarded by Hrothgar. The following night,

however, Heorot's ordeal continued as it was attacked by Grendel's vengeful mother, who attacked the palace in her turn and captured Aeschere, the king's best friend. Beowulf, Hrothgar and their men followed the ogress's bloody trail and eventually found the monsters' hideout, an ominous pond on a mountainside. Beowulf put on armour to confront Grendel's mother alone in a large hall underneath the water. After a ferocious fight, the prince managed to overcome the ogress with a gigantic sword

that he took from weapons he found there. Having saved the kingdom of the Danes once again, Beowulf returned home and gave his uncle and suzerain Hygelac the rewards that he had received from Hrothgar: the King of the Geats then involved Beowulf in the governance of the kingdom, and after Hygelac's death – historically confirmed as taking place in the 6th century – his nephew came to the throne. After a reign of 50 years, the ageing King Beowulf had to confront a dragon who was enraged by the theft of a precious cup from his lair and was now ravaging the kingdom. Equipped with a special shield, Beowulf and a small group of men headed to the cave where the dragon kept his treasure. Beowulf squared up to the dragon and, with the help of the young Wiglaf, managed to topple the monster – but not without receiving a fatal wound. As he lay dying, the king ordered the construction of his own funeral pyre and memorial, before naming Wiglaf as his heir. The poem ends with a description of Beowulf's funeral and the tributes paid to him by the Geats. Beowulf was buried with the dragon's treasure.

Tolkien was fascinated by the poetic qualities of *Beowulf*, which he discovered at a young age. In 1936, after his appointment as Professor of Anglo-Saxon in Oxford, he gave a famous lecture on *Beowulf* to the British Academy (*Beowulf: The Monsters and the Critics*), in which he highlighted its literary value. This poem was one of Tolkien's foremost inspirations as a writer, and several elements from *Beowulf* are redeployed in his corpus, and most particularly in *The Hobbit*. In Chapter 5, for example, Gollum's eyes light up with an unsettling glow when he realizes that Bilbo Baggins has recovered the One Ring that he himself had lost: this glow is similar to the light emanating from Grendel's eyes in *Beowulf* during his last night-time attack on Heorot (lines 724–727). In Chapter 12 of the novel, Bilbo's theft of a cup from the Dragon Smaug's treasure trove, and the resulting fury of the monster, recall the episode in Beowulf in which a man steals a golden cup from the dragon in order to take it to his master. This robbery unleashes the dragon's fury when he wakes up and prompts him to exact a terrible revenge (lines 2215–2220, 2287–2319). Finally, the name of the Arkenstone is derived from the Old English *eorclanstän*, meaning 'precious stone'; it appears once in *Beowulf*, in its plural form, in a passage about King Hygelac (lines 1202–1209).

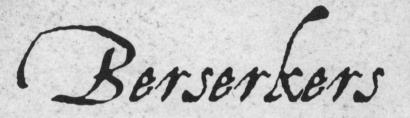

Berserkers

'*He came alone, and in bear's shape; and he seemed to have grown almost to giant-size in his wrath. The roar of his voice was like drums and guns; and he tossed wolves and goblins from his path like straws and feathers.*' (The Hobbit, Ch. 18).

The berserker, a warrior-beast prone to deadly frenzies that rendered him impervious to ordinary weapons, was a recurring figure in the Scandinavian sagas. He often served as the enemy that the hero of a saga had to overcome, although sometimes he could also play the role of an invaluable ally. A berserker would fly into a rage at the start of a fight, emitting bestial cries and acting extravagantly, as described by Snorri Sturluson in his *Ynglinga Saga*:

'[Odin's] men, in contrast, went without a *broigne* [coat of armour] and they were as furious as dogs or wolves; they would bite their shield and they were as strong as bears or bulls; they killed other people but no fire nor could hurt them. This was known as the "fury of the warrior-beasts".'

Berserkers' immunity to sharp weapons is sometimes considered a natural consequence of their frenzy, but some sagas described them blunting their enemies' weapons with a curse or even a mere glance. Some berserkers seem to have been endowed with even more remarkable powers, such as the capacity to change shape (these were called *hamrammr* in Old Norse). In contrast, several stories, such as one in *Gesta Danorum* by Saxo Grammaticus, stated that berserkers were vulnerable to blunt-force weapons such as hammers and bludgeons. Once a berserker's rage subsided, he would be overcome by a physical and mental stupor that would leave him vulnerable for several days.

Berserker means 'bear's shirt' in Old Norse, as they were reputed to wear a bearskin when they went into battle. Several sagas use the synonym *úlfheðinn* ('wolf's tunic'), recalling the transformation of Sigmund and his son Sinfjötli into wolves when they put on magic wolfskins in *The Völsunga Saga*.

In *The Hobbit*, Beorn embodies the essence of the berserker. Gandalf introduces him as a dangerous character who is easily riled

and should never be crossed in any circumstances. His name means 'warrior' in Old English, but it also resembles the Old Norse *björn*, or 'bear', thus connecting him to the famous berserker Bödvar Bjarki, one of the heroes of the *Hrólf Kraki Saga*. Like Bödvar Bjarki, Beorn came from the mountains and was capable of assuming the form of a giant bear, which gave him astonishing powers and rendered him virtually invulnerable. At the Battle of the Five Armies, Beorn went to the rescue of Thorin II Oakenshield, just as Bödvar Bjarki protected King Hrólf in the guise of a bear in the battle against the army of Skuld and King Hjörvard. However, the Battle of the Five Armies ended with the victory of the Free Peoples, whereas Hrólf's army was defeated in the Saga, as the spell that enabled Bödvar to transform himself was inadvertently broken by one of his companions.

Tolkien created other characters who are sometimes possessed by a violent rage reminiscent of that of the Berserkers. Such was the case with King Théoden at the Battle of Pelennor Fields, where he was so inflamed by the belligerent fury of his ancestors that he acquired a valour verging on madness. The Haradrim cavalry was overwhelmed by his full-bodied onslaught and fled after the death of their chief. Only an intervention by the Witch-King of Angmar was capable of stopping and defeating him. Even more surprising was Samwise Gamgee's reaction when he realized that he and Frodo Baggins had been lured into a trap by Gollum's scheming. Sam was overcome with anger and attacked Gollum in a blind fury, heedless of his own safety and that of Frodo. It took Gollum's disappearance into a hole to bring him back to his senses for a moment – long enough to realize that his master was in mortal danger. On seeing Frodo at the mercy of Shelob, Sam charged at the Spider, shrieking, and struck him with colossal force, wounding him and forcing him to flee. After the departure of his enemies, Sam found himself drained of all strength and he could only approach the unconscious Frodo on hands and knees.

Tolkien used these different characters to present various approaches to the myth of the Berserkers, from the archetypal figure of the skin-changer (Beorn) to the extraordinary fearlessness of a Hobbit, who for a fleeting instant became the equal of the greatest heroes of Middle-earth.

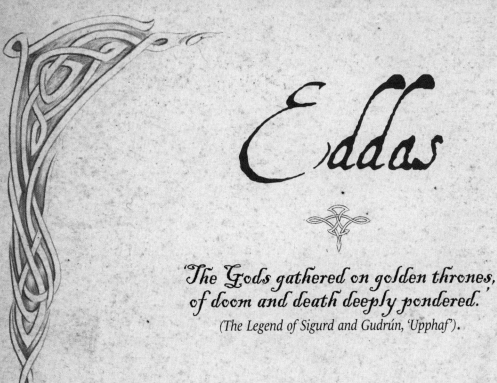

Eddas

*'The Gods gathered on golden thrones,
of doom and death deeply pondered.'*
(The Legend of Sigurd and Gudrún, 'Upphaf').

The *Eddas* comprise two manuscripts written in Old Norse that date from the 13th century but are based on older, orally transmitted legends and stories. The meaning of the word 'Edda' has long been a subject of debate, but nowadays most experts agree that it means 'superstition, or creed'. The first manuscript, known as the Poetic or the Elder Edda, gathers together some thirty poems drawn from the Codex Regius, an ancient late 13th-century manuscript that somehow came into the hands as Brynjólfur Sveinsson, who was Bishop of Skálholt, in Iceland, from 1639 to 1674. This Codex consists of mythological poems, such as the *Völuspá*, and the heroic sagas, such as the *Brot af Sigurðarkviðu* ('Fragment of the Lay (song) of Sigurd'), the *Sigurðarkviða hin skamma* ('Short Lay of Sigurd') and the *Guðrúnarkviða I, II* and *III* ('The Three Lays of Gudrún'). The second manuscript, the *Prose Edda*, is also called the *Snorri Edda*, after its author, Snorri Sturluson.

The *Prose Edda* is like a poetry textbook, throwing light on Nordic mythology in the *Gylfaginning*, ('Tricking of Gylfi') and explaining skaldic aesthetics in the *Skáldskaparmál* ('Language of Poetry'), particularly the significance of the *heitir* (metonymies) and *kenning* (periphrases) used in place of common nouns and proper names. Finally, in the *Háttatal*, Sturluson presents the different verse forms used in Old Norse poetry, based on numbers of syllables and on assonances, consonances and alliterations. Between them, the two Eddas represent the primary source of the Nordic myths and legends known to us today, and ever since their rediscovery in the 17th century, they have inspired countless creative artists in various fields. Many experts, including Tolkien, consider that the term 'Edda' used by Sturluson to describe his work has been wrongly applied to the *Poetic Edda*, which is unrelated to the *Prose Edda*.

Tolkien was a passionate linguist. He started studying Icelandic literature in 1913 and came to master Old Norse so well that he taught it at Oxford University from 1926 to 1939, in parallel with his courses in Anglo-Saxon. He also created a club, the Coalbiters, whose very name was a periphrasis designating layabouts (a term probably applied ironically to this group of professors) who sat twiddling their thumbs by the fireplace and were in danger of swallowing the embers. Nevertheless, the club had the serious purpose of emphasizing the importance of the Old Norse language and of Nordic literature in Germanic studies.

Like William Morris, Tolkien believed that Nordic legends should occupy the same place for the English that the story of Troy occupies for the Greeks. Like the Finnish *Kalevala*, the Eddas constitute a link

The meaning of the word 'Edda' has long been a subject of debate, but nowadays most experts agree that it means 'superstition, or creed'.

between the past and the present, thereby establishing a cultural continuity, however incomplete. As far as Tolkien was concerned, the Norman invasion marked an irreparable rupture in English culture and its language, and so it was hardly surprising that he was so enthusiastic about these examples of stories that had remained intact over time. *The Lord of the Rings* was his attempt to create a comparable mythology for the English.

Both the Eddas and *Beowulf* provided Tolkien with ideas for the names of his characters. Gandalf, for example, was called Olórin, 'the Visionary', in Valinor; Gandalf, in the Shire; Mithrandir, 'the Grey Pilgrim', among the Elves and in Gondor; and Tharkûn, 'the Grey Man' (or 'the Man with the Stick' in another version), among the Dwarves. Like the periphrases (*kenning*) of the Nordic legends, these descriptive names serve to pinpoint a person's most prominent features. Likewise, Galadriel/Alatáriel means 'Young Girl Crowned with a Radiant Garland', in reference to the character's hair. The Eddas also use *heitir*, metonyms in which a part, such as an object, serves to denote a whole, such as a character. Tolkien used this device, in his turn, as when he gave Beleg the nickname Strongbow.

The *Völuspá* ('Prophecy of a Seeress'), written in Old Norse alliterative stanzas known as *fornyrðislag*, is the first work in the *Poetic Edda* and is undoubtedly the best-known story in the collection, and the one that has provided the most artistic inspiration, including for Wagner (although Tolkien found his interpretation of the texts annoying). In this work, the prophetess Völva describes her visions, from primordial times to Ragnarök, the final fate of the gods. This poem had a particularly strong influence on Tolkien, as he himself explained in a letter. He was

fascinated by the sounds of some of the names therein, as well as the emotions that they aroused in him. The *Dvergatal* ('Catalogue of Dwarves') in the *Völuspá*, for example, led Tolkien to reproduce these Dwarf names in *The Hobbit* (with the exception of Balin, whose etymology is unclear). Tolkien teases his readers and critics, however, as characters' names are not necessarily related to their personal traits or destiny, even though certain features do appear to be linked to their Old Norse names: thus, Bombur ('Potbelly') was renowned for his rotundity, while, Glóin ('Radiance') was skilled at lighting fires (as was his brother Oin – whose name is, however, completely unconnected with this talent). Although the Dwarves in *The Hobbit* show some similarities with the *dvergar*, they are not totally identical. Tolkien reserved the right to use these names simply as a starting point for characters and situations, and then to deviate from their original meanings. Thorin's sobriquet of Oakenshield, derived from the Old Norse *Eikinskjaldi*, was also taken from the *Völuspá*, but the reasons for its attribution are different in the two stories. The Eddas exerted a lasting influence on Tolkien, who admired their capacity to draw the reader in with their lively style and rhythmic poetry. Unlike epics, which take their time to build up a tragedy, Old Norse poetry valued concision and sought, as Tolkien put it, to illuminate a situation like a bolt of lightning. This influence was not limited to the Legendarium. Tolkien similarly explored themes from Icelandic poetry

in the same style as the originals by writing two alliterative poems of his own in modern English, published as *The Legend of Sigurd and Gudrún*. In the *New Lay of the Völsung*, Tolkien went back to the prophecies of the seer in the *Völuspá*, as well as recounting episodes from the the Niflung cycle, particularly *Frá dauða Sinfjötla* ('the Death of Sinfjötli'), *Reginsmál* ('the Lay of Regin') and *Fáfnismál* ('the Lay of Fáfnir'), together with episodes from the 13th-century Scandinavian *Völsungasaga* ('Saga of the Völsung'). The seeress had prophesized the fate of the gods and the birth of a mortal who would slay the Serpent and so overcome Evil, and Odin thus fathered several children. The Serpent-slayer would see the light of day within the Völsung lineage. Tolkien also described the misadventures of Odin, Loki and Hoenir, which led to the curse of the Dwarf Andvari's gold. He told of the retrieval of Grímnir's sword by King Völsung's son, Sigmund, before the king's death, and of the incestuous love between Sigmund and his twin sister Signý, whose own son Sinfjötli would be poisoned by the queen. Sigmund married Princess Sigrlinn but had to fight against a king's seven sons who had all laid claim to her hand; he was eventually struck down by a one-eyed warrior. Sigrlinn subsequently gave birth to Sigurd, who was brought up by Regin, while Sigrlinn, now remarried, preserved the pieces of Grímnir's broken sword. Regin pushed Sigurd into fighting against Fáfnir, his brother, now transformed into a dragon. The sword Gram was forged from

fragments of Grímnir's sword. Sigurd killed the dragon and, after tasting its blood, he acquired the gift of understanding the language of the birds. Sigurd was betrothed to Brynhild the Valkyrie but, after drinking a love potion, he married Princess Gudrún instead. Brynhild got her revenge, however, and Sigurd was killed in his bed. *The New Lay of Gudrún* recounts the adventures of the princess after Sigurd's death and her later marriage to Atli, the king of the Huns, as told in the *Atlakviða* ('Lay of Atli') and the *Atlamál hin groenlenzku* ('Greenlander Lay of Atli').

Eucatastrophe

"'The Eagles! The Eagles!" he shouted. "The Eagles are coming!"' (The Hobbit, Ch. 17).

This arrival of the Eagles towards the end of *The Hobbit* is more than merely a plot twist. The birds appeared just at the moment when Bilbo Baggins was overcome with foreboding that the Goblins were gaining the upper hand in the battle at the Gate. However, the arrival in extremis of his allies revived his spirits and 'made his heart leap'. In his excitement, he started to jump for joy and wave his arms in the air.

Tolkien saw this rekindling of hope, in both the hero and the reader, as crucial to his intentions in *The Hobbit*. He considered such moments of positive shared emotion as the main purpose and most noble function of successful fairy stories, even though this feature is played down in the simplified formats of many traditional tales.

Tolkien wanted to repair this omission and restore the rightful place of this essential device in the very heart of his story. He called this kind of decisive moment a eucatastrophe. This neologism is derived from the Greek εὖ ('fortunately') and κατασροφή ('conclusion') and conveys the idea of a brutal but positive upheaval. It denotes an abrupt shift that turns around a story mired in a desperate, disastrous situation to give back to the hero (and the reader) the hope that they had lost.

A eucatastrophe is therefore neither a pleasant interlude nor a final triumph. It is a specific moment, as emotionally powerful as the irruption of a catastrophe, in the sense that a eucatastrophe 'pierces you with a joy that brings tears', as Tolkien indicated in one of his letters. Whereas catastrophe engulfs us in sadness and anxiety, eucatastrophe overwhelms us with joy and hope.

This is exactly what Bilbo felt when he saw the 'dark shapes small yet majestic against the distant glow'.

Faërie

'For most of them (together with their scattered relations in the hills and mountains) were descended from the ancient tribes that never went to Faerie in the West.' *(The Hobbit, Ch. 8).*

Faërie, refers to Eldamar, the land of the Elves, situated beyond the seas, in the West. The Elves awoke in the Far East of Middle-earth and then undertook a Great Journey westward to Valinor, the holy land, at the invitation of its inhabitants, angelic spirits known as the Valar. Some of these Elves stopped off en route, giving rise, most notably, to the Silvan Elves of Doriath and Mirkwood, while others ventured beyond the Great Sea. Once they reached Eldamar, the Elves founded three great cities: Tirion and Alqualondë in Aman and Avallónë on the island of Tol Eressëa. The Elves thrived in both body and soul in this environment, under the auspices of the Valar. They refined their language and invented the Sarati and Tengwar writing systems, as well as producing craftwork so wondrous that nothing like it had ever been seen before (and it would still be celebrated in song in later Ages). These marvels aroused the envy of Melkor, the dark Vala and master of Sauron, who sneaked out of Faërie to go to Middle-earth, taking with him the Silmarils, three jewels enclosing divine light. Some of the Elves followed him in order to recover these treasures, and these exiles considered Faërie a land of redemption; most of them would only regain it at the end of the First Age, after Morgoth's defeat by the Valar. In the Second Age, the Men of Númenor, urged on by Sauron, became obsessed with occupying Faërie, seeing it as a means of obtaining immortality. However, just as Faërie was being invaded by the Numenorean fleet, the world, which had been flat until then, became curved, leaving Faërie out of reach of mortals. Only a few chosen figures – among them, Gandalf the Wizard, the Elves Galadriel and Elrond, and the bearers of the One Ring, the Hobbits Bilbo and Frodo Baggins – would have the chance to go to Faërie, at the end of the War of the Ring.

In the 1930s, Tolkien gave a lecture on fairy tales in which he explained his concept of Faërie: as well as being a place, Faërie denoted the enchantment associated with fairies. It was the Perilous Realm in which fairies and elves were in their element, and it was dangerous for humans because it was where some of their deepest and most natural desires were fulfilled. So, anybody who ventured into Faërie could explore other spaces and other times, and enter into communion with other living beings or understand the language of the birds, beasts and trees. Faërie thus represented a far bigger and more indeterminate place than the Blessed Realms of the Valar.

Faërie was not only home to fantastic creatures, however, as it contained everything

that could be found in the whole wide world: nature, objects and living beings. It was at one and the same time our world and another world – or, to be more precise, it was our world in a state of enchantment, when everything familiar seemed to be bathed in a new light. Faërie may have been an imaginative construct, but it was no less real for that. For anybody who penetrated and explored it, it was no illusion or dream or figment of the imagination. It was a state of the world that revealed truths that could not be accessed by other means. Literary works that are set in Faerie (such as fairy tales) can provide insights or offer a way in. This other world idea recalls those of Celtic legends, particularly Sir Orfeo, where a person inside that world can experience a long period of time that goes by far more quickly in the everyday world.

The term Faërie was directly borrowed from Old French, although it had an Old English equivalent: 'faerie'. It refers to both the realms and the activities typical of fairies, whom Tolkien, in his lecture, associated with the elves of the Nordic and Germanic traditions. Tolkien generally preferred the more archaic term 'Faërie' to the modern English 'fairy', as he found its resonances to be deeper and more substantial.

For Tolkien, fantasy was the art of creating a secondary world – or the art of sub-creation.

The legends of Middle-earth, which are themselves portals to Eldamar and Valinor, provide the reader with an exploration of Faërie that reflect Tolkien's own sensibility and aesthetics. They cast light on his vision of the Elves and of a world that responds to mankind's deepest wishes, along the lines of fairy stories. Thus, the Elven legends of the Elder Days, which Tolkien called *The Silmarillion*, have the same characteristics as the Perilous Realms of Faërie. Similarly, Bilbo's adventure and the Hobbits' experiences in the Elven kingdom of Lórien during the War of the Ring strongly evoke Faërie. Tolkien also recounted a completely different type of journey into Faërie in a short story that fell beyond the remit of his Legendarium: *Smith of Wootton Major*.

Each of these stories invites the reader to experience another world and another time that reveal a joy that surpasses the limits of our ordinary world.

Faërie refers to Eldamar, the land of the Elves, situated beyond the seas, in the West.

Riddles

'A box without hinges, key, or lid,
Yet golden treasure inside is hid.' (The Hobbit, Ch. 5).

Although Bilbo Baggins was diving into the unknown when he left the tranquillity of the Shire to accompany Thorin and Company, he himself was a mystery to many of the creatures who crossed his path. Tolkien symbolized the uncertainties aroused by these confrontations with the unknown by shrouding them with riddles. Bilbo's riddling encounters with his troll captors and, later on, Smaug the Dragon serve to frame the astonishing episode of the duel of riddles between Bilbo and Gollum. The meeting with the three trolls – the very first of Bilbo's adventures – was notable for a riddle that was as surprising as it was involuntary. When asked by the trolls who have taken him captive whether there were any other creatures like him thereabouts, Bilbo replied, 'Yes, lots' and then 'No, none at all, not one.' This turnaround could be explained by Bilbo's desire to avoid betraying his companions, but the trolls took his words literally and successfully solved it when they captured the various Dwarves that had come

to Bilbo's rescue: there was no other Hobbit, but there were plenty of dwarves! The lessons to be drawn from this episode encourage caution. Not only do riddles reveal more than their creator could imagine, they are also dangerous: if Bilbo had introduced himself straightforwardly, he would probably have been freed… and his companions would not have found themselves at the mercy of the trolls! Tolkien set up a symmetry with this involuntary riddle in Bilbo's later meeting with Smaug. By then, he was a seasoned adventurer and understood that his sole chance of survival was to maintain the Dragon's attention in order to avoid being gobbled up on the spot. Thus, he deliberately introduced himself in the form of riddles that dramatized the most glorious episodes of his adventure.

For all Bilbo's cunning, however, his riddles gave more away to the Dragon than he thought, as they led Smaug to guess that the inhabitants of Lake-town had come to the assistance of the Dwarves during their

expedition. Smaug subsequently resolved to lay waste to Lake-town.

The dual nature of riddles became most evident, however, on the crossing of the Misty Mountains. Bilbo was separated from his friends in the Goblins' caves, in the heart of the mountains, when he came across

Bilbo's riddling encounters with his troll captors and, later on, Smaug the Dragon serve to frame the astonishing episode of the duel of riddles between Bilbo and Gollum.

Gollum, a strange creature who had lived in these subterranean depths for hundreds of years. This time, the initial introductions were uneventful, with Bilbo declining to give his name or answer questions about himself. The two only came to really know each other over the course of a memorable duel of riddles in which the stakes were nothing less than Bilbo's survival: if he won, Gollum would show him the exit; if he lost, Gollum would eat him. The dangers inherent in the riddle are thus thrust into the foreground.

This long exchange of riddles also provides the reader with an opportunity to learn more about these two characters. Riddle-games were commonplace among the Hobbits, in keeping with a social life that was rural and festive, revolving around traditional get-togethers (story-telling, singsongs, riddling

contests) that would still be recognizable to a mid-20th-century reader. As for Gollum, this duel allowed him to escape being categorized as an outright evil monster. Over the course of the contest, this sad character finds himself obliged to evoke the time in which he was less lonely, wicked and devious. Above all, this episode tells us about the customs of his people and their astonishing similarities with Hobbit society: a shared practice of riddling duels (equally codified, or indeed sacred), a comparable way of thinking and the construction of underground homes all represent connections between the two peoples, as Gandalf would observe later on when he wondered about Gollum's origins.

Tolkien dug deep into his medieval Germanic sources to dream up this duel, although the ninety-six riddles in the *Exeter Book*, the most important of all the Old English manuscripts, are also worthy of mention. The riddles in this medieval compendium often concern an animal, a familiar object, nature or natural phenomena, along the same lines of those exchanged between Bilbo and Gollum during their confrontation. Furthermore, the contest in another Old English text, *The Second Dialogue of Solomon and Saturn*, offers up a riddle reminiscent of one of Gollum's, while another is close to one of the riddles posed by Gestumblindi (the god Odin in disguise) to King Heidrek in the *Saga of Hervör and Heiðrekr*. There is also a striking resemblance between Bilbo's encounter with

Gollum and the *Vafþrúðnismál* ('Sayings of Vafthrúdnir'), a story in the *Poetic Edda* that also has a scene with a riddling duel involving Odin. Both these confrontations start after an appraisal of the opponent's courage. Furthermore, the stakes are the same (life or death) and victory is stolen by means of a fake riddle, a question without a conundrum. Riddling duels were thus an integral part of the imaginary world of Scandinavia, but Tolkien's riddles drew on a wide variety of other medieval sources as well.

Scandinavian sagas

'Fathoms thirty fell the fearful cliff
whence the dragon bowed him drinking thirsty.'
(The Legend of Sigurd and Gudrún, 'Regin').

The sagas are stories in Old Norse prose, mainly written down in Iceland between the 12th and 15th centuries. The word 'saga' comes from the verb *segja*, ('to recount'). They are often interspersed with passages in verse that purport to be direct accounts by the story's protagonists or witnesses to the events described therein. The sagas generally relate the actions of an individual or family of note, and they invariably begin with a list of the main characters' ancestors and significant facts about their lives. They also often conclude with references to these characters' most illustrious descendants, thereby rooting them in Scandinavian history.

There are five main types of sagas. The oldest are the royal sagas (*Konungasögur*), which revolve around Scandinavian kings. The best known of these is the *Heimskringla*, written by Snorri Sturluson, the compiler of the *Prose Edda*, which tells of the first kings of Norway up to the reign of Magnus Erlingsson. The Sagas of Icelanders (*Íslendingasögur*) focus on the first generations of the colonizers of Iceland, from the 9th to the 11th century, whose heroes were renowned for their bravery and political astuteness, as well as their Viking expeditions. *The Saga of Eiríkr the Red* and the *Saga of Burnt Njáll* are two celebrated examples of this category. The Contemporary Sagas (*Samtíðarsögur*) describe events that took place in their authors' own lifetime, and they include the Sagas of the Bishops of Iceland, written after the island's conversion to Christianity at the start of the 11th century. The most famous Contemporary Saga is the *Sturlunga Saga*, which recounts the bloody power struggles between the island's various chiefs that led to its annexation by Norway. The Legendary Sagas (*Fornaldarsögur*) describe the exploits of heroes from ancient times, while also drawing heavily on mythological elements and fantastic beasts. Their stories mainly unfold in Scandinavia or the part of Russia that was colonized by the Varangians. The

most well known of these stories is the *Völsunga Saga*, which culminates in the life of Sigurd, the slayer of the dragon Fáfnir. Finally, there were also Chivalric Sagas (*Riddarasögur*), which were adaptations of *chansons de geste* and stories about the Round Table. Courtly love, notable by its absence in the other sagas, takes on an important role here.

Tolkien became fascinated by the Scandinavian sagas at an early age, initially through translations by William Morris, particularly his Story of the *Volsungs and Niblungs*. Tolkien used to read extracts from this book to his friends Rob Gilson, Geoffrey Bache Smith and Christopher Wiseman. Subsequent examination of the original texts gave Tolkien the opportunity to learn the ancient Scandinavian language Old Norse. After becoming a lecturer, Tolkien founded the Viking Club with a colleague at Leeds University, E.V. Gordon. This club was open to both professors and students, who would meet up to drink beer, sing and read the sagas. After his appointment as Professor of Anglo-Saxon at Oxford University, Tolkien created another club, the Coalbiters (after a description of men in the sagas who stayed by a hearth throughout the day). This time, membership was confined to teaching staff, and its purpose was to read the Icelandic sagas together in their original versions.

Tolkien's academic work often led him to compare the texts of the Icelandic sagas with those of their Anglo-Saxon equivalents, but he also went a stage further. When his literary and linguistic research met a dead end, he trusted in his own imagination to unify and reorganize the material in the Eddas and the Legendary Sagas that told the story of Sigurd, the slayer of the dragon Fáfnir. Thus, in the 1930s, he wrote two long alliterative poems about the story of the Völsung family, from which Sigurd was descended, and the subsequent conflicts between the Goths and the Huns, in which Gudrún, Sigurd's widow, was involved. These poems, accompanied by other texts, are now available in the collection entitled *The Legend of Sigurd and Gudrún*. Furthermore, Tolkien integrated characters and events from the sagas into the stories that would make up his Legendarium. For example, Túrin Turambar and Mîm the petty-dwarf were largely inspired by Sigurd and Fáfnir's brother (and Sigurd's surrogate father), the dwarf Regin, in the *Thidrekssaga*. Some elements reappear in different contexts, so that the scene in which the sword Gram is reforged by Regin echoes both Túrin's reforging of the sword Anglachel (which he renamed Gurthang) and the reconstruction by Rivendell's Dwarf blacksmiths of the sword Narsil (subsequently renamed Andúril) in *The Lord of the Rings*. Other passages in the latter book draw inspiration from the sagas: for example, the Barrow-wights evoke the Icelandic *draugar* who haunted burial mounds and sometimes guarded treasure contained within them, as in the case of the *draugr* Kárr the Old in the *Saga of Grettir*.

The Hobbit is similarly permeated with Scandinavian influences. The very names of Gandalf and most of the Dwarves of Thorin and Company hark directly back to the Eddas, while trolls frequently crop up in the Legendary Sagas as the worst of all the monsters, in hideously deformed human bodies. Heroes have to draw on both ingenuity and courage to defeat them, as in the case of Gestr, who overcame Kolbjörn and his giant guests in the *Saga of Bárðr*. Beorn, in his turn, was directly inspired by the hero of the *Saga of Hrólf Kraki*, in terms of his temperament and his powers. Both have the ability to turn into bears, which makes them even more fearsome in a combat situation. These powers of metamorphosis are often portrayed in the sagas, where they are described by the adjective *hamrammr*.

The fourth riddle that Gollum asks Bilbo Baggins is adapted from the riddling contest between King Heidrek and Odin, in the guise of Gestumblindi, in the Saga of Hervör and King Heiðrekr. The contest between Gollum and Bilbo also ends in the same way as its legendary model, with a question that has an answer known only by the questioner. Gollum, like Heidrek, forces his wily opponent to flee, but does not succeed in killing him. Finally, the scene in which Bilbo is confronted by Smaug features an element taken from the *Völsunga Saga*. Like Sigurd in the face of the dragon Fáfnir, Bilbo avoids telling Smaug his real name and answers his questions with riddles. The narrator of *The Hobbit* comments that it is wise not to give away one's true identity to a dragon. Sigurd takes the same approach and thus prevents the dying Fáfnir from putting a curse on him or his family.

So, the Scandinavian sagas exerted a considerable influence on Tolkien's work. He himself went as far as referring to *The Hobbit* as the *Saga of the Three Jewels and the Rings of Power*, and his friend C.S. Lewis also used the term to describe the closing chapters of Bilbo's adventures.

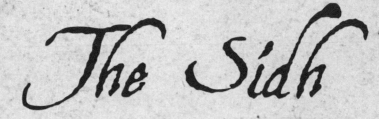

The Sídh

'The king's cave was his palace, and the strong place of his treasure, and the fortress of his people against their enemies.'
(The Hobbit, Ch. 8).

The Síd, or Sídh in modern Gaelic, denotes the Otherworld. The primary meaning of the word is 'peace', but it has a secondary meaning of 'mound, hillock' (as found in countless toponyms) that is related to the Irish concept of the Great Beyond and the legends of the Tuatha Dé Danann. The Sídh is situated beyond the sea, but any body of water (such as a lake or river) can provide access to it. Thus, to reach the Otherworld, it is necessary to cross the ocean or penetrate the depths of a lake or the source of a river. As for the Tuatha Dé Danann, they were a mythical Irish fairy people who took refuge underground when they were defeated by the Gaels. The Sídh can therefore be found under burial mounds, tumuli, and other extrusions, thus corresponding to the sense of 'hillock'. It was a wondrous land which human beings were incapable of entering on their own. Another feature of the Sídh is its existence outside time: any mortal who manages to venture into the Otherworld will discover, to their cost, that time passes far more slowly there than in the world of mortals, and that if they return to that world, years or even centuries will have gone by in their absence.

Even though the Elves in *The Silmarillion* are closer to the Tuatha Dé Danann than those in *The Hobbit*, there is no doubt that the latter were inspired by Irish fairy creatures, particularly as regards their habitat. The first Elven dwelling that Bilbo Baggins and his companions came across was Rivendell, where Elrond the Half-elf lived in the Last Homely House West of the Mountains. When Thorin and company approached Rivendell, there was no indication of its whereabouts, and Gandalf had to use all his guile to find the way.

Rivendell was hidden at the bottom of a craggy valley beyond a stream. Once they had settled in under Elrond's roof, the travellers received food and medical care, their

The Síd, or Sídh in modern Gaelic, denotes the Otherworld. The primary meaning of the word is 'peace', but it has a secondary meaning of 'mound, hillock' (as found in countless toponyms) that is related to the Irish concept of the Great Beyond.

clothes were mended and their spirits were raised by the telling of stories and legends. However, the time spent in Rivendell is given short shrift in the story because, as the narrator explains, there is not much to tell about happy times: the Company stayed for at least two weeks with Elrond but the chapter about that is less than ten pages long – whereas the six weeks between the start of their adventure and their arrival in Rivendell fill more than fifty pages.

The second fairy dwelling described in *The Hobbit* was that of Thranduil in Mirkwood. After vainly trying to participate in the Elves' feast in the forest and then escaping from the Spiders (thanks to Bilbo), the Dwarves were captured by the Elves and taken to Thranduil's palace. They walked through the forest, crossed an enchanted river via a bridge and finally came to the gates of an enormous grotto in the side of a hill shrouded in vegetation. Although Thranduil and his subjects lived

underground, the narrator stresses that this settlement bore no resemblance to the goblins' caves, which were smaller and shallower, and with unhealthier air to boot. This underground palace was difficult to penetrate as it was protected by magic gates, and even though the One Ring enabled Bilbo to escape captivity, he soon realized that leaving the confines of the palace was a difficult and dangerous undertaking as he would have to sneak behind the Elves and risk giving himself away. However, Bilbo was no longer suffering from the pangs of hunger that had previously driven him to pilfer food wherever he could. The Dwarves were also being fed in their imprisonment, which was a welcome change to the days prior to their capture. This is not to say that Bilbo was having a whale of a time, but it is worth noting that the 'week or two' between the capture of the Dwarves and Bilbo's discovery of Thorin occupy a mere two pages. Once again, there is a marked contrast between the time period of a particular episode and the number of words devoted to it. The relevant chapter, the ninth, is punctuated by vague indications of time but it is never entirely clear how long the Dwarves and Bilbo stayed with the Elves – and, moreover, most of the chapter is devoted to their escape, which took place in a single night.

Both Rivendell and Thranduil's palace display several characteristics of the Irish Sídh. They are set beside a river, hidden in plain sight, and they offer food and rest, even in

unwelcoming circumstances. Time seems to pass at a slower pace than on the outside. So, even in *The Hobbit*, which sometimes strays from the Legendarium of Middle-earth in terms of both form and content, Tolkien firmly placed his elves in the lineage of the Irish Tuatha Dé Danann. He later developed these features of the Sídh still further in *The Lord of the Rings*, where the feeling of time being distorted during the Fellowship of the Ring's stay in Lórien gave rise to a discussion of moon phases.

Sir Orfeo

"Sir Orfeo was a king of old,
in England lordship high did hold;
valour he had and hardihood,
a courteous king whose gifts were good."
(Sir Gawain and the Green Knight, Pearl and Sir Orfeo, Ch. 3).

Sir Orfeo is an English poem from the late 13th century that integrates Greek and Irish influences in a verse form very popular in Brittany at that time: the lay. The poem purports to be a retelling of the Orpheus myth but its story displays undeniable similarities with that of *The Wooing of Etain*, a text from the Irish Mythological Cycle. Although *Sir Orfeo* borrowed the names of both the Greek hero and his wife Eurydice – spelt Heurodis here, as well as her captivity in the underworld, there are also many elements of the Irish tale, such as Heurodis's capture by the Fairy King and Orfeo's ruse of using a solemn promise to rescue her. Finally, the poem evokes the tradition of the Breton lay, a combination of romance and fantasy that had been made famous by the *Lays of Marie de France*.

In this poem, Sir Orfeo was the King of England and a friend to musicians and harpists (he himself was a harpist beyond compare). His wife was the beautiful Heurodis, who had a vision of the King of the Elves while asleep under a tree. He told her that he was going to take her with him because he wanted her as his queen. Despite the protection of Orfeo and his soldiers, Heurodis disappeared. The grief-stricken Orfeo appointed a steward to take charge of the kingdom and then departed from the court, leaving everything behind except his harp. For a whole ten years, he wandered in the woods, occasionally spotting the Fairy King and his entourage but never managing to catch up with them. One day, he came across a group of women hunting with sparrowhawks and he saw his wife among them. He followed them and introduced

himself as a minstrel in the Fairy King's castle. The king initially expressed his annoyance at this intrusion but he was eventually so won over by the stranger's musical artistry that he promised Orfeo a reward of his own choice. Orfeo asked for Heurodis, and as the King of the Elves was bound by his promise, he allowed her to leave. On his return to his own kingdom, Orfeo tested the loyalty of his steward by hiding his identity and declaring that he had found the king's harp next to a corpse.

The poem purports to be a retelling of the Orpheus myth but its story displays undeniable similarities with that of The Wooing of Etain, a text from the Irish Mythological Cycle.

Seeing the steward's distress on hearing this news, Orfeo revealed himself and order was fully restored.

In any reckoning of the works that could have influenced Tolkien, *Sir Orfeo* is not the first to spring to mind, as it is a medieval Celtic poem and Tolkien is more readily associated with Germanic literature, particularly *Beowulf*. However, he published a critical edition of *Sir Orfeo* in 1944 at his own expense, and he also translated it into modern English. It therefore seems perfectly natural to find images derived from *Sir Orfeo* in *The Hobbit*, particularly the first appearance of the Elves in Mirkwood: in the middle of attempting to cross a river, Bilbo and his companions vainly tried to kill a black stag that was running towards them. They then heard the distant sounds of hunting horns and dogs, before crossing the path of a doe and her fawns.

There is no mention of a white doe in *Sir Orfeo*, but it was a common theme in Celtic literature. The colour white was associated with the fairy world, particularly in the *Mabinogion*, a collection of medieval Welsh stories. In the story *Pwyll, Prince of Dyfed*, it is not the doe hunted by Arawn that is white but rather the Lord of Annwvyn's pack of hounds, which are white with scarlet ears, thereby indicating the latter's origins in the Otherworld. Furthermore, the hunting of a white doe as a prelude to an encounter with fairies appears in several stories in the *Matter of Britain*, such as *Erec and Enide* and *Perceval, the Story of the Grail* by Chrétien de Troyes and several of Marie de France's lays. Thorin and Company only heard the hunt from a distance in the forest and did not take part, and this is highly reminiscent of a scene in which Orfeo saw the Fairy King and his entourage from afar without succeeding in joining them. Similarly, just like the Dwarves with the Elves, Orfeo saw the fairies several times but was unable to reach them. The influence of *Sir Orfeo* on *The Hobbit* is not confined to images of this type, however. There is one crucial difference between *Sir Orfeo* and the *Lays of Marie de France*: in all her stories, Marie presents the Otherworld as benevolent, even blessed. In contrast, the

Fairy King in *Sir Orfeo* is cruel and arbitrary, capable of stealing Heurodis from her husband on a whim, and his court is a terrifying place full of corpses. So the Otherworld takes on the precise meaning of the world of the dead. The Fairy King cannot be trusted to keep his word, and Orfeo has to admonish him to respect his promise of a reward for the music – even if the reward chosen involves Heurodis. Of course, Thranduil's court is not the same as the Otherworld in Sir Orfeo, but, of all the fairy beings encountered by Bilbo Baggins on his adventures, Thranduil is the least likeable, and the reader can never be sure whether he is friend or foe.

Tolkien had numerous references for fairies at his disposal, from the Tuatha Dé Danann of Irish mythology to the flower fairies of C.M. Barker, from the fairies of Shakespeare to the creatures of medieval folklore. While the Elves of Rivendell may recall the cheeky fairies of *A Midsummer Night's Dream*, Elrond is closer to the Tuatha Dé Danann and Thranduil is an avatar of the Fairy King, a powerful lord whose goodwill is questionable and whose decisions are sometimes arbitrary.

Songs

'And suddenly first one and then another began to sing
as they played, deep-throated singing of the dwarves
in the deep places of their ancient homes' (The Hobbit, Ch. 1).

Almost all the chapters of *The Hobbit* include lyrics from one or more songs, as well as references to other songs and pieces of music. Everybody seemed to sing in Middle-earth: the Dwarves of Thorin and Company; the Hobbit Bilbo Baggins; The Elves of Rivendell and Mirkwood; The Men of Lake-town; even the Goblins of the Misty Mountains... Music was highly valued, as evident from the instruments that the Dwarves led by Thorin Oakenshield took with them when they invited themselves for tea in Bilbo's house (even though they were about to set off on a long and dangerous expedition). There were violins, flutes, clarinets, a drum, as well as large viols and a harp. And when they recovered the Dragon Smaug's treasure, Fili and Kili almost immediately picked up harps and filled the cave with melodies.

Tolkien conceived his sub-creation as a world in which music and singing played a central role. In his creation story, the Ainulindalë,

recorded in *The Silmarillion*, Ilúvatar was the god who created the world – and this creation was materialized through the singing of the Ainur, which evoked musical instruments. Thus, singing in Eä, the physical world, was a means to connect with this primordial energy. Music was woven into the very soul of the world and acted as its driving force. Singing became a bulwark against despair and left open a potential eucatastrophe. This scenario recurs constantly in the Legendarium: when all seems lost, the hero lets loose with song, in defiance of all fear and gloom, and inexplicably, a new and hitherto unimaginable course of action opens up for him. Music and song in Middle-earth are evidence of the process of fragmentation that runs through Tolkien's entire work; they may all hark back to the same creation story, but they manifest themselves in various forms, including the most banal. Not all songs have the same value, therefore. They range from the playful ditty of the Dwarves threatening to

break the plates of the panic-stricken Hobbit to the solemn chant that marked the return of the King under the Mountain. Songs also served a dramatic purpose: *The Hobbit* was aimed at children and so it was important not to rack up the tension too much. Tolkien used various stylistic devices to slow down the action, including songs and the direct intervention of the narrator (often with humorous touches). The incorporation of song lyrics served to dedramatize situations that might otherwise have been too frightening. The Goblins' songs, as well as those of Bilbo in his confrontation with the Spiders in Mirkwood, are perfect examples of this strategy, as in both cases they lighten the tone in an extremely dangerous situation. The onomatopoeia and heavy dialect of the Goblins' utterances make them seem somewhat ridiculous, and the maliciousness of the Spiders is similarly softened by the disparaging humour with which Bilbo addresses them.

Songs also enabled Tolkien to impress on his readers the cultural richness of Middle-earth. The songs that he introduced into the story sometimes alluded to events that were not explicitly recounted. When Thorin and Company arrived in Lake-town, the local Men launched into an ancient song in honour of the King under the Mountain – which makes us realize that the Dwarves' kingdom was sufficiently important for neighbouring Men to know and remember songs about it several generations later. Anything that was put into song was worth retaining, and singing acted as a vector of memory for the societies of Elves, Dwarves and Men alike. It provided a direct route to their cultural heritage. When the Dwarves sang before the Battle of the Five Armies, Bilbo noticed that their music was not the same as that of the Elves.

The cosmogonic dimension of music and song is less marked in *The Hobbit* than in other texts from the Legendarium that were written at the same time. This is partly due to the variations that appeared in Tolkien's depiction of Middle-earth as he developed the story. In *The Lord of the Rings*, he again used singing in a number of ways, as in the case of Tom Bombadil's song, which was light-hearted in a moment of danger but, when shrouded in magic, served to loosen the grip of Old Man Willow.

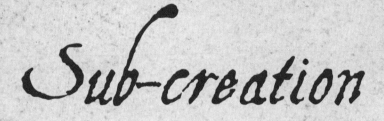

Sub-creation

'We may make the rare and terrible blue moon to shine; or we may make woods to spring with silver leaves and rams to wear fleeces of gold, and put hot fire into the belly of the cold worm. But in such "fantasy", as it is called, new form is made; Faerie begins; Man becomes a sub-creator.'

(The Monsters and the Critics and Other Essays, p. 154).

Middle-earth, the setting for the story of *The Hobbit*, is what Tolkien called a 'sub-creation'. In his essay *On Fairy-Stories*, he explained his concept of secondary creation. Man is a creature of God who can create in his own right, but his creations will always be secondary to the primary creation of God. An artist's sub-creation therefore stands within the context of divine creation, participating in and adding to it, albeit on a very modest scale. The hierarchy of the initial creation and sub-creation – of the primary (real) world and the secondary (imagined) world – is immutable, as the former provides the inspiration for the latter. Accordingly, Tolkien's main focus in his sub-creation was the achievement of the reality that was required to make the secondary world convincing,

despite the presence of fantastic elements and bizarre creatures.

Tolkien explained that such creatures would be implausible in our primary world, but could be perfectly credible in a secondary one, providing they were appropriately conceived and realized. It is therefore possible to answer the perennial children's question 'Is it true?' by replying: 'What [it] relates is "true": it accords with the laws of that world.' (*The Monsters and the Critics*, p. 192) And it is true in that world because, like the primary world, it respects its own laws; providing its constituent parts adhere to those laws, then plausibility – and the essential feeling of reality – can be sustained.

Sub-creation is therefore an art that has to find a subtle balance between the reality of

the primary world in which we live and the secondary world dreamed up by an artist's imagination. And the precision with which Tolkien constructed the secondary world of Middle-earth may be unequalled. He was a passionate linguist who started inventing languages at an early age, and Middle-earth and its inhabitants served to give them a setting in which they could flourish. Next came all the myths and history of a world that had developed over the Ages. The end

Middle-earth, the setting for the story of The Hobbit, is what Tolkien called a 'sub-creation'.

result was a world with its own calendar, its own gods and its own languages. It is the delicate balance between distance from our own world and familiar references that make the secondary world of Middle-earth – where the trusty oak grows alongside the fantastic mallorn – so convincing. In short, a secondary world can accommodate even the most far-fetched notions as long as it is conceived in a manner that makes it believable. This

credibility was crucial to Tolkien's thinking, as it meant that his readers would not be obliged to fall back on a 'willing suspension of disbelief'.

If a sub-creation is successful, then readers are free to immerse themselves in a secondary world and ingenuously believe in its existence in some other place or time. This is secondary belief, which will not question the existence of elves or trolls because such creatures are not presented as fantastic in this world – they belong to it, just as the reader belongs to the primary world. If the sub-creation fails and there is no secondary belief, the reader can resort to a suspension of disbelief and make an abstraction of the parts that they find unconvincing. This requires an effort on the part of a reader, and it constitutes a roundabout way of accessing the secondary world – one that Tolkien considered the mark of an author's failure. Sub-creation therefore demands painstaking work and contemplation. And, like the road that takes us ever further onward (which Bilbo warned his nephew Frodo about), and like Niggle's painting that started as a single leaf and expanded endlessly, a sub-creation that achieves a sufficiently credible secondary world can take, as in the case of Tolkien, a whole lifetime – and more.

Victorian literature

'As for the rest of the tale it is, as the Habit suggests, derived from (previously digested) epic, mythology, and fairy-story – not, however, Victorian in authorship, as a rule to which George Macdonald is the chief exception.' (Letters, no. 25).

The term 'Victorian' is applied to British literature that saw the light of day during the reign of Queen Victoria (1837–1901). A great number of famous novels were written in this period, in various literary genres, including many outstanding explorations of the fantastic. The fairy story may have been the dominant form in this field, but full-length novels also delved into this other world, and fantasy began to emerge as a full-blown genre in its own right.

Fairy stories were particularly close to Tolkien's heart. He devoted his Andrew Lang Lecture to this subject and developed his ideas still further in the essay *On Fairy Stories*. Tolkien, who was born in 1892, grew up with these stories, most particularly Andrew Lang's collections of Fairy Books, published between 1889 and 1910. Moreover, the tales of the Brothers Grimm had been translated into English for the first time in 1823 and they had given rise to a long lineage of fairy stories. The top authors in this field included not only Andrew Lang but also George MacDonald and William Morris – and all three had a strong impact on the young Tolkien.

Andrew Lang (1844–1912) was, like the Brothers Grimm, a compiler of stories, but he also wrote his own. Like so many English children, Tolkien was nurtured by these stories, as evident in his later work, which

features references to tales collected by Lang. *Snow-White and Rose-Red* had already been retold by the Brothers Grimm before it was included by Andrew Lang in *The Red Fairy Book* of 1890. In this story, a prince was put under a spell and imprisoned in the form of a bear. This transformation recurs in Beorn, the skin-changer. Even more strikingly, there are two cases of rings that bestow invisibility in Lang's collection: in *The Enchanted Ring* and *The Dragon of the North*. Tolkien also acknowledged his debt to previous depictions of goblins, such as those of George MacDonald (1824–1905) in *The Princess and the Goblin* and its sequel *The Princess and Curdie*, although Tolkien did not share his predecessor's predilection for horror. In fact, Tolkien's vision of goblins changed over time, and in later years he disowned his poem *Goblin Feet*, which was published in 1917. Similarly, his enthusiasm for MacDonald's stories waned with the passing of time, and when he was asked to write an introduction to the latter's story *The Golden Key*, he eventually came up with a story of his own, *Smith of Wootton Major*. Nevertheless, MacDonald's influence on Tolkien's work is undeniable, particularly in *The Hobbit*, which was written well before *The Lord of the Rings*. For example, the character of Galion, King Thranduil's butler, who gets

drunk with the captain of the guards, brings to mind a butler in MacDonald's work who helps himself to wine from a king's cellar.

As for William Morris (1834–1896), he described a forest in his novel *A Tale of the House of the Wolfings* that was called Mirkwood (the forest originally called Greenwood the Great, which was crossed by Thorin and Company in *The Hobbit*)[1]. Morris also referred at one point to the expression 'roots of the mountain' which crops up in one of Gollum's riddles. More generally, however, it was Morris's literary style that most inspired Tolkien. Both writers described a world with a medieval atmosphere in enormous detail. In fact, Morris was the first to set a story in an entirely invented world, a world of fantasy.

Tolkien, like Morris before him, extolled a simple life in a rural environment devoid of any type of industry. This aspect of the Shire is developed more explicitly in *The Lord of the Rings* than in *The Hobbit*, for in the later work the land of the Hobbits has to confront the intrusion of the outside world in the form of Saruman, who symbolizes the dangers of industry. This theme of encroachment on an idyllic setting had already been touched upon, however, in Tolkien's first novel, through Bilbo's travels in the Wilderland. It is also possible to see echoes of the work of John Ruskin (1819–1900), the art critic and champion of the Pre-Raphaelites, whose *King of the Golden River* put nature to the fore.

The contrast between a hero's home ground where everything is safe and familiar and the

---

1 - From Tolkien's reply to a letter written under a pseudonym that appeared in The Observer *on 16 January 1938, containing questions about the origins of Hobbits*

outside world, with all its dangers, is a classic theme of fairy stories. This transition obliges the hero to embark on a rite of passage that will ultimately increase his moral stature. Another classic trope appears in *The Hobbit*: the passage through a forest, where the hero has to confront his fears and test his courage. Mirkwood represented the final obstacle between the Company and their destination of Erebor. According to Vladimir Propp in his *Morphology of the Folktale*, a hero embarks on his journey into the unknown after being either invited or forbidden to do so, and this pattern is reflected in The Hobbit when first Gandalf and then the Dwarves recruit Bilbo for their quest.

Forests often crop up in fairy stories. They appear in several tales of the Brothers Grimm, as well as in another of Tolkien's favourites from the Victorian Era: *Puss-cat Mew* (1869) by E.H. Knatchbull-Hugessen, which recounts the adventures of Joe Brown in a scary forest.

Fairy stories were not the only influence on Tolkien's work, however. Adventure stories were also extremely popular in Victorian times and beyond, and Rudyard Kipling, the author of *The Jungle Book*, and H. Rider Haggard, the creator of Allan Quatermain, would also have been references (Tolkien specifically acknowledged his debt to Haggard). Quatermain, like Bilbo, was confronted by an unknown world in which he had to learn to survive. Furthermore, it has been said that Haggard's most emblematic novel, *She*, established the archetype for the female adversary that Tolkien would draw on for his depiction of the spider Shelob.

Wastelands

'There was little grass, and before long there was neither bush nor tree, and only broken and blackened stumps to speak of ones long vanished. They were come to the Desolation of the Dragon, and they were come at the waning of the year.'

(The Hobbit, Ch. 11).

The myth of the Wasteland seems to date back to the mythology of the Insular Celts, who attributed a kingdom's sterility to a curse on its king that could only be lifted through the intervention of a hero. This situation can be found, for example, in the Irish legend of *Echtrae Airt meic Cuinn*, which was first written down in the 14th century. It starts with the adventures of the High King of Ireland Conn Cétchathach, who married the witch Bécuma and brought infertility to the kingdom as a result. He set off to the lands of the West to find a remedy for this curse and eventually came to an island, where he saw the niece of the god/king of the Otherworld, Manannan Mac Lir. After attending a banquet, Conn went back home and banished his wife, thereby seemingly dispelling the misfortune.

Another variation on the theme of the Wasteland crops up in the Arthurian legends, in which the Fisher King, the guardian of the Grail, is rendered impotent by a groin injury. In Chrétien de Troyes's unfinished romance, *Perceval, the Story of the Grail*, this injury causes his kingdom to become barren. The Fisher King could only be cured if Perceval were to ask him about the Grail, which the knight failed to do on his first visit, as his upbringing forbade him to be so inquisitive. The story is cut off before Perceval returns to the king's castle. The anonymous author of the First Continuation to this romance tells how Gauvain (Gawain) partially puts the kingdom to rights, while the later Continuations recount the subsequent adventures of Perceval, who ends up accomplishing his healing mission.

This mystical link between a king and the natural habitat of his kingdom can also be seen in Tolkien's work. As soon as Aragorn was crowned at the end of *The Lord of the Rings*, Gondor regained its fertility and a sapling of the White Tree was discovered, marking the kingdom's rebirth. When the Hobbits returned to Bree, Gandalf informed the innkeeper Barliman Butterbur that old roads would be reopened, evil creatures would be expelled and abandoned lands would be repopulated. The previous barrenness was not directly caused by a curse but rather was the result of evil creatures capable of ravaging a country and, by their mere presence, causing even the land itself to suffer. The Brown Lands, which ran alongside the Anduin, formed one of the first deserts that the Fellowship of the Ring passed through on their journey to the South. This area had once been the Entwives' Garden, but it had been reduced by the war to arid hills devoid of all vegetation. Further south, the desert plain of Dagorlad, which extended right to the gates of Mordor, had been irretrievably disfigured and polluted by the relentless labouring of Sauron's slaves. Similarly, the rocks and pebbles of the desert around Barad-dûr, which Frodo Baggins and Samwise Gamgee had to climb to reach Mount Doom, were further signs of Sauron's malevolence.

The Dragons in Tolkien's work display the same destructive power over nature. They were almost wiped out at the end of the First Age, but they multiplied in the deserts of the North and then went on to attack the Dwarves and chase them out of the Grey Mountains. At the time of the Sack of Erebor, the enormous valley that divided the Grey Mountains into two chains to the east was called the Withered Heath and played host to countless Dragons. When Thorin and Company finally approached the Lonely Mountain, they witnessed the devastation that the Dragons had inflicted on the surrounding land, which came to be known as the Desolation of Smaug. The oldest participants in the Quest of Erebor could still remember the exuberance of these plains, but they were now barren and lifeless, with only blackened tree stumps as vestiges of their former lushness. The atmosphere was so oppressive that the members of the expedition were plunged into despair. Smaug's death dispelled this baleful degradation, however. In their eagerness to spread the news, the birds that lived on the edge of the Desolation of Smaug flew in whole flocks to the Lonely Mountain and Dale. After the Battle of the Five Armies, peace and prosperity were restored and the Dwarf peoples and the Men of Dale thrived side by side.

Sources

Characters

Azog and Bolg
The Hobbit, ch. 1, 4 and 17; *The Lord of the Rings*, app. A, III

Baggins Family
The Hobbit, ch. 1, 5 and 20; *The Lord of the Rings*, I, 1–3; VI, 3 and 8–9; apps. B and C

Balin
The Hobbit, passim; The Lord of the Rings, II, 1–2 and 4–5; app. A

Bard
The History of the Hobbit, XIII, i and XV, b; *The Annotated Hobbit*, ch. 14–18; *The Lord of the Rings*, II, 1

Beorn
The History of the Hobbit, VII, Plot Notes F, XVIII; *The Hobbit*, ch. 7 and 17; *J.R.R. Tolkien: Artist and Illustrator*, nos. 114 and 116; *Pictures by J.R.R. Tolkien*, no. 10; *The Lord of the Rings*, II, 1 and 8; app. B

Bilbo Baggins
The Hobbit, passim; The Lord of the Rings, I, 1; II, 1–2; VI, 9

Carc and Roäc
The Hobbit, ch. 15–17

Dáin II Ironfoot
The Hobbit, ch. 15–18; *The Lord of the Rings*, app. A, III

Elrond
Unfinished Tales, II, 1 and 4; IV, 3; *The Hobbit*, chs. 3 and 19; *Letters*, nos. 131, 183 and 211; *The Peoples of Middle-earth*, XII–XIII; *The Lord of the Rings*, I, 11 *and passim; The Silmarillion*, ch. 24; 'Of the Rings of Power and the Third Age'

Galadriel
Unfinished Tales, II, 4; *Letters*, nos. 142, 213 and 320; *The Lord of the Rings*, II, 6–8; *The Silmarillion, passim*

Gandalf
Unfinished Tales, IV, 2; *The Hobbit, passim; The Lord of the Rings, passim; The Silmarillion*, 'Valaquenta' and 'Of the Rings of Power and the Third Age'

Girion
The History of the Hobbit, XIV; *The Hobbit*, chs. 12 and 18; The Lord of the Rings, app. B

Gollum
The Annotated Hobbit, ch. 5; *The Lord of the Rings*, passim

Legolas
Letters, no. 211; *The Lord of the Rings*, II, 2 and 6; III, 1–2; V, 2; VI, 6; app. B

Line of Durin
The Annotated Hobbit, passim; *The Lord of the Rings*, apps. A, III and B

Necromancer
Unfinished Tales, III, 3; *Letters*, passim; *The Hobbit*, ch. 1, 7 and 19; *The Lord of the Rings*, passim; *The Silmarillion*, 'Of the Rings of Power and the Third Age'

Radagast
Unfinished Tales, IV, 2; *The History of the Hobbit*, VII, vi; *The Annotated Hobbit*, ch. 7; *The Lord of the Rings*, II, 2–3; *The Silmarillion*, 'Of the Rings of Power and the Third Age'

Saruman
Unfinished Tales, IV, 2; *The Lord of the Rings*, passim

Smaug
Unfinished Tales, III, 3; *The Hobbit*, chs. 1 and 11–14; *The Lord of the Rings*, apps. A–B

Thorin and Company
The History of the Hobbit, add. iv; *The Annotated Hobbit*, passim; *The Lord of the Rings*, apps. A, III and B

Thorin II Oakenshield
Unfinished Tales, III, 3; *The History of the Hobbit*, V; *The Annotated Hobbit*, ch. 1 and passim; *The Lord of the Rings*, II, 2; app. A

Thráin II
The Annotated Hobbit, chs. 1, 7, 10 and 15; *The Lord of the Rings*, apps. A, III and B

Thranduil
The Hobbit, ch. 3–5; *The Lord of the Rings*, II, 2–3; II, 7; app. B; *The Silmarillion*, ch. 23

Thrór
The Annotated Hobbit, chs. 1, 7, 10 and 15; *The Lord of the Rings*, apps. A, III and B

Tom, Bert and William
The Annotated Hobbit, ch. 2; *The Lord of the Rings*, I, 12.

Took Family
The Hobbit, ch. 1; *The Lord of the Rings*, Prologue, II, 2; III, 1 and 3–4; V, 1; VI, 8; apps. B and C

White Council
Unfinished Tales, II, 4; *The Annotated Hobbit*, app. A; *The Lord of the Rings*, app. B; *The Silmarillion*, 'Of the Rings of Power and the Third Age'

Peoples and creatures

Dragons
The Children of Húrin, passim; *The Shaping of Middle-earth*, III, 18; *The Hobbit*, chs. 1, 12 and 14; *The Lord of the Rings*, apps. A, III and B; *The Silmarillion*, chs. 13, 20–21 and 24

Dwarves
Unfinished Tales, III, 3; *The Annotated Hobbit*, passim; *Letters*, nos. 138 and 176; *The

Lord of the Rings, apps. A, III; B and F; *The Silmarillion*, chs. 2, 10 and 22; 'Of the Rings of Power and the Third Age'; *The War of the Jewels*, II, 13

Eagles

Unfinished Tales, I, 1; II, 1–2 and 4; *The Hobbit*, chs. 6–7 and 17–18; *Letters*, no. 210; *The Lost Road*, II, 6; *The Lord of the Rings*, I, 7 and *passim*; *The Silmarillion*, ch. 1 and *passim*; *The War of the Jewels*, I

Elves

The Hobbit, chs. 3, 8–10, 14 and *passim*; *The Book of Lost Tales*, I, 1 and *passim*; II, 3–4; *Morgoth's Ring*, III, 2; *The Silmarillion*, ch. 3 and *passim*; 'Of the Rings of Power and the Third Age'; *The War of the Jewels*, IV

Goblins / Orcs

The Annotated Hobbit, chs. 4 and 17; *Letters*, nos. 144 and 151; *The Lord of the Rings*, *passim*; *The Silmarillion*, *passim*

Hobbits

The History of the Hobbit, introduction; *The Annotated Hobbit*, *passim*; *The Lord of the Rings*, prologue and app. F; *Letters*, nos. 19, 25 and 131

Men

Unfinished Tales, II, 1–3; *The Hobbit*, chs. 2, 7 and 10; *Morgoth's Ring*, IV; *The Lord of the Rings*, I, 9; II, 2; *The Silmarillion*, chs. 12 and 17

Spiders

The Hobbit, chs. 8–9; *The Lord of the Rings*, IV, 9–10; V, 1; app. B; *The Silmarillion*, chs. 8–11, 16 and 19

Stone-giants

The Hobbit, ch. 4; *Letters*, no. 306

Trolls

The Annotated Hobbit, ch. 2; *Letters*, no. 153; *The Monsters and the Critics and Other Essays*, 'Beowulf: the Monsters and the Critics'; *The Lord of the Rings*, III, 4; apps. A, B and F; *The Silmarillion*, ch. 20

Wargs

The Hobbit, chs. 6–9; *Letters*, no. 306; *The Lord of the Rings*, II, 4; *The Silmarillion*, ch. 19

Wizards

Unfinished Tales, IV, 2; *The Hobbit*, *passim*; *The Lord of the Rings*, *passim*; *The Silmarillion*, 'Of the Rings of Power and the Third Age'

Woodmen

The Hobbit, ch. 6; *The Lord of the Rings*, I, 2; app. B

Languages and writing systems

Elvish

The Monsters and the Critics and Other Essays, 'A Secret Vice'; *The Peoples of Middle-earth*, XI–XII; *The Lost Road*, II, 5; III; *The Lord of the Rings*, app. E; *The Silmarillion*, chs. 13 and 15; *The War of the Jewels*, IV

Khuzdul

The Lord of the Rings, apps. E and F; *The Silmarillion*, ch. 4

Old Norse

The Hobbit, passim; The Lord of the Rings, apps. E and F

Runes

The Annotated Hobbit, chs. 1, 3 and 11; app. B; *Letters,* nos. 15, 112 and 118; *The Lord of the Rings,* app. E

Tengwar

The Annotated Hobbit, ch. 12; *J.R.R. Tolkien: Artist and Illustrator,* ill. no. 133; *Pictures* by J.R.R. Tolkien, no. 17; *The Lord of the Rings,* app. E

Objects and constructions

Arkenstone

The History of the Hobbit, XIV, ii; *The Hobbit,* ch. 12–13 and 15–18; *The Lord of the Rings,* app. A, III

Glamdring and Orcrist

The Hobbit, chs. 2–4, 6, 10 and 18; *The Lord of the Rings,* II, 3–5; III, 6; VI, 7

Mithril

The Hobbit, chs. 3 and 13; *The Lord of the Rings,* II, 4–6; app. A, III

One Ring

The Hobbit, ch. 5; *The Lord of the Rings, passim; The Silmarillion,* 'Of the Rings of Power and the Third Age'

Pipes and pipe-weed

Unfinished Tales, III, 4; *The Annotated Hobbit, passim; The Lord of the Rings,* III, 8–9; V, 8

The Red Book of Westmarch

The Adventures of Tom Bombadil, preface; *The Hobbit,* ch. 19; *The Lord of the Rings, passim*

Smials

The Hobbit, ch. 1; *The Lord of the Rings,* prologue, I, 2; III, 8; app. F

Sting

The Hobbit, chs. 2, 5, 8, 10 and 19; *The Lord of the Rings,* prologue; II, 3–6 and 9–10; IV, 1, 4 and 9–10; VI, 1–4 and 6

Thrór's Map

Unfinished Tales, III, 3; *The Annotated Hobbit,* ch. 1, app. A

Places

Anduin

Unfinished Tales, II, 4 and app. A, III, 1; *The Hobbit,* ch. 7; *The Lord of the Rings,* I, 6 and 8–9 and *passim; The Silmarillion,* ch. 3

Arnor

Unfinished Tales, III, 1 and 4; IV, 3; *The Lord of the Rings,* prologue, II, 2; III, 11; V, 9 and *passim,* app. A, III; *The Silmarillion,* 'Akallabêth' and 'Of the Rings of Power and the Third Age'

Bag End

The Hobbit, chs. 1, 2 and 19; *The Lord of the Rings,* prologue, I, 1 and 3; VI, 8 and 9

Notable events

The Ages of Middle-earth
Letters, nos. 131, 211 and 256; *Morgoth's Ring*, II; *The Lord of the Rings*, app. B; *The War of the Jewels*, I and III, 5

Battle of the Five Armies
The Annotated Hobbit, chs. 17–18

Quest of Erebor
Unfinished Tales, III, 3; *The Annotated Hobbit*, app. A; *The Lord of the Rings*, app. A, III

Sack of Doriath
The Children of Húrin, passim; *The Hobbit*, chs. 8–10 and 14–18; *The Book of Lost Tales*, II, 1–2 and 4; *The Silmarillion*, chs. 4, 10, 13 and 15–22

Sack of Erebor
The Hobbit, ch. 1; *The Lord of the Rings*, apps. A and B

War of the Ring
The Hobbit, passim; *The Lord of the Rings*, passim

War of the Dwarves and the Orcs
The Lord of the Rings, app. A, III

Sources of inspiration

Beowulf
The Hobbit, chs. 5 and 12–13; *Letters*, nos. 25 and 183; *The Monsters and the Critics and Other Essays*, 'Beowulf: the Monsters and the Critics'

Berserkers
The History of the Hobbit, VII; *The Hobbit*, chs. 7 and 18; *Letters*, no. 144; *The Monsters and the Critics and Other Essays*, 'On Translating Beowulf'; *The Lord of the Rings*, IV, 9–10; V, 5–6

Eddas
The Children of Húrin, passim; *The Annotated Hobbit*, ch. 1; app. A; *The Legend of Sigurd and Gudrún*, passim; *Letters* nos. 295 and 297; *The Peoples of Middle-earth*, II, 11; *The Lord of the Rings*, IV, 5; *The Silmarillion*, ch. 21

Eucatastrophe
The Hobbit, ch. 17; *Letters*, no. 89; *The Monsters and the Critics and Other Essays*, 'On Fairy-Stories'

Faërie
The Hobbit, chs. 3 and 8; *The Monsters and the Critics and Other Essays*, 'On Fairy-Stories'; *The Lord of the Rings*, II, 6

Riddles
The Hobbit, ch. 5; *The Lord of the Rings*, I, 2

Scandinavian Sagas
The History of the Hobbit, I (b); *The Annotated Hobbit*, introduction, chs. 5, 7, 12 and 15; *The Legend of Sigurd and Gudrún*, passim; *Letters*, nos. 125, 126, 199 and 281; *The Lord of the Rings: A Reader's Companion*, I, 7, 10; *The Monsters and the Critics and Other Essays*, 'Beowulf: the Monsters and the Critics' and 'On Fairy-Stories'

Selective bibliography

Works by J.R.R. Tolkien

The Adventures of Tom Bombadil and Other Verses from the Red Book, ed. Christina Scull and Wayne G. Gammon, London, HarperCollins, 2011

The Lord of the Rings: The Fellowship of the Ring, London, HarperCollins 2011

The Lord of the Rings: The Two Towers, London, HarperCollins 2011

The Lord of the Rings: The Return of the King, London, HarperCollins 2011

Beowulf and the Critics, ed. Michael D.C. Drout, Tempe, Arizona, Arizona Center for Medieval and Renaissance Studies 2011 (2nd edition)

The Book of Lost Tales, part one (History of Middle-earth vol. 1), ed. Christopher Tolkien, London, George Allen & Unwin 1983

The Hobbit, London, George Allen & Unwin 1978 (4th edition)

The Lays of Beleriand (History of Middle-earth volume 3), ed. Christopher Tolkien, London, George Allen & Unwin 1985

The Legend of Sigurd and Gudrún, ed. Christopher Tolkien, London, HarperCollins, 2009

The Letters of J.R.R. Tolkien, ed. Humphrey Carpenter and Christopher Tolkien, London, HarperCollins 1981

The Lost Road (History of Middle-earth volume 5), ed. Christopher Tolkien, London, Unwin Hyman 1987

The Monsters and the Critics and Other Essays, London, George Allen & Unwin, 1984

Morgoth's Ring (History of Middle-earth volume 10), ed. Christopher Tolkien, George Allen & Unwin 1993

The Peoples of Middle-earth (History of Middle-earth vol. 12), ed. Christopher Tolkien, London, HarperCollins 1996

The Return of the Shadow, (History of Middle-earth vol. 6), ed. Christopher Tolkien, London, Unwin Hyman 1988

Roverandom, ed. Christina Scull and Wayne G. Hammond, London, HarperCollins 1998

Sauron Defeated (History of Middle-earth vol. 9), ed. Christopher Tolkien, London, HarperCollins 1992

The Shaping of Middle-earth (History of Middle-earth vol. 4), ed. Christopher Tolkien, London, Unwin Hyman 1986

The Silmarillion, London, George Allen & Unwin, London, 1977

Sir Gawain and the Green Knight, Pearl and Sir Orfeo, ed. Christopher Tolkien, London, HarperCollins 2006

Smith of Wootton Major, ed. Verlyn Flieger, London, HarperCollins 2015

Tales from the Perilous Realm, London, HarperCollins 2008

Tolkien on Fairy-Stories, ed. Verlyn Flieger and Douglas A. Anderson, London, HarperCollins 2014

The Treason of Isengard (History of Middle-earth vol. 7) ed. Christopher Tolkien, London, Unwind Hyman 1989

Unfinished Tales of Númenor and Middle-earth, ed. Christopher Tolkien, London, George Allen & Unwin 1980

The War of the Jewels (History of Middle-earth vol. 11), ed. Christopher Tolkien, London, HarperCollins 1994

The War of the Ring (History of Middle-earth vol. 9), ed. Christopher Tolkien, London, Unwin Hyman 1990

Other Works

Anderson, Douglas A. (ed.), *The Annotated Hobbit*, Boston, Houghton Mifflin 2002

Atherton, Mark, *There and Back Again: J.R.R. Tolkien and the Origins of the Hobbit*, London, I.B. Tauris 2012

Blackham, Robert S., *The Roots of Middle-earth*, Stroud, Tempus 2006

Bratman, David, 'In Search of the Shire", *Mallorn* no. 37, Tolkien Society 1999

Burns, Marjorie, *Perilous Realms: Celtic and Norse in Tolkien's Middle-earth*, Toronto, University of Toronto Press 2005

Carpenter, Humphrey, *J.R.R. Tolkien: A Biography*, London, George Allen & Unwin 1977

Fimi, Dimitra, *Tolkien, Race and Cultural History from Faeries to Hobbits*, Basingstoke, Palgrave Macmillan 2008

Fisher, Jason, *Tolkien and the Study of his Sources*, Jefferson, NC, McFarland 2011

Garth, John, *The Worlds of J.R.R. Tolkien: The Places that Inspired Middle-earth*, London, Frances Lincoln, 2020

Garth, John, *Tolkien and the Great War, The Threshold of Middle-earth*, London, HarperCollins 2003

Foster, Robert and Ted Nasmith, *The Complete Guide to Middle-earth: The Definitive guide to the World of J.R.R. Tolkien*, London, HarperCollins 2022

Gilliver, Peter, Jeremy Marshall and Edmund Weiner, *The Ring of Words: Tolkien and the Oxford English Dictionary*, Oxford, Oxford University Press 2006

Hammond, Wayne G and Douglas A. Anderson, *J.R.R. Tolkien: A Descriptive Bibliography*, Winchester, St Paul's Bibliographies 1993

Hammond, Wayne G., and Christina Scull, *The Art of the Hobbit*, London, HarperCollins 2013

Hammond, Wayne G., and Christina Scull, *The Art of the Lord of the Rings*, London, HarperCollins 2014

Hammond Wayne G., and Christina Scull, *J.R.R. Tolkien Artist and Illustrator*, London, HarperCollins 1995

Hammond Wayne G., and Christina Scull, *The Lord of the Ring's: A Reader's Companion*, London, HarperCollins 2014 (2nd edition)

Howe, John, *A Middle-earth Traveller: Sketches from Bag End to Mordor*, London, HarperCollins 2018

Hynes, Gerard, '"Beneath the Earth's dark keel": Tolkien and Geology' in *Tolkien Studies* vol. 9 (2012)

Larrington, Carolyn, *The Norse Myths: A Guide to the Gods and Goddesses*, London, Thames & Hudson 2017

Lee, Stuart and Elizabeth Solopova, *The Keys of Middle-earth*, Basingstoke, Palgrave Macmillan, Basingstoke 2015 (2nd edition)

Lyons, Mathew, *There and Back Again: In the Footsteps of J.R.R. Tolkien*, London, Cadogan 2004

Mellwaine, Catherine, *Tolkien: Maker of Middle-earth*, Oxford, Bodleian Publishing 2018

Morris, William, *A Tale of the House of the Wolfings and All the Kindreds of the Mark*, London, Reeves and Turner 1889

Olsen, Corey, *Exploring J.R.R. Tolkien's The Hobbit*, Boston, Houghton Mifflin 2012

Orchard, Andy, *Pride and Prodigies: Studies in the Monsters of the Beowulf Manuscript*, Toronto, University of Toronto Press 2003

Phelpstead, Carl, *Tolkien and Wales: Language, Literature and Identity*, Cardiff, University of Wales Press 2011

Ratcliff, John D., *The History of the Hobbit*, London, HarperCollins 2007

Sabo, Deborah, 'Archaeology and the Sense of History in J.R.R. Tolkien's Middle-earth", *Mythlore* vol. 21, no 1 (Fall/Winter 2007)

Scull, Christina, 'The Influence of Archaeology and History on Tolkien's World' in *Scholarship and Fantasy: Proceedings of the Tolkien Phenomenon*, ed. K.J. Battarbee, Turku, University of Turku Press 1993

Scull, Christina, and Wayne G. Hammond, *The J.R.R. Tolkien Companion and Guide: Reader's Guide*, London, HarperCollins 2017

Shippey, Tom, *The Road to Middle-earth: How J.R.R. Tolkien created a new mythology*, London, HarperCollins 2005 (expanded edition)

Simek, Rudolf, *Dictionary of Norse Mythology*, trans. Angela Hall, Cambridge, D.S. Brewer 1993

Tolkien, John and Priscilla, *The Tolkien Family Album*, Boston, Houghton Mifflin 1992

Wyke-Smith, Edward, *The Marvellous Land of Snergs*, Garden City NY, Dover Publications 2006

Wynn Fonstad, Karen, and Christopher Tolkien, *The Atlas of Tolkien's Middle-earth*, London, HarperCollins 2017

Translations of Tolkien's Works

French:

Ledoux, François (trs.), *Bilbo Le Hobbit,* Le Livre de Poche, Paris 2012

Lauzon, Daniel (trs.) *Le Hobbit*, Christian Bourgois Éditeur, Paris 2012

Lauzon, Daniel (trs.) *Le Seigneur des Anneaux*, Christian Bourgois Éditeur, Paris 2014–16

German:

Carroux, Margaret (trs.) *Der Herr der Ringe*, Stuttgart, Hobbit Presse 1969–70

Scherf, Walter (trs.), *Kleiner Hobbit under der grosse Zauberer*, Recklinghausern, Paulus Verlag 1957

Italian:

Alliata, Vicky, *Il signore degli anelli*, Rome, Astrolabio 1967

Jeronimidis, Elena, *Lo Hobbit, o la Reconquista del Tesoro*, Milan, Adelphi Edizioni 1973

Spanish:

Domènech, Luis, *El señor de los anillos*, Barcelona, Ediciones Minotauro, 1977–90

Figuerna Manuel, *El hobbit*, Barcelona, Circulo de Lectores 1984

List of authors of articles in this book

Bador, Damien: Eagles, Berserkers, Wilderland, Elrond, Rivendell, Old Norse, Runes, Scandinavian Sagas, Wasteland, Thorin II Oakenshield

Bes, Elisa: Azog and Bolg, Stone Giants

Boissay, Solveig: Bilbo Baggins, The Shire, Baggins family, Took family, Legolas, Victorian literature, Sub-creation, Tom, Bert and William

Bories, Benjamin: The One Ring, Beowulf, Carc and Roäc, Sting, Dol Guldur, Mirkwood, Glamdring

Brémont, Aurélie: Sídh, Sir Orfeo

Brice, Lucie: Lake-town, Woodmen, Gondolin, Thranduil, Wargs

Carbon, Julien: Anduin, Arnor, Bree, Erebor

Coudurier-Abaléa, Gaëlle: Eddas, Saruman

Escarbassière, Romain: War of Dwarves and Goblins, Dale, Misty Mountains

Hamon, Gwenc'hlan: White Council, Riddles, Eucatastrophe, Wizards, Necromancer

Marlair, Sébastien: Ages of Middle-earth, Faërie, Middle-earth, Hobbits

Morelle, Audrey: Bard, Goblins, Arkenstone, Radagast, Smials

Paulino, Romain: Spiders, Galadriel, Mithril

Potot, Coralie: Beorn, Songs, Bag End, Elves, Elvish, Girion, Men, Sack of Doriath, Tengwar

Stocker, Vivien: Thrór's map, Dragons, Quest of Erebor, Gandalf, Gollum, Khuzdul, Red Book of Westmarch, Sack of Erebor, Smaug, Trolls

Vigot, Dominique: Balin, Battle of the Five Armies, Dáin II Ironfoot, War of the Ring, Line of Durin, Dwarves, Pipes and pipeweed, Thorin and Company, Thráin II, Thrór

Index

Page numbers in **bold** refer to
main entries

A

Aglarond 81
Ainur 244, 302
Aiwendil *see* Radagast
Alatar 149
Alatáriel *see* Galadriel
Aletsch Glacier 140, 230
Alqualondë 115, 285
Aman 45, 285
Amdír 116
Amlaith 199
Amon Sûl 199
Amor 246
Amroth, King 46, 239
Anárion 41, 198
Ancalagon the Black 103, 104, 112
Anduin River 55, 74, 97, 110, 128,
    152, 180, 186, **196–7**, 209, 219, 222,
    227, 228, 238
Anduin Valley 115, 152
Andúril 176
Angband 116, 218
Angerthas Erebor 205
Anglachel 176
Anglo-Saxon runes 164, 165, 167
The Annals of Valinor 173
Annatar 41

Annúminas 199
Ar-Pharazôn 112, 133, 246
Arador 142
Aragorn 42, 44, 50, 51, 56, 59, 95, 97,
    113, 137, 142, 176, 185, 197, 232,
    235, 236, 248, 263–7
Aragorn II 199
Arathorn II 42
Ardgalen 218
Argeleb II, King 199, 235
Arkenstone 20, 27–8, 33, 54, 84–6,
    92, **172–3**, 180, 210, 250, 258, 259,
    268, 276
Arnor 41, 44, 128, 133, 157, 197,
    198–9, 202, 211, 218, 248
Arthedain 199, 202, 232, 235, 236
Arthurian legends 52, 176, 189,
    311–12
Arwen Undómiel 44, 45, 185, 232,
    267
Ash Mountains 219, 238
Aulë 244
Avari 115, 156
Azanulbizar 20, 240, 269
    Battle of 21, 22, 40, 83, 87, 108,
    228, 261, 269, 270
Azog 20–2, 39, 40, 62, 87, 93, 108,
    120, 228, 260–1, 268, 269, 270

B

Bag End 23, 24, 32, 79, 80, 81, 88,
    128, 163, 180, 182, 185, 187, 189,
    200–1, 234, 236, 254, 263
Baggins, Bilbo 23, 24, 25, 26, 27, 28,
    30, **32–6**, 37, 39, 40, 41, 46, 50, 53,
    54, 56, 58, 59, 66, 69, 75, 76, 78, 79,
    80–2, 84–6, 94, 95, 96, 97, 98, 99,
    102, 103, 110, 114, 117, 122, 126,
    128, 129, 133, 135, 137, 139–40,
    141–2, 145, 150, 151, 152, 162, 168,
    169, 172–3, 176, 177, 178, 179, 180,
    182, 184, 187, 188–9, 190, 200, 204,
    206, 207, 211, 214, 219, 223, 228,
    232, 236, 246, 248, 250, 252, 254,
    255, 256, 257, 262–3, 276, 283, 285,
    288, 289–91, 295, 296, 297, 300,
    301, 302
Baggins, Bungo 23, 32, 97, 200
Baggins, Drogo 23
Baggins, Frodo 23, 24, 34, 41, 44,
    46, 50, 51, 57, 70, 80, 95, 96, 97,
    113, 117, 124, 126, 137–8, 177, 180,
    184–5, 187, 189, 200–1, 203, 214,
    232, 236, 246, 248, 252, 263–6, 267,
    278, 285, 312
Baggins family 23–4, 200, 234
Bain 28
Balar 107
Balin 25–6, 26, 37, 62, 79, 80, 87, 88,
    92, 94, 205, 271, 281

Illustrations by:

Sandrine Gestin: pp. 23, 33, 34, 46, 51, 64, 67, 75, 77, 78, 86, 89, 90, 96, 121, 142, 146, 180, 183, 185, 189, 204, 205, 209, 211, 220, 222, 223, 234, 241, 264, 265, 269, 275, 292, 293, 299

Xavier Sanchez: p. 13, 18, 21, 22, 26, 27, 42, 43, 53, 55, 60, 61, 68, 69, 71, 73, 81, 92, 93, 95, 99, 100, 104, 108, 109, 113, 115, 125, 127, 129, 134, 135, 149, 152, 153, 154, 157, 170, 172, 176, 177, 178, 190, 193, 194, 213, 217, 242, 247, 251, 258, 259, 272, 289, 309, 313, 326

Artworks by **Leslie Boulay**